Women
As
Winners

TRANSACTIONAL ANALYSIS FOR
PERSONAL GROWTH

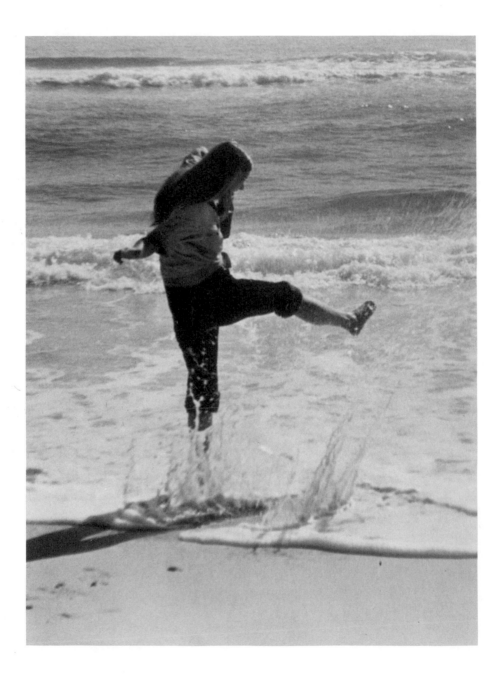

Women As Winners

TRANSACTIONAL ANALYSIS FOR PERSONAL GROWTH

DOROTHY JONGEWARD
DRU SCOTT

ADDISON-WESLEY
PUBLISHING COMPANY

Reading, Massachusetts
Menlo Park, California
London
Amsterdam • Don Mills, Ontario
Sydney

Library of Congress Cataloging in Publication Data

Jongeward, Dorothy.
   Women as winners.

   Bibliography: p.
   Includes index.
      1. Women—Psychology.   2. Transactional analysis.
I. Scott, Dru, joint author.   II. Title.
HQ1206.J66   155.6'33   76-421
ISBN 0-201-03386-0
ISBN 0-201-03435-2 pbk.

Third printing, August 1976

This book is dedicated to each one of the several thousands of women

who have been close to us,
who have trusted us, and
who have shared their lives and experiences with us

in their search for self.

Foreword

I am delighted with *Women As Winners*. It is a happy, useful book for women and men who want women to be all they can be.

Women do not have to be inferior or feel inferior. They do not have to sit around in groups playing "Ain't It Awful" about men or society or parents. As Jongeward and Scott state, each woman can know her past in order to decide whether she wants to go on along the same paths or to make changes now.

This book is a valuable tool for women who are about to decide to be productive, to be important, to use their brains, and to learn new and interesting skills. I believe it is equally valuable for the women I teach and treat. They are therapists who are already successful professionals, but still many of them have trouble allowing themselves to be winners.

Many female therapists learned in early childhood that they should have been male, because that was what Father or Mother really wanted. So they decided to compete, to use their brains, to be "tomboys"; they worked hard to prove they were as good as boys. Sometimes, as is explained in this book, they then believed that there was no way they could ever be successful girls (and later, women)—their hair was too curly or not curly enough, they were too big or too ugly. And so they continued to work hard, to get good grades and good jobs, but they still had troubles. If they married, they felt guilty, because "real women" did not "neglect their homes." They worked harder on the job and at home. I am amazed, for example, at the number of female psychiatrists who continue to do their own housework because "that is what women are supposed to do." They apologize to their husbands for working. They apologize to their children, and any time one of the children has a problem, they feel extra guilty. "If I'd been home as I should have been. . . ." At our workshops, they tell me what a treat it is to have four whole weeks without having to cook. One woman who said that earns $40,000 a year. Her husband, whose income is approximately the same, has never cooked a meal for her. And neither of them had considered hiring a good cook.

The therapists who do not marry are often ashamed—they let their parents down, they are not "real" women, and secretly they believe they were too "unfemale" to attract a husband. Married or unmarried, M.D. or Ph.D. or M.S.W., these women still believe, in their archaic childhood feelings, that they still are not what they should be.

It is my hope that all women will seek their autonomy and that women who choose motherhood will come to recognize that the authentic, autonomous woman makes a lovely mother for the men and women of the future.

And I have another hope—that this book is used as a high school and college text, so that our new women learn early in their lives that they can *decide for themselves* who they are and who they want to be.

Mary Edwards Goulding, M.S.W.

Preface

Women As Winners is a practical and positive book for women and men who are ready to better understand the dynamic and perplexing changes facing women. It is for people who are ready to help women move in positive directions toward wholeness.

Prepared or not, aware or not, women are coping with rapid change. Today's complex living with broken homes, longevity, smaller families, and more opportunities in the market place compels women to reach further to attain what they are capable of attaining.

More than a decade ago Betty Friedan's heated and controversial book *The Feminine Mystique* energized a conscious awakening among many women. As a result, a bevy of books on women graces the shelves of your local bookstore. The goals of this book complement some of these books and challenge others. Its uniqueness lies in the fact that it is very personal. It offers few answers. However, it does offer psychological tools and thought-provoking experiences to help you to discover your own answers, to set your own goals, and to solve your own problems. It is a beginning which offers a fresh perspective.

Women As Winners is written to meet special needs:

- It will give people insight, awareness, and understanding into women's past and present circumstances, the psychological limitations set on their self-images, and the learned compulsions which shape their life stories.

- It will help to heal or soften the barriers that exist among women. Many things cut women away from one another—the generations, their quest for men, and what they learn to believe is their proper role. Because of these chasms we want to build bridges to better understanding between younger and older women, between women who have money or the financial support of men and low-income and single women, between women who campaign for equal pay for equal work and those who choose homemaking as a full-time career.

- It will increase understanding between women and men. We would like men to understand the psychology of women and what can happen for men if women have more choices. We want to encourage men to support and facilitate the potentials of the women in their lives and to gain satisfaction and happiness out of seeing women grow. We fully realize that many of the patterns and problems discussed in this book could just as well be those of men, since men and women are much more alike than they are different.[1] However, the focus of this book is on women.

- It supplies challenging questions, experiences, and how-to ideas for personal growth. These techniques, which we call *Steps to Awareness*, are helpful to anyone taking the time to do them. A useful mix of techniques and theory threads throughout the book.

- It supplies tools for insight, understanding, and change. The tools of Transactional Analysis supplemented with Gestalt experiences offer clear psychological and experiential frames of reference. People can put them to use to examine their own personal feelings and opinions about women and to move toward positive growth. Without complicated psychiatric jargon, they help to answer the questions, "Who am I?" and "Where am I going with my life?" They open up new options for new directions.

From Dr. Eric Berne, the originator of TA,* we draw from two meaningful approaches:

Script analysis: the study of life dramas people feel compelled to live out, whether they are joyful, banal, or tragic; whether they are winning, nonwinning, or losing.

Structural analysis: the study of individual personality in terms of three sources of thoughts, feelings, and actions called the Parent ego state, the Adult ego state, and the Child ego state.

From Dr. Frederick Perls, who popularized Gestalt therapy,[2] we draw on his unique role-playing technique and his emphasis on closure—bringing unresolved emotional problems to resolution. When practiced, these methods help people reclaim unknown parts of their personalities. They help people become more integrated into a unified whole, or gestalt. For instance, it helps a man, who may have suppressed his emotions, to learn to acknowledge his need to cry. It helps a woman, who may have suppressed

---

* For a complete list of Eric Berne's and others' writings on TA, contact: International Transactional Analysis Association, 1772 Vallejo Street, San Francisco, CA 94123. This address should also be used for inquiries about TA training and ITAA membership.

her expressiveness, to be assertive in a direct and constructive way about what she wants.

TA and Gestalt techniques as used in this book are in no way substitutes for needed therapy. People who are disturbed enough to not function well or who are plagued with unhappiness need to seek outside help. However, using these practical tools wisely, people can fulfill more of their unique potential. This individual growth can lead to further personal emancipation. For women, this means emancipation from the boundaries they have set for themselves in the past. For men, this means emancipation from the restricted ideas they have held about women. For both men and women, it means the freedom to choose. It means learning to think in new ways about who and what women and men can be and how they can relate more honestly, openly, and directly.

In *Women As Winners* we are advocating neither marriage nor the single life, neither careers nor homemaking, neither children nor childlessness, neither lesbianism nor heterosexuality. We *are* advocating more meaningful choices—choices that society and circumstances have not allowed women to make before and choices that some women have not allowed themselves to make.

In the past, many women received messages which somehow caused them to think of themselves as less—as weak, dependent, or helpless. Pressures bore down on women to conform, to be who *other people wanted them to be,* to be who *other people thought they should be.*

Women today are actively reaching out to discover themselves, to know themselves, and to be themselves. This book helps with that journey. Every woman can be more herself, more authentic. She can be more the winner she was born to be.

We wish to thank all of the talented people with whom we have studied. In particular, we appreciate the associations, learnings, skills, and writings of Eric Berne, M.D., Mary McClure Goulding, M.S.W., and Frederick Perls, M.D. A most special thanks goes to our dedicated and effective assistants, Jean Fisher, Debra Smith, and Sandy McPartlon.

Orinda, California   D. J.
San Francisco, California   D. S.
April 1976

Contents

1

Women Caught in Change   1

2

The Time of Your Life   19

3

Once Upon a Time . . .   37

4

Mirror, Mirror, on the Wall   61

5

Someone Touched Me   89

6

The Watchful Inner Eye 109

Steps to Awareness

7

Sugar and Spice 129

Steps to Awareness

8

Losing to Win 153

Steps to Awareness

9

Not for Parents Only   177

Steps to Awareness

10

The Capable Woman   193

Steps to Awareness

11

Thinking Straight About Women   223

12

A Hundred Years Hence   243

13

Daring to Dream   271

14

Living Your Dream   291

1

Women Caught in Change

- What new challenges do today's women face?
- How do these changes affect women?
- What is a winning woman like?

When it's snowing and I put on all the galoshes
While he reads the paper,
Then I want to become a
Women's Liberation Movement woman.
And when it's snowing and he looks for the taxi
While I wait in the lobby,
Then I don't.
And when it's vacation and I'm in charge of
mosquito bites and poison ivy and car
sickness
While he's in charge of swimming,
Then I want to become a
Women's Liberation Movement woman.
And when it's vacation and he carries the trunk
and the overnight bag and the extra blankets
While I carry the wig case,
Then I don't.
And when it's three in the morning and the baby
definitely needs a glass of water and I have
to get up and bring it
While he keeps my place warm,
Then I want to become a
Women's Liberation Movement woman.
And when it's three in the morning and there is
definitely a murderer-rapist in the vestibule
and he has to get up and catch him
While I keep his place warm,
Then I don't.

Judith Viorst[1]

Your life is touched in some way each day by the conflicts that confront modern women. Change, accompanied by the inevitable way it alters choices, most often results in discomfort. Not only do women feel turmoil at a personal level about what they want and who they should be, but they also are confronted by pressures from the outside. Mere mention of the topic "Women" is likely to spark an instant debate, with everyone chiming in as somewhat of an expert.

These inner and outer conflicts are generated as rapidly changing circumstances rub against tradition-bound attitudes. They contribute to many women's unrealistic, sometimes confused, self-image. The result of this mix of slowly changing attitudes and rapidly changing circumstances is that modern women's roles and life-styles are being pushed and pulled in all directions:

"Get married."	"Stay home where you belong."
"Get a job."	"Be more of a *real* woman."
"Don't have children."	"Be yourself."
"Have a family."	"Be sexy."
"Keep your freedom."	"Don't do it."

In response to the forces that tug and tear at them, women are often set against not only men, but also one another. Some women staunchly defend their traditional roles. Some smolder in anger, discontented with their lot. Others turn their backs on women's problems. But probably most feel perplexed and confused. They realize that something significant is happening to women, but the problems remain muddled.

Expanding Women's Roles

Women's traditional roles of mothers and homemakers will always be important ones. For women who choose them, these roles may always be *the* most important. However, there are women who, without rejecting the value of parenting, either need or want to widen their spectrum of possibilities.

As a result, many women, even though they have had few female models, are breaking new ground. Some have found their way into what has always been considered "men's work"—hauling garbage for the city, piloting jets for the Navy, climbing poles for the telephone company, switching rails for the railroad line, chairing corporate boards, directing traffic at busy intersections, and starting their own businesses.

Women interested in doing "more" may or may not decide against parenthood. Some experience a great sense of fulfillment relating to children. As Abigail Heyman writes:

> When I was a little girl I thought that playing with dolls was stupid and that playing games like the boys did was really exciting. Later I thought I liked man-conversation better, that girl-talk was stupid. Now it seems to me that girls were talking about real things like dolls and babies and love. We've been denying that the really important talk is important. We've been putting ourselves down.[2]

About This Book

The need today is not only to call attention to the conflicts and problems facing women, but also to offer a fresh perspective—a new way to view change and growth. This book helps with both.

In addition to portraying the issues women face and how these problems touch your life, this book also gives you practical and positive ways to change if you choose to. This is a book about choices and possibilities. It is about women and men enjoying more options and taking more responsibility for their own lives. It is about dreaming dreams, finding the freedom to share those dreams, and learning how to make those dreams come true.

WHAT IS HAPPENING TO THE WOMEN IN YOUR LIFE?

Each of the 108 million women in the United States—51% of the population—is unique. Even though each woman sees her life from a private vantage point, a common thread runs through the lives of many. Few women are prepared for the realities life deals them. What actually happens is often a far cry from what they learned to expect. Some feel content with their lives, but many are struggling to define themselves more clearly. They are searching to understand their own uniqueness, their own potentials, their own relationships, and their own destinies.

In the next few pages, seven women we know talk about some of the problems and challenges they have faced. Each of these seven represents many of the thousands of women who have shared their lives with us. Although both the women and their problems are real, we have altered the names and some of the details to protect their privacy.

Some of these stories may sound familiar to you. You may feel saddened or angered by what they say. Some may not interest you. However, most will offer you new insights.

The statistics included in our comments following each interview may surprise you. They clearly show that women have *not* "come a long way." These facts are here because accurate information is the best way to dispel myths and misunderstandings.

As you glimpse into the lives of these women, think about the women in *your* life. Ask yourself:

Is this woman

someone who needs my support?

someone who needs my understanding?

someone I know and work with?
    my neighbor?
    my wife?
    my daughter?
    my mother?
or . . . . .
    someone like me?

Edna—An Unexpected Divorce

I thought that Cliff and I had an ideal marriage. We'd been together for more than 12 years and never had a really bad fight. During the last five years of our marriage, however, I noticed that Cliff and I were spending less and less time together, and we seemed to have fewer and fewer things in common. When the two of us did go out to dinner alone, we'd sit for long stretches, saying nothing to each other.

But even with these signals, I was stunned when he told me he wanted a divorce. I thought I'd been an ideal wife. Cliff had wanted me to stay home with the children, and I was very happy to do this. We entertained frequently, and I spent a lot of time with company people. I always felt that this was my share in Cliff's success. But it didn't prepare me to make my own way. Somehow it seemed only right that he do his part and support me financially. But the alimony didn't even last a year.

When we were first separated, I kept buttonholing my friends for reassurance that Cliff was mistreating me. I went out with one man after another. I know I was just trying to get even with Cliff—to show him that I was still a desirable woman. But this soon got to be a hassle. Frankly, I began to feel like a middle-age adolescent going through all the problems of dating.

Now, after going through a lot of soul searching and getting some good help, I've decided that the best thing for me to do is to make a life for myself. Maybe I'll share it with someone else and maybe I won't. There is little point in my holding a grudge against Cliff any longer—especially the resentment I had about bringing up the kids alone. And why should I turn this divorce into a personal defeat? Those feelings don't help me or the kids. Pinning the blame on one of us hasn't helped, but the urge gets to me once in awhile.

In the year and a half since our divorce became final, I've still had some trouble accepting the fact that I'm a divorced woman. But I've taken a step to get over that, too. Just as I was about to get into the shower one morning last week, I slipped my familiar wedding ring off my finger. I had finally granted myself full custody of me.

September 1975 is a milestone date. It marks the first time in American history that there were more than one million divorces in a year's time.[3] Some women, like Edna, emerge from the upheaval of divorce stronger as individuals. Others do not.

The reasons for divorce are varied and complex, yet most brides believe that they will never have to face such a major change. Although the divorce rate almost doubled between 1960 and 1972,[4] most women are not prepared either emotionally or economically to handle this event.

New challenges confront the children of divorced parents. Sometimes they are ping-pong balls between angry and hurt parents. Sometimes they fare better with one caring parent. Most frequently, they stay with their mothers, and their fathers move on to rear other men's children. How prepared are most women to rear their children alone?

In addition to the crucial question of children, divorce always involves the question of money. Gaining wealth through alimony is a myth for all but a handful of women. A wealthy woman may suffer mental anguish after a divorce, but at least she knows where her next meal is coming from.

The middle-income woman is hit hard financially in a divorce. Often she has elected to stay home with the children, and as a consequence is ill-prepared for working outside her home when the marriage is over. In fact, contrary to common opinion, the sharpest rise in divorce is among women like Edna who do not have jobs outside their homes. Research shows this trend particularly predominant among young women. By 1970 the youngest women in the population who worked actually had *more* intact first marriages than those without jobs.[5]

An ex-husband is also beset by financial problems. If he remarries, his income is spread between two families. In addition, he may carry a burden of guilt, feeling that he encouraged his first wife to be a full-time homemaker and that now she cannot support herself.

Not having the luxury of choice, the low-income woman usually works during her married life. When she divorces, she certainly cannot count on alimony or even child support. Typically, she has held a low-paying job, and neither her experience nor education has prepared her to move upward. Since her financial needs demand that she work, she finds it almost impossible to quit and get the education and training she needs for a better-paying job. In addition—educated or not—she finds few well-paying jobs open to women.

Most divorced women experience emotional pain. For many, however, the problem of financial independence surfaces as the crucial issue.

Martha—Unprepared for a Life of Employment

I've stood behind the cash register in this little dress shop for more years than I care to remember. I guess I never expected to have to work for a living. But was I ever startled the other day to realize that I've been working for more than 47 years. I couldn't believe it!

When I was a little girl, my father said that it would be a good idea to have a job to fall back on, just in case. But I never really thought about work very seriously. I got my first job at 17 and planned to work only a few years, until I got married. Then I worked after I married just to help us get started.

But when I was widowed at 32, I had to keep on working to support myself and my two daughters. I feel proud of myself because I managed to put them through school and help them in college. But somewhere I got the idea I would be able to live on Social Security when I got older. It never dawned on me that I'd get only $190 a month. That just doesn't go very far. So here I am, 64, and still working.

I hate the thought of being a burden to my children. But somehow, I was always too busy with the daily pressures of earning a living and taking care of my family to sit down and think about what I wanted to do and what my future would be. I surely want each of my daughters to take time to prepare for her future.

When Martha married, she certainly did not expect to become a widow. Yet three out of four wives will be widowed[6]—most in their mid-50s.[7] And two-thirds of all widows live below the poverty line.[8] In fact, *more than half of all women will live their last days in poverty.*

The yearly income for women 65 years and older is $2119. Only $177 a month[9] provides no luxuries. In fact, it does not even provide a minimum standard of living.

Although women are often portrayed as controlling the wealth in the United States, the life of an average elderly woman paints a very different picture. Rather than basking in the luxury of alimony or insurance payments or clipping coupons, she far more likely lives in a retirement hotel, buys six eggs at a time at a Ma and Pa corner grocery store, cooks her meals on a hot plate, and in extreme cases fills out her diet with dog food. In short, most women are unaware of and totally unprepared for the widowhood and poverty which are now the destiny of a majority of them.

Jeanette—Conflicting Attitudes About Sex

Jack and I went together for more than two years. When I was 19, I decided that sex was not a good enough reason to get married. So he and I decided to live together. When I told my parents about it, they cut me off from the family. Mom said, "We don't want to have anything to do with a girl who lives in sin. Why, he'll never marry you if you give him his way now. After all, since Jack has the milk, why should he buy the cow?"

Their attitude really hurt me, but I didn't believe that I was doing anything immoral. If Jack and I ever want children, we'll get married. Any children we have will have a "legal" mother and father.

I'm 24 now, and I have a good job at a commercial design company. I'd like to open my own business, and I'd be good at it, too. But I need some extra money to get started.

The money part really frustrates me. When I was 15, my parents set up a $10,000 trust for me. But just recently they've added a clause stating that I must be married to get the money. Can you believe it!

Well, I've thought it over, and money isn't a good enough reason to get married either. My parents still hardly speak to me. I don't want to hurt them, but I'm responsible for my life now. I feel that I must do what is right for me, not for them.

Even though most people still choose marriage, the number of marriages began to decline in 1973.[10] Increasingly, couples are testing this tradition. Some no longer see legal bonds as necessary to cement or validate their emotional bonds. In addition, more reliable birth-control methods have immeasurably widened the options available to women.

As a result, many young women are facing a rapid change in sexual mores. Some are making thoughtful choices. Others are conforming to peer pressure that "everybody's doing it."

This drastic change often widens the generation gap. Many parents feel distressed and suffer pangs of guilt for "not having done a good job." Rather than looking at the individual character of the people involved, they tend to judge their children on the basis of tradition.

Some young people can talk over their current problems with their parents. But some, like Jeanette, are caught in a situation in which the generations are unable to understand each other.

Debbie—Needing More Than College to Help Out Financially

Grant just got word that he's been laid off. When he left college with his degree in aeronautical engineering, we both thought we'd always be rolling in clover. Now he doesn't think there's a chance for him to get another job in aerospace for at least a year.

I'd really like to be able to support the family so Grant can get some new training. But who cares about my ten-year-old college degree in French literature? The best I can do is get a job as a sales clerk or receptionist. I've never thought much about what a woman could earn, but I know it certainly won't keep a family of five afloat. Just when Grant needs me the most, I'm the least able to help.

Debbie's anxieties are real. She is not prepared for paid employment. But even if she were, she probably wouldn't be able to earn a living wage for her family.

Contrary to common belief, even a college degree may not ensure a woman a decent living. In 1973 a woman with a college degree earned $350 a year *less* than a man with an eighth-grade education.[11] The trend has worsened. Only three years earlier, she earned $600 *more* than a man with an eighth-grade education.[12]

Even with the same educational backgrounds, women and men do not earn the same money. The average educational level for both women and men workers in the United States is 12.4 years.[13] Yet women working full time average $6300 a year, whereas men average $11,200. A typical woman earns less than 57% of what her male colleague earns.[14] Although 58% of all working men earn $10,000 or more a year, only 14% of all working women earn this amount.[15] In fact, 96% of all people earning over $15,000 a year are men.[16]

Look at what women earn for each dollar men earn.[17]

1955	1970	1973
64¢	59¢	57¢

Comparison of Women's and Men's Earnings

In addition to the widening earnings gap, it is hard for a woman to earn a salary large enough to support a family.

Despite the low pay they receive, nine out of ten American girls will work,[18] mostly because they need the money. Almost two out of every

three working women are widowed, single, divorced, or married to unemployed men or those who earn less than $7000 a year.[19]

Single women will work more than 45 years outside the home. Widowed or divorced women will work slightly more than 40 years. Married
women who don't have children will work 35 years. And even a woman
who married and has children will work 20 to 30 years outside her home.[20]
Most have not prepared themselves for these years of paid employment.
Also, most are not aware that their paychecks shrink because they are
women.

**STEPS TO
AWARENESS**

Helping Women

The following exercise is the first of several. You can use these "steps to awareness" to strengthen your insight. You may want to do them as you go along,
or you may prefer to come back later and do those that particularly fit your own
situation.

If Debbie were a woman in your life, what would you say to her?

What would be some useful things for you to do to help her solve the problem
of her husband's being laid off?

If she lived in your community, what are the best places she could go for information or counseling?

Doris—Hooked on Drugs

Sure my son Joey was in a bit of trouble, but it wasn't that much. I guess all teenage boys are bound to sow a few wild oats. I just didn't understand why I was so nervous all the time. I had a faithful and devoted husband. My other son wanted to be a lawyer. But still so many of my days seemed empty.

I first started taking a tranquilizer every once in awhile, just to take the rough edges off my feelings and to help when I felt really down. I just wanted something to help tide me over. Then with the menopause and everything else happening, I started taking more. I soon found that I couldn't stand the thought of going through the day without taking my little blue pills.

Many women feel depressed without knowing why. As a result, they turn to chemicals to relieve the symptoms. In fact, middle-age women like Doris are the most frequent users of tranquilizers and antidepressants in the United States.[21] Although men outnumber women in the consumption of barbiturates and narcotics, women consume minor tranquilizers—most prescribed by doctors—at almost twice the rate of men.[22] Yet it is unrealistic to assume that the high use of drugs among women is justified by an equally high number of "nervous" or "stress-ridden" women. Physicians, frustrated about treating vague symptoms, often order drugs to take the edge off bad feelings. Many unknowingly contribute to women's covering up rather than curing their underlying problems.

But tranquilizers and antidepressants are only a small part of the drug problem of modern women. Alcoholism is no longer "a man's problem." Of the eight to ten million alcoholics in the United States, at least two million are women.[23] These figures do not include the estimated 15 to 20 million more who hide themselves from the public eye. Since women at home can mask their drinking problems more easily than men away at work can, they make up an even larger proportion of this invisible group. The invisible woman alcoholic is often hidden, sheltered, and "protected" by her family. She may start her morning with gin concealed in orange juice or vodka concealed in tomato juice. As she sips her way through the day, she struggles frantically to maintain an image of respectability and to hide an ever-increasing number of empty liquor bottles in the family garbage can.

One taxi driver attested to this problem and the casual attitude toward it when he was asked how he made a living in the suburbs. He replied with a shrug, "Well, I spend most of my mornings taking bottles to housewives."

Ramona—Breaking Into a Traditional Man's World

*After years of being a legal secretary, I was glad just to get into law
school. I know that if I were a Caucasian woman, I'd have had a harder
time getting in. The class work was challenging, but that wasn't the
hardest part.*

*Some people resent my getting into law school as part of a special
La Raza program. They tell me that my spot "should have gone to a man."
They take me seriously as a Chicana, but not as a woman.*

*When I first got the job with this firm, the secretaries all but ignored
me. My new business cards were misprinted with "Ramon," a man's
name. When clients phoned, they couldn't believe that I was a lawyer.*

*When I graduated, 17 out of 309 law students were women. This
year that number increased to 70 women. In 1964 there were 2100 women
law school students. And in 1974 there were 21,000. That's a good
beginning.*

Ramona has seen changes in one of the most difficult professions for
women to enter. For decades less than 2% of all lawyers were women. Now
women of all races are entering that field.

Medicine has also been notorious for its male bias. Most medical schools
maintained a 10% quota system and routinely rejected brilliant female
students in favor of their more mediocre brothers, arguing, "the investment
is too expensive for someone who might get pregnant." One young woman
premed student voiced the change that has begun to occur: "Eight years
ago my cousin, who was at the top of her class, was turned down because
the quota was filled and they feared she might get married. Today, women
are 20% of my class. My family doesn't quite understand why I'm doing
this, and I get tired of some of the double-meaning jokes, but all in all I'm
doing all right."

The problem of the small number of women admitted to medical school
is not new. The American Medical Women's Association was founded in
1915.

Barbara—Having Communication Problems with Her Husband

*I never thought Jerry would take my success this way. When the bank
started opening up opportunities for women to take management training,
I was thrilled. And I thought he would be, too. But he's not. He's really
upset. It was OK for me to work as long as I wasn't really serious about*

it. But now that I've made a commitment to a career with the bank, he's really pushed out of shape. We won't even be in the same fields. But he says I'm putting him down and that I'll just turn into one of those bitchy career women. He feels that he's not being a man unless he's doing something more important than his wife. I really feel caught in a bind. I want a better job, but I want Jerry to be happy too.

Barbara was not prepared for her husband's attitude toward her career advancement. Many men accept society's image of manliness. Rather than taking pride in the women in their lives and facilitating their opportunities to grow, these men learn to fear successful women. The lack of objective basis for their feelings reflects the distress of the "delicate ego."[24] They learn that in order to feel OK as men, they must always appear superior, even if it is to the detriment of someone else's growth, their own personal relationships, or their own health.

The seven women you have met in these pages are not alone in their problems, even though they may sometimes feel that way. Other women have other types of problems. Perhaps you know someone like:

- Denise, who loves her children but feels alone and trapped in the suburbs.
- Stephanie, who was ostracized by the office staff when she revealed her lesbianism.
- Helene, who assumed almost total responsibility for a handicapped child.
- Thelma, who was abandoned by her boyfriend and must now seek an abortion alone.
- Mary Lou, who needs to work but is unable to find good care for her two-year-old daughter.

Most women feel the pressure of change in some way in their lives. Some, like Edna, Martha, Jeanette, and Ramona, are learning to adapt to those changes. Others, like Debbie, Doris, and Barbara, are in some way frustrated about change. At one time or another, each of us yearns for the simple, clearcut patterns of yesterday. But yesterdays never return.

We might ask, "Why were so many of these women ill-prepared for reality?" or "Why was it hard to step out of a traditional female role?" Two reasons emerge as paramount: (1) women's low or incomplete self-images, and (2) the way women learn to see themselves in relationship to men.

14

STEPS TO
AWARENESS

Looking At Your Life

Think about yourself (or, if you are a man, about an important woman in your life).

If your story appeared here, what would be the title?

How would your story read? Jot down a few ideas.

What were you best prepared for? Family responsibilities? Career? Other?

Least prepared for?

What facts are relevant to your situation?

Do you need to find out more information?

_____

NO ONE WINS THE BATTLE OF THE SEXES

Many women refrain from solving their problems because they believe that
to do so would mean hurting men. One twentieth-century woman voiced
this one-up, one-down seesaw belief with, "I would never take a job where
I earned more than Bob. If I start being really successful, that means I'm
making him less of a man." She makes the assumption that there is only
so much human strength and talent; by expressing as much as she can,
she takes away from the man in her life.

For centuries, men and women have made the assumption that the
best way for them to relate is in this seesaw manner. As one partner grows,
the other must shrink. If one is good, the other is bad. If one is superior,
the other is inferior.

More than 2400 years ago, Pythagoras taught:

There is a good principle which has created order, light, and man,
and a bad principle which created chaos, darkness, and women.[25]

And 200 years ago, Napoleon Bonaparte reaffirmed this belief:

Nature intended women to be our slaves . . . they are our property; we
are not theirs. They belong to us, just as a tree that bears fruit belongs
to a gardener. What a mad idea to demand equality for women!
Women are nothing but machines for producing children.[26]

The classic struggle between "top dog" and "underdog" further illustrates this see-saw phenomenon. To exist, underdogs must sharpen their
wits, manicure their manipulative skills, and devote their energies to developing devious strategies for power. In order to gain power over other
people, underdogs often try to end up looking as if they are losing. The
price for such playacting is high in terms of loss of personal dignity and
integrity. For example,

The woman who is angry at her husband for not talking with her or
confiding in her may go out and run up unreasonable bills on their
charge account.
This hurts both of them.

The woman who quits her job every time her husband wants to move
for his career advancement may get even. She may subtly annoy him
by staying 30 pounds overweight, despite his continual nagging.
Both lose a potentially close and sharing relationship.

The woman who stands behind her famous man, organizing the meetings, correcting the papers, planning the campaigns, or writing the

book, may then cash in her resentments in private with, "You'd still be a nobody if it weren't for me."

Both suffer the pain of the lack of authentic achievement.

The woman who complains, "I have a headache" or "I'm too tired," may be withholding sex from the man in her life in order to experience power.

They both lose out on sexual closeness.

Such cat-and-mouse games between a man and woman destroy their capacities to relate to each other from the full spectrum of themselves. Instead, they spend their time making power plays. They maintain false identities of who's right and who's wrong, who's strong and who's weak, who's superior and who's inferior. It is a tragic waste to invest energy in exploitation and deviousness rather than in open honesty and genuinely caring encounters.

This old frame of reference is win/lose. A new frame of reference is win/win. A part of every woman or man wants to win—to be open, honest, genuine, and direct. However, people who have learned a limited or poor self-image may not know how to win. They look like they want to lose. They are closed and untrue to themselves. What they have learned to want may actually hurt them.

Real winners—people who are self-actualizing and who respond authentically to life—do not need losers. Women winning does not mean that men must lose, any more than men winning should mean that women must lose. If women have more options, so too will men. More choices for women means more choices for men. For example, it has long been acceptable for a married woman to quit her job and stay at home, explaining, "I'm tired of working. I'm going to relax and do something different for a while." Yet how many married men—no matter how tired or pressured— would be greeted with the same degree of acceptance if they announced, "I'm tired of working. I'm going to stay home with the family for a while."?

Winning ways are not tied to any set of circumstances. Instead, they help people to deal effectively with life's problems and possibilities. In the past, many women learned to think of themselves as losers or at least to act like losers. What are women as winners like?

WINNING AS A WOMAN

Winners have different potentials. Achievement is not the most important thing. Authenticity is. The authentic woman experiences the reality of herself by knowing herself, being herself, and becoming a credible, responsive person. She actualizes her own unprecedented uniqueness and appreciates the uniqueness of others.

She does not dedicate her life to a concept of what she imagines she *should* be. Rather, she *is herself* and as such does not use her energy putting on a performance, maintaining pretense, and manipulating others with games. A winner can reveal herself instead of only projecting images that please, provoke, or entice others. She is aware that there is a difference between being loving and acting loving, between being stupid and acting stupid, between being knowledgeable and acting knowledgeable. She does not need to hide behind a mask. She throws off unrealistic self-images of inferiority or superiority. Autonomy does not frighten a winner.

Everyone has moments of autonomy, if only fleeting. However, a winner is able to sustain her autonomy over ever-increasing periods of time. She may lose ground occasionally. She may even fail. Yet in spite of setbacks, a winner maintains a basic faith in herself.

A winner is not afraid to do her own thinking and to use her own knowledge. She can separate fact from opinion and doesn't pretend to have all the answers. She listens to others, evaluates what they say, but comes to her own conclusions. Although she can admire and respect other people, she is not totally defined, demolished, bound, or awed by them.

A winner does not play "helpless," nor does she play blaming games. Instead, she assumes responsibility for her own life. She does not give others a false authority over her. She's her own boss and knows it.

A winner's timing is right. She responds appropriately to the situation. Her response is appropriate when it is related to the message sent and preserves the significance, worth, well-being, and dignity of the people involved. She knows that for everything there is a season and for every activity a time.

A time to be aggressive and a time to be passive,
A time to be together and a time to be alone,
A time to fight and a time to love,
A time to work and a time to play,
A time to cry and a time to laugh,
A time to confront and a time to withdraw,
A time to speak and a time to be silent,
A time to hurry and a time to wait.[27]

To a winner, time is precious. She does not kill it. She lives it here and now. Living in the now does not mean that she foolishly ignores her own past history or fails to prepare for her future. Rather, she knows her past, is aware and alive in the present, and looks forward to the future.

A winner learns to know her feelings and limitations and is not afraid of them. She is not stopped by her own contradictions and ambivalences. She knows when she is angry and can listen when others are angry with her. She can give and receive affection. She is able to love and be loved.

A winner can be spontaneous. She does not have to respond in predetermined, rigid ways. She can change her plans when the situation calls for it. A winner has a zest for life. She does not get her security by controlling others. She does not set herself up to lose. Instead, she enjoys work, play, food, other people, sex, and the world of nature. Without guilt she enjoys her own accomplishments. Without envy she enjoys the accomplishments of others.

Although a winner can freely enjoy herself, she can also postpone enjoyment. She can discipline herself in the present to enhance her enjoyment in the future. She is not afraid to go after what she wants, but she does so in appropriate ways. She gets what she wants without hurting herself or others.

A winner cares about the world and its peoples. She is not isolated from the general problems of society. She is concerned, compassionate, and committed to improving the quality of life. Even in the face of national and international adversity, she does not see herself as totally powerless. The winning woman does what she can to make the world a better place.[28]

2

The Time
of
Your Life

- In what ways can time be used?
- What is the waiting game, and how is it played?
- How have *you* been programmed to use *your* life's time?

EPITAPH

I have served my quiet term of
desperation:
diapers and dishpans,
egg salad sandwiches for the social.
I spilled sweet smiles in the sisterly
sanctity of the lodge hall, and
covered my knees with modesty as became
the Village Lawyer's Wife.
I won the prizes old women poets
and retired schoolteachers strive for,
building a house around my sorrows,
rearranging rooms to infinity in my restlessness.
Unhappiness seeped silently into my sand
until the sand was fenced and refenced and even
the cactus curled, withered and died.
I have been to eighty and back again
these nine years. But I have been advised
the believable world does not end at
-30-

Sara Rath[1]

For Sara Rath, as for all of us, life is an interval of time. We all need to fill our time in some way; otherwise, boredom and deterioration set in. But what shall we do with our time?

Shall we, like Sara, spend our time with diapers, dishpans, and egg salad sandwiches for the social?

Shall we find someone to love and someone to love us? Or someone to hurt and someone to hurt us?

Shall we spend our time trying? Trying to just get by? Trying to be perfect? Trying to stay eternally young?

Shall we fade into a corner and daydream our time away?

And in the end, what will we look back on with pride, with sorrow or regret, with joy, with humiliation, with guilt? Will we look at our lives and say, "Good show"? Or, like Sara, will we consider our lives "quiet terms of desperation"?

Your Epitaph

Most of us have an inkling of the essence of what our lives are about. Each person's life has a theme—a thread. The succinct theme of your life sums up what the time of your life ends up meaning. It is your epitaph.

WE STRUCTURE OUR TIME

Eric Berne observed that most people structure their time in six different ways: withdrawal, rituals, pastimes, games, activities, or intimacy. Looking at time in this manner gives a woman a particularly useful framework for clarifying what she values.

Withdrawals. A woman may withdraw into her adolescent daydreams of being carried away into the sunset by a championship football player on a white horse. Or, she may withdraw for needed time in self-reflection, re-thinking, and creative fantasies.

Rituals. A woman may structure her time with highly predictable, stereo-typed rituals, such as meetings on Mondays, bridge on Tuesdays, and sex on Friday nights. Or, she may use rituals to commemorate and give signifi-cance to important events in her life, such as marriage, childbirth, gradua-tion, or promotions.

Pastimes. A woman may engage in conversations about innocuous subjects, repeating information that does not lead to change. Such topics might include which detergent to use, shopping, or working conditions. Or, she may use pastimes to grease the wheels of social exchange and to open up acquaintances with a variety of people.

Games. A woman may play games without being aware of what she is doing. Using disguised means to put down herself and others, she reinforces negative feelings she learned in childhood.

In every game there is a plausible exchange on the surface and the *real*, though unaware, exchange underneath. This ulterior (real) message leads to someone's feeling bad—the payoff for the game. For example, a woman who as a child was always picked on may now unknowingly play *Kick Me* by being late for appointments, getting bawled out, and then feeling bad. She may also play *Blemish* by pointing out inconsequential flaws in a friend's appearance, encouraging her friend to feel bad, and then feeling superior herself. At other times she may play *I'm Only Trying to Help You* by cleaning up her daughter's desk top without being asked, suffering her daughter's wrath and frustration, and then feeling hurt. Or, rather than play these games she may develop open, honest relationships, clearly aware of other people here and now.

Activities. A woman may spend her time getting a job done, just "to keep busy." She may unnecessarily straighten, shift, and sort away her time without any end result in mind. Or, she may meet the challenge of activities that require her to use and even expand her unique potentials.

Intimacy. A woman may feel that intimacy means having sexual relations with the men she meets. Or, she may recognize that the true basis for intimacy is an open, honest, game-free encounter that may or may not involve a sexual exchange. She may also recognize that authentic relationships with other women open up new dimensions in the quality of her life's time.

**STEPS TO
AWARENESS**

Your Use of Time

Consider how you spent your time yesterday. Thinking of the day as a pie, divide it into six pieces. Make each piece represent the amount of time you spent in a particular manner.

Does your use of time look like this?

Or this?

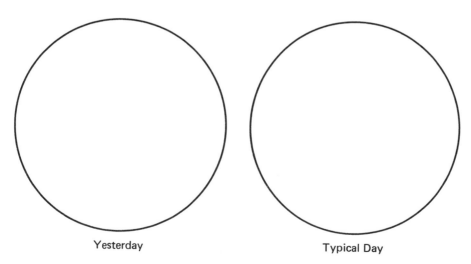

Now diagram the way you spent yesterday. Then diagram a typical day in your life.

Yesterday   Typical Day

What use of your life's time would you like to minimize? What would you like to expand? Now draw the way you'd like to structure your time.

What would you need to do to make the changes you want?

_____

Messages About Time

All children hear messages about time. "Hurry up, you're going to be late." "She's as slow as molasses." "Time is money." "Everything comes to the one who waits." You probably heard how you should spend your time.

**STEPS TO
AWARENESS**

Your Messages About Time

When you were growing up, what messages or mottoes did you hear about time? List those you recall now and add to the list as you remember others.

How did you *feel* in response to these messages?

In what ways do you structure your time *now* that reflect those things you heard?

Are these ways of investing your time helping or hindering you now?

What do you want to do differently?

Some Women Wait

Carol spent her life's time waiting—waiting for something to happen in the future. She believed that somehow, in some way, life would be better "when."

Carol was totally bored with high school. She particularly hated her math classes, often spending her time sneaking looks at the movie magazines tucked in her textbooks. She took only those subjects she had to in order to get by, but she spent a great deal of her time in front of the bathroom mirror, worrying about how she looked. Her last year in school dragged on interminably. As she sat absentmindedly in each class, she dreamed of the day she'd graduate. She could hardly wait to get out of school.

During this last year in high school, Carol began to plan her wedding. She was dating a young man in his second year of college, and marrying him became the center of her thoughts. She could hardly wait to get married.

The week after graduation, Carol walked down the aisle in the lace wedding gown she had dreamed of so often. And soon after that, she found part-time work in a department store to help support her husband while he finished college. But she detested her job. She could hardly wait for the day she could quit and start a family.

Carol eventually did quit her job, and her first baby arrived within a year and a half; her second, two years after that. For a while her entire life centered on her home, her husband's job, and her two children. Even though she seemed to have everything she had always wanted, she sometimes complained, "I can hardly wait till the kids grow up."

When the children finally reached their teens, a vague feeling of loneliness settled over Carol. She felt that no one paid any attention to her any more—either to her looks or the way she kept house. When their first child left home, Carol's feelings of loneliness intensified, and she tried to fill her time by having coffee with neighbors, shopping, and cleaning. And by the time their second child left home, she began suffering more severe depression. Without understanding why, she felt finished and useless. Life seemed to hold little meaning. She frequently sighed, "I just don't know what to do with myself. I have so much time on my hands now."

This "waiting" theme runs like a thread through the lives of many women. They wait for an outside person or outside influence to come along and make their lives better—to rescue them. In the meantime, their lives are passing by, and they may not ever be rescued. Vivian talks about this theme.

You know, I really like my job, and I find teaching third grade very satisfying. It feels good seeing those little kids develop. Even after the eight years I've been teaching, I still see new and good things happening. Although I get to feeling down now and then, this job has really helped me pass the time. But if the right man came along today, I'd be most happy to give it all up. In fact, I really don't want to do anything too definite about buying an apartment or a house or setting aside money for my retirement, because I just can't imagine turning 35 and not being married.

Like Vivian, some single women cannot imagine living without a man. Even though the facts show that more women are remaining single,[2] some still bide their time, waiting.

The Waiting Game[3]

Are you waiting for something? If so, what are you waiting for?

For the right person to come along?
For the children to grow up?
For the right affair?
To finish your education?
For your ship to come in?
For a better job?
To quit working?
To find the end of the rainbow?
To move into a more exclusive neighborhood?
For something bad to happen?
To pay for the good times you've had?
For someone else to change?
For someone else to make the decision?
For someone to discover you?
For what?

What is the probability that what you are waiting for will really happen?

What is happening while you are waiting?

Where do you think you will end up?

What can you do today to *stop waiting* and start getting what you want?

WE FOLLOW PSYCHOLOGICAL BLUEPRINTS

Whether passively waiting or actively growing, a person is unconsciously following a personal psychological script—a life plan designed in childhood. Eric Berne defines a script as: "... an ongoing program, developed in early childhood under parental influence, which directs the individual's behavior in the most important aspects of his [or her] life."[4]

Personal scripts are like blueprints for life. Unless we become aware of our scripts, we will go through life, unquestioningly clutching the old blueprints no matter how outdated or ill-fitting they are.

Each of us has our unique script. It is formed from a number of influences: inherited capabilities, environmental circumstances, cultural expectations, and most important, the recognition and messages received from significant authority figures.

Each person's script contains all of the elements of a stage drama. A drama—whether it is a play or a person's life script—progresses through various scenes and acts. And of course in life, as in a play, there is a final curtain.

As we follow our scripts, we play roles, act out themes, and select a cast of supporting characters. We rehearse and deliver dialogue. We even wear costumes appropriate to our character and designed to intrigue the audience. For example, a woman scripted to seduce men is likely to wear a "fitting" costume.

An important part of every play is its theme. So it is with individual scripts. Carol and Vivian followed the waiting theme. Here are some other life themes women have revealed to us. See if they fit any of the women (or men) in your life:

Working my fingers to the bone

Being strong

Suffering silently

Being seen and not heard

Waiting for someone to help me

Maintaining the family image

Keeping a stiff upper lip

Saving myself for someone special

Sacrificing myself for others

Working hard but never succeeding

Surrendering to others

Being the power behind the throne

Acting dumb

Always taking care of others

Giving my all for a cause

Taking a back seat

Always there when someone needs help

Being bitchy

Trying hard to please everybody, to be perfect, to do everything, to stay young, to always look beautiful

One woman discovered that her script theme was echoed in the old, popular song, "I Want To Be Happy, But I Can't Be Happy Till I Make You Happy, Too." She felt that she could not ever be happy unless the people around her were happy. As a result, she scurried about looking for unhappy souls, trying to get them to smile and feel better. At parties, she was attracted to people who looked sad, and she tried hard to cheer them up. Before leaving on a business trip, she made elaborate arrangements so that her husband would be happy while she was gone. At work she told jokes and poked fun at her co-workers, trying to keep everyone laughing. But since it was such an impossible task to keep everyone happy, she felt depressed much of the time. According to her script, she did not deserve to be happy in her own right.

The theme of a significant number of women is being smart only in a clever and devious way, not in a straightforward manner. These women learn that if they exhibit too many brains, they are likely not to be attractive to men. This same old theme shows up again and again—but sometimes in radically new attire.

A young woman student visited an authority on women's problems to collect information for a Master's thesis on women. The student arrived wearing a long, flowered dress, an army jacket and boots, and had a piece of towel tied around her long, unkempt hair. During the interview she was asked, "How are things with you? How are you getting along in graduate school?" The young woman looked up and without hesitation said, "It's really rough, particularly in graduate school, because if I show my brains, the guys ignore me."

Even though this young woman's costume was not traditional, her script was.

**STEPS TO
AWARENESS**

Parts of Your Script

Here is a chance to begin to examine your own script. Find a quiet, private place. Close your eyes and turn your awareness inward. Imagine yourself as very, very old—almost 100. Picture how you look, where you are, and who is with you. Savor the image for awhile.

Now imagine that somehow you know this is your last day. Allow your life to pass before your eyes as if on a stage or a movie screen. Be aware of the sights, sounds, feelings, smells, people, and situations that you experience.

After you have given yourself time to do this exercise, ask yourself:

- What is the title of my play?

- What is the theme?

- Who are the supporting characters? What parts do they play?

- Where is the scene? Does it change often, or does it remain pretty much the same?

- What is the turning point of the play?

- What happens in the final scene?

- What is the audience reaction to my play? Do I get a standing ovation? Does the audience clap politely? Fall asleep? Get up and leave?

- What did I regret doing?

- What did I regret *not* doing?

- What am I really glad I did?

- Is there something I'd like to change or do more of?

Sometimes a person must face death before facing life to its fullest.

Scripts take different turns.

- Constructive messages that are realistic in terms of the person's potential lead to *constructive and winning scripts.*
- Banal, empty messages that instruct a person to go nowhere lead to circular or *nonwinning scripts.*
- Hurtful, distorted messages, and in extreme cases death messages lead to *destructive or losing scripts.*

Scripts are not only of different kinds, but are also delivered with different intensities. Some scripts and messages are little more than suggestions or ideas delivered to a child in a rather soft manner. The child may not make decisions about these messages until he or she is a few years old. Later in life these messages may be relatively easy to evaluate and to accept or reject. At the other extreme are those scripts which authority figures deliver with a great deal of intensity, perhaps even cruelty. Some of these messages are passed on by withholding approval and affection or inflicting physical pain unless the stated or implied rules are followed. The child makes decisions early and tends to stick by them.

These kinds of scripts result in very hard personality patterns which later are literally harder to undo. People with such intense scripts often require outside help. In the process of evaluation, even people with softer, but still negative, scripts can benefit from bouncing them off other people. It helps anybody to gather ideas, opinions, and facts in order to clarify, evaluate, and make new decisions. Understanding congruence puts a handle on this idea.

Congruence and Scripts

A mark of winning scripts is *congruence.* A person's body, mind, and value system work together. There is a unity to what a person thinks, feels, and does. People who are congruent live what they speak. They laugh when they are happy, love when they are affectionate, turn red when they are angry. They also think. They think about their lives and where they are going. They know what they feel and do. They widen their winning streaks.

The congruent person lives a balance of thinking, feeling, and doing. Balance can be portrayed like this:

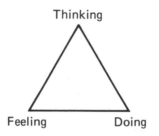

On the other hand, a mark of nonwinners and losers is *incongruence.* A person who is incongruent may feel affectionate and think it is all right to express that affection, but then does it through clenched teeth. Another incongruent person may think idealistic thoughts and feel righteous, but then work to keep "those people" out of the neighborhood. This person's doing is out of balance with thinking and feeling.

One woman whose feeling was out of balance and dysfunctional gave her flu-stricken friend public health statistics rather than comfort. She let her thinking totally govern her actions rather than considering feelings too.

Another woman whose thinking was dysfunctional fell madly in love with a succession of men who promised her the world but who ended up using and mistreating her. She let her feelings govern her actions, without putting her thinker in gear.

Still another woman whose doing was dysfunctional felt lonely and left out at a party. She kept on thinking about why she felt lonely, but rather than doing anything about it, she busily bustled around the kitchen, emptying ashtrays and picking up empty glasses. Her doing was out of balance with her thinking and feeling.

Degrees of congruence or incongruence are important aspects of each person's psychological life plan. The following questions can help you look at this part of your psychological script.

Balance in Your Life

When you consider *your* thinking, feeling, and doing, do you see one area not functioning as well as the others?

If so, what are two things you can do to bring your life into better balance?

How can you start bringing these things into your life this week?

You may want to keep these three elements in mind as you think about your life and the lives of women portrayed in this book.

THE SLEEPING BEAUTY SCRIPT

Women like Carol and Vivian feel and do, but they do not think enough. Their scripts follow a waiting theme like that of Sleeping Beauty. Does the following description of the Sleeping Beauty script fit any of the women in your life?

As a typical Sleeping Beauty script[5] develops, a little girl learns to think of herself as a future mommy—to the exclusion of any other possibilities. Her first toys, most likely baby dolls, reinforce this script. Later, she spends her time playing with her miniature ironing board, sink, stove, refrigerator, and dust mop. If she starts showing an interest in trucks or erector sets, she is often whisked back to her household items, with the admonishment, "That's not for girls."

By the time she is 10 to 12, she picks up the idea that she must attract boys. At this point, whatever her age, a discernible change occurs in her behavior.

She centers her interest on her appearance and spends hours locked in a bathroom. Hair, makeup, and clothes consume an abnormal amount of her time. She pages through magazines, looking for the exact equipment she needs to improve the bait. Madison Avenue appears in her life and appeals to her passion to be odorless, pimpleless, and alluring.

Even at this early age, she starts her process of going to sleep. She sleeps in terms of physical and social development.

So while other young people her age are roughhousing in a swimming pool, Sleeping Beauty is likely to be reclining on a nearby lounge chair. Sleeping Beauty does not get applause for taking an active part, so she becomes a spectator. She doesn't want to swim or splash in the water because it will ruin her hairdo, her eye makeup, and the image she is beginning to project of herself as the passively feminine, alluring young woman. As she sits at poolside, she may even raise one knee slightly to show off a budding calf. She feels that this makes her look like the beautiful women in the suntan lotion ads.

By the age of from 14 to 16, Sleeping Beauty has usually firmed up her life goals. At this point she sleeps. Instead of developing her academic skills or other unique talents, she stops struggling in math class. She doesn't take chemistry or physics, which are "for boys." She defends herself with, "Who needs it? I'm just going to get married anyway."

Sleeping Beauty and her brother may overhear their parents discussing the family's tight budget situation. Since there is enough money to send only one child to college, they conclude that "a college education is important for Johnny because he'll have to earn a living" and that an education for Sissy is nice but not really important. "After all, money for college is a waste if a girl is just going to get married." The children may accept these unquestioningly, even though most women will probably work 20 to 45 years in paid employment.

Sleeping Beauty almost always verbalizes her script. "Why should I study? I can get by without knowing all that stuff." She may use her anticipated status as wife and mother to rationalize her failure to develop on her own. "I'm just going to be a housewife."

If Sleeping Beauty does go to college, it is to get an M.R.S. degree. She does not think seriously about college as a means of developing a career or enhancing her own potential. She sleeps instead of learning.

A woman living out a Sleeping Beauty life drama sleeps in an almost literal sense as she waits for her rescue. This script gives her little purpose for living beyond her 40th year—when she will still have half of her life-time to go. When her life plan comes to its premature conclusion, she ends up feeling useless and sometimes even suicidal.

The Sleeping Beauty Script Is Out of Date

There was a time when this script satisfied a large number of women. How-ever, times have changed so rapidly that women with such scripts *now* often find their lives deeply troubled. Some advise their daughters, "What-ever you do, don't do what I did."

The average American woman's life now is very different from what it was around 1900. Then, women married at age 22 and produced large families, often giving birth until their menopause. Many women centered their goals exclusively on childrearing and homemaking. Extra hands were needed to work the land, and children were an economic asset. However, at that time a woman's life expectancy was less than 50 years.

Today's woman can expect to live nearly 80 years. She is likely to marry by the time she is 20 and to produce two children before she is 30. The following graph points out the dramatic change since 1900.

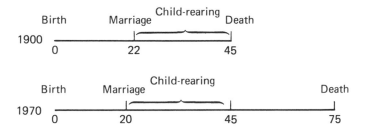

Lifetime of the Average American Woman: Then and Now [6]

The woman who has a Sleeping Beauty script often finds that her script runs out when she is in her 40s and *actually in the prime of her life.* The primary reasons for her existence have grown up and walked out the door. Like many people who retire from jobs, she feels finished, with nothing important to do.

Women are experiencing these feelings younger and younger. Some act them out by becoming runaway wives. In the past, men deserted their families more frequently than women did. Now twice as many women as men run away from a marriage. Common elements in the lives of these women are that their marriages are about ten years old, that their children are growing up, and that they are running away from someone, not run-ning to anyone.[7]

Sleeping Beauty Can Change

Sleeping Beauty can wake up and embrace her own existence. She can turn on to herself and reach for a richer, more satisfying, and more productive life. Awareness is the first step. Once Sleeping Beauty understands her script, she can take action.

She can:

- Stop waiting for someone or something to give direction to her life.
- Stop investing time in depression.

She can also:

- Start writing a new script, now that the old one has run out.
- Start setting fresh life goals that extend through her old age.
- Start learning again, opening her mind to a variety of people and experiences.
- Start figuring out what to do *right now* to add zest to her life.
- Start learning to enjoy her life no matter what her age—16, 46, or 86.

To start to change her script, Sleeping Beauty can ask herself:

- What am I doing now that I really enjoy?
- What do I seem to be good at?
- Do I have or do I need to acquire salable skills?
- What can I do right now to begin to establish fresh life goals?
- What specific plans can I make for my 50th year, 70th year, 100th year?

Sleeping Beauty is just one of a number of scripts that many women live out. In the next chapter, you will be reading about other scripts, including Cinderella, Little Red Riding Hood, and Mother Hubbard. You will also be discovering more about how women can become aware of the life dramas they unknowingly live out.

Living their lives as they were taught rather than discovering themselves and becoming themselves is common to many of the life dramas women act out. Putting on "acts" robs women of experiencing the richness of their full potential. Abraham Maslow observes that if people fail to develop their talents, if they live dull, uninteresting lives, if they do not develop workable methods of relating to other people, they know at some level that they have wronged themselves for it. Our real guilt results from our failure to live up to our own potential.[8]

As you read the next chapters, ask yourself, "How much of *my* life is based on compulsion and how much on choice?"

3

Once Upon a Time...

- What is your own personal script?
- How do women sometimes play the roles of Persecutor, Rescuer, and Victim instead of being authentic?
- In what ways are women's scripts like fairy tales?

Just for fun, take a few minutes to write a fairy tale which has a beginning, a middle, and a conclusion. Start your story:

"Once upon a time, there was a little . . .

When ———— grew up, . . .

And the story ended when. . . ."

When you have completed your story, lay it aside while you read more about how some lives are lived like fairy-tale themes. You will be coming back to *your* story toward the end of this chapter.

SCRIPTS ARE LIKE FAIRY TALES

Many women live out scripts that resemble the stories found in folklore, fairy tales, and mythology. Literature depicts women playing such parts as poor little match girls, babes in the woods, wicked witches, tyrannical step-mothers, would-be princesses, and young innocents who set about to rescue frogs in ponds and beasts in castles.

Do you know a woman whose life resembles any of the following?

- *Cinderella*, who learns to accept suffering while doing menial chores as she looks for a man who will rescue her from her awful drudgery;

- *Beauty* (and the Beast), who learns to feel self-righteous and virtuous in comparison to men and who believes in the magic of the love of a good woman;

- *Lady Atlas*, who learns to carry a huge load of miseries and to martyr herself at the altar of ingratitude;

- *Mother Hubbard*, who learns to take care of everyone else's needs but neglects her own and consequently seeks solace for herself from her cupboard or refrigerator;

- *Little Red Riding Hood*, who learns to entice men and then rebuke them as she treads her way through forests, parks, or lonely streets.

Women Play Roles

Whether a woman has learned to follow the script of a Little Red Riding Hood, Beauty and the Beast, or any of dozens of others, she plays her part from a favorite role. Classical roles in any drama are those of victim, rescuer, and persecutor. These roles can be phony script roles play-acted to fit the character, or they can be real.

Real victims suffer from life's real tragedies and real injustices. But phony Victims* not only solicit trouble, they thrive on it. They tenaciously hang on to problems no matter who tries to help. For example, women who follow the Sleeping Beauty script described in Chapter 2 often play Victim roles. They sleep and become helpless. They wait for someone to wake them up, rescue them, and get them going.

---

* Phony roles will be capitalized throughout this book.

Phony Rescuers offer help to others, but only to a certain point. The person they "help" never completely stops needing them. They basically assume that others are not-OK and foster dependency. In contrast, real rescuers help others become independent. No one is put down. No dependency is fostered. No strings are attached.

Phony Persecutors enjoy pointing a finger at problems and catching people in mistakes, but don't contribute to solutions. If you have heard someone say, "I hate to tell you this, but . . ." and smile while delivering the bad news, you may have been observing a phony Persecutor in action. Some people who act as limit setters, taskmasters, and critics are legitimate. Yet they may be seen as Persecutors by people who have learned to play the Victim role.

Steve Karpman has shown how these same three roles are acted out in everyday life. His drama triangle[1] not only portrays these roles, but also shows how people switch from one to another. For example, a woman playing a phony Rescuer may regularly volunteer to help out on different committees. Yet she ends up persecuting each committee head at the last minute by not producing the needed work. Thus she switches from Rescuer to Persecutor. When the committee heads get mad at her, she moves to the Victim's corner. Around they all go.

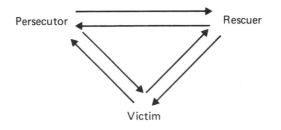

Karpman Drama Triangle

Another common script role is that of Seducer. Sometimes a Seducer plays a Victim role—for example, by acting helpless. But this is not always true. A Seducer may lay the bait by flirting, while having no intention of delivering the goods. Later comes a switch to the Persecutor or Rescuer role.

The following fairy tales parallel some women's lives.[2] As you read them, see if you can identify script roles and the switching of these roles.

In addition to roles, these scripts reflect the need for a better balance of thinking, feeling, and doing. As you read through each story, be aware that in most of these scripts, the women are not thinking enough. To encourage more "thinking," we have provided a list of questions and ideas after each script description.

CINDERELLA LOOKS FOR A FELLA

Cinderella not only loses her own good mother by death, desertion, or divorce, but also is cast off by her father. He chooses to marry a cold, demanding, bossy woman who rules him with an iron will and creates a pain-filled life for both him and his poor daughter. In this new and unhappy situation, Cinderella becomes melancholy and spends most of her time sitting alone "in the cinders." She cannot be happy until something or someone brings change and excitement to her life.

A real-life Cinderella, just like her fairy-tale counterpart, tends to have a strong "until" theme in her script. She cannot get away from the ashes *until* someone helps her out. She cannot meet the man of her dreams *until* someone fixes it up for her. She enjoys the ball, but only *until* midnight. She suffers the torments of her cruel stepsisters and stepmother *until* someone betters her position. She will not stop living poorly *until* she marries.

Her father, unhappy in his own marriage relationship, likely has a girlfriend on the side—perhaps a mistress. This "other" woman serves an important role for Cinderella even though, as Eric Berne points out, her own motives may be questionable.[3] Just why is this fairy godmother so interested in getting Cinderella out of the house? Perhaps it is because with Cinderella gone to the ball, she and Cindy's father can be alone, at least until midnight.

It takes a Rescue from her fairy godmother to get Cinderella into the "right" clothes, at the "right" place, at the "right" time. For some real-life Cinderellas, the "right" time and place frequently turn out to be Friday night at a swinging cocktail lounge in the city's financial district.

Though Cinderella is deluded into thinking that her Prince Charming will surely help her to live happily ever after, she has learned from her father an attraction to not-OK men. Fairy-tale Cinderella's ineffectual prince acts stupid—much more like a frog prince than a true prince. He forgets to get Cinderella's address, her telephone number, or even her name. He wants to marry her, even though he barely knows her. And then he sends another fellow around to see if the shoe fits. Even though this errand boy is straight and insists that Cinderella take her turn at the shoe while others scorn her, she pays him little mind, and his part in her cast of characters is fleeting.[4]

In her life drama, Cinderella first takes the Victim role. She learns to feel kicked, put upon, and bewildered. She plays the games of *Kick Me, Poor Me, Why Does This Always Happen To Me?*, and *See How Hard I*

Try. Later she becomes a coquettish teaser, playing *Try And Catch Me* with her prince and *I've Got A Secret* with her sisters. Finally, she surprises her Persecutors with *Now She Tells Us!* Then she switches to the Rescuer role, finding husbands for her mean sisters, whom she forgives, playing *What Would You Do Without Me?* and *Aren't You Glad I'm Such A Nice Girl?*

One real-life Cinderella told her story like this:

When I was a little girl, I really felt happy. But my mom and dad didn't get along and finally divorced. Mom had to struggle 'cause she didn't have any way to earn money, and Dad struggled to try to come through with child support.

Dad remarried when I was around 12. His new wife had a family of her own. He couldn't support me and his new family. So, since my mother's health was failing, it was easy to talk her into letting me go and live with him. Everyone agreed it would be a lot easier. But I never felt accepted by them. No matter what I did, it was never good enough. I got all the hand-me-downs. And it seemed like all the dirty jobs around the house were given to me. I got so I just wanted to be left alone.

Then I started to spend a lot of time with my mother's sister, Aunt Rosie. She kept in close touch with Dad and was about the only relative I could turn to. I don't know what I'd have done without Aunt Rosie. She made me clothes and seemed like the only source of comfort in a miserable time.

I really had a strong feeling that there was something better for me some place, if I could just find it. How I wanted to get out of that house! One night at a party, I met Peter. We hit it off right away. He was considered a real catch, and I had admired him from afar for quite a while. But I couldn't believe I'd ever meet him or that he would take an interest in me. Six months later, we married. Was my stepmother ever surprised!

I worked at the variety store while Peter finished up college. But now, after several years, I'm beginning to feel that he's never going to finish. He starts in one subject and then drops out and takes up a whole new major. I don't really like my job all that much, but I guess I'll have to put up with it until Peter finds his niche and gets settled in his career.

Many a Cinderella has a job, but it is likely to be at the lowest level within an organization. She may carefully file papers and reports that no one is interested in seeing again. Symbolically sweeping the "organizational hearth," she never aspires to move into a managerial or professional position, even if she has potential. Instead, she tends to feel that she does "other people's dirty work." Because she does her job and often does it well, people sometimes make demands on her time and talents. This gives her more cause for feeling victimized.

Although she may work very hard, her motives to achieve within the organization lie dormant. She clings to her illusion that some day, some way, she will be whisked away from this boring job. Or, she explains, "I know I hate this job, but I don't intend to be here long." She marks time; her life is in limbo while she looks for her prince.

Questions about career development are likely to annoy Cinderella. In fact, she may pooh-pooh equal opportunity for women. Sometimes she even expresses contempt for women interested in upward mobility: "Those pushy women make me sick." Later, if and when she's left her job, she may go back and visit the women she worked with. Even though she once felt they pushed her around, she remembers them kindly, sending them flowers and bringing cakes on their birthdays.

Some Cinderellas, however, invest many years of their life's time in low-level, nonchallenging jobs, believing that a better life is waiting somewhere out there. One such woman, who had marked time in the same position for 17 years, lamented, "I'd leave this job tomorrow if I could get married." Even though her past programming might have been well intentioned, holding such a delusion paralyzes her personal possibilities.

What Can a Cinderella Do?

She can:
- Stop living in the future.
- Stop looking for a rescue.
- Stop living through others.
- Stop marking time.
- Stop waiting *until*.

She can also:
- Start living now.
- Start developing her own potentials.
- Start setting realistic goals for her own accomplishments.
- Start going where men who like themselves and like women are likely to be.

- Start accepting that she can be her own fairy godmother for whatever goals she sets.

To start to change her script, Cinderella can ask herself:

- Do I *have* to let people push me around so I can then forgive my tormentors?
- How can I figure out ways to get what I want for myself?
- *If* I *never* find the right man, what am I going to do with my life and my time?
- Where do I expect to be in this organization in two years?
  In five years?
  In ten years?
- Will I be satisfied if my job keeps on going like it is now for the next ten years?
- What do I expect after the ball is over?

BEAUTY TENDS HER BEAST

Beauty is a Rescuer, programmed with the delusion that all a beastly man needs is a good woman. She unthinkingly utters, "Once he gets married to the right girl, I know he'll settle down." Or, "All he needs is the love of a good woman."

Beauty's father was probably not-OK; he needed, or appeared to need, reformation or transformation. Perhaps he was an alcoholic who needed to be rescued every Friday night by Beauty's mother. When the local bartender called with, "Mrs. Smith, your husband is causing trouble here again," she bundled Beauty into the car, and off they went to collect their troublesome man. Beauty and her mother received approval for being patient and long-suffering with their imperfect man.

Beauty's script leads her to believe that she and women in general represent the virtuous and pure sex. She believes that her magical Rescuer powers will transform not-OK men into handsome princes.

Not surprisingly, Beauty feels uncomfortable with happy, successful men. She knows neither how to pass time with a pleasant conversation nor how to behave. She is much more at ease with men who treat her like dirt. She knows what to say to them, how to act with them, and how to proceed with her drama. The dialogue and the direction of the plot are painful but clear.

One day Beauty finds herself "in love" with a fellow who has a problem. He may be a job loser, a chronic grouch, irresponsible, or addicted to alcohol or other drugs. But she still believes that his life with her will somehow make him better. Beauty and her Beast walk down the aisle. She waits for her magic to work its wonders.

After several years of futile attempts at reform, Beauty realizes that her Beast is not going to change. As a Rescuer, she has invested many years in the game *I'm Only Trying To Help You,* a phony rescue doomed to failure. Or, she may persecute with *I Told You So.* "If you keep drinking, you'll lose your job" soon becomes "I told you you'd lose your job."

At this time she may decide to martyr herself: "I've given this man the best years of my life, and this is what I get in return." Or, she may decide to unload this Beast and to look for someone else. But since Beauty is a Rescuer, she needs a Beast in order to complete her script. Here is how one Beauty moved through this script:

At 39, Sally divorced for the third time. Even though her father was an alcoholic, she chose as her first husband a man who was much like him. During their engagement, she said many times that she knew he would settle down just as soon as he had a home and a family. "All he needs is someone like me to take care of him." Three years of unhappy married life convinced Sally to give up trying to convert her drunken husband. She divorced him, declaring emphatically, "I'll never again marry a man who drinks."

She kept her promise. Husband number two was a felon. In and out of jail, he could never hold a steady job. Within four years, Sally decided to divorce him. This time she swore, "I'll never again marry a guy in trouble with the law. What a hassle."

Husband number three was neither an alcoholic nor a felon. He was a chronic gambler. Their marriage was a story of unpaid bills and fending off creditors. After seven years of living in financial chaos, Sally gave up trying to reform her third husband and divorced him.

Even after three bad marriages, Sally said of her new boyfriend, whom she described as a hypochondriac, "I know he would feel better if he would just settle down with a nice home and family."

Even though the facts seem obvious, Sally took a long time to see that she was just trading in one kind of beast for another. She had to give up the belief that each new marriage was a change for the better. She had to give up the belief that somehow, some way, she could transform beastly men into handsome princes.

Another, and perhaps more common, variation of the Beauty and the Beast script is reported by a woman concerned about her sister's unhappy life. She writes in a letter:

Beverly often dreamed as a small child of having a home with pale blue walls and just the right furniture. She also pictured a small garden outside. And somewhere in the picture was a husband who was going to make all this come true.

When Beverly met Bill during her second year in college, she felt immediately that he was the man to fill the spot in her dreams. She knew he had been reared in an unloving home situation and recognized that he did not accept love. Bev believed in the back of her mind that this would automatically change when she married him. Her love would change Bill into a different person. He would become the man in her dreams—her prince.

Even before they got married, Bev quit school in order to support Bill. When he was drafted, she followed him from base to base. Finally, they married. She later confessed that she felt she had "trapped" him because he hated the Army so much. She continued to follow him from base to base, living in small, dumpy apartments and decorating each place they lived in with bright curtains and flowers and little colored bottles on the window sills. No matter where they lived, she worked hard to create the illusion of her dream house.

When Bill got out of the service, Bev began to realize that her love wasn't a magic potion after all. Bill was still the same uncaring person he had been before they were married. He went back to college, but after three years changed his major and is now in another degree program. Bev is still working to support them. She works, takes care of the bills and groceries, fixes lunch—because he won't eat if it's not fixed for him—takes care of him, and takes care of everything else as well!

They're now in debt, and their small, one-bedroom apartment is in a run-down part of the city. She sees nothing that resembles her dream-house in the suburbs. Beverly is finally realizing that things are not going to work out the way she believed. But she feels she can't leave, because she talked him into marrying her.

What Can a Beauty Do?

Like Beverly, Beauties have disrupted personal lives. They are likely to work in low-level, low-paying jobs to support someone else's bad habits. They do not channel their energies toward developing their own skills, potentials, and talents, but instead either resign themselves to tending a beast or move from beast to beast, trying to find one who is more susceptible to their magic powers. In the meantime, their lives are passing by. A Beauty *can* change.

She can:

- Stop collecting people with problems.
- Stop rescuing people who don't want it, are not ready for it, don't respond to it.
- Stop believing that no matter how bad things are, everything will turn out all right in the end.

She can also:

- Start letting other people run their own lives.
- Start thinking and solving problems rather than depending on her magical power, "the love of a good woman."
- Start getting acquainted with happy, successful men, learning to be comfortable in conversations with them, and learning to appreciate their OKness.
- Start expecting to enjoy relationships with men.
- Start enjoying life and developing her personal talents.
- Start believing that she *deserves* a happy life.

To start to change her script, Beauty can ask herself:

- Is there anything similar about the men I'm attracted to?
- What are men like who like themselves and who feel good to be around?
- What would I do with my time if I weren't spending so much of it taking care of someone else?
- What are three things I'd really like to do for myself?

LADY ATLAS CARRIES A BURDEN OF MISERIES

In Greek mythology, Atlas displeased Zeus, the father of the Gods, and thus was doomed to hold the vault of Heaven on his shoulders. Even though in an encounter with Hercules he had the chance to give up his burden, he took it back. A modern-day Lady Atlas also bears the miseries and troubles of the world on her back, yet does nothing to get rid of them.

Lady Atlas is likely to repeat her trouble-filled story over and over again. Perhaps she is burdened with money problems, troublesome children, an unfaithful husband, or bodily aches and pains. She sighs a lot.

One Lady Atlas stood over the stove, stirring the evening's pot of stew and bemoaning her suffering for the sake of her ungrateful children and husband. They in turn played their parts, frequently complaining about the stew she cooked every Wednesday night despite their protests of not liking it.

Parents often suppress their own needs in order to care for their totally helpless infants. But a Lady Atlas never gives up this role. Even as her children grow up and become less dependent, Lady Atlas unknowingly develops ways to maintain a dependency relationship. She plays the part of the woebegone, eversuffering mother. For example, a Lady Atlas may not allow her children to bother her in the kitchen. But then she later laments, "No one lifts a finger to help me fix a meal." Or, she may give her son two shirts. Then, when he wears the green one, she expresses her disappointment with, "So you didn't like the blue shirt I gave you!"

A Lady Atlas in the office heads up 17 committees, among them the awards committee, the clean-up committee, the bond campaign, and the employee council. She takes on more and more responsibility. Finally, somebody suggests that she hire an assistant. "Oh, no," she says, shrugging off the suggestion, "it takes more time to train someone than it does to do it myself. If you want anything done right, you have to do it yourself."

A Lady Atlas supervisor may not completely train her subordinates. Then she complains, "I guess I'll have to stay late again so that this project gets out on time."

As a child, Lady Atlas probably was rewarded for working hard and "acting busy," but not for finishing her chores. You can recognize a grown-up Lady Atlas by her refusal to take action to solve her problems. She reacts to her troubles by suffering, often conspicuously, and wringing out every possible misery from each situation. She would not give up her problems for the world. After all, if her miseries all dropped away, what would remain of her script? What would she say to her friends? Think of the new scenes and acts she would have to learn!

Lady Atlas sees herself as a Victim. For example, she plays *Poor Me* games with a "woe is me" theme: *Ain't It Awful?*, *Harried Housewife*, and *Why Does This Always Happen To Me?* As the *third* large sack of groceries she wrestles out of the car trunk spills cans and cartons over the driveway, she wails, "Why does this always happen to me!"

Lady Atlas plays games like *Kick Me* and *Stupid* that eventually put her down. However, the people around her often end up feeling persecuted. She blames others for her troubles with the games of *If It Weren't For You* . . . and *See What You've Done To Me*. Her games, as well as her roles, reveal the suffering theme. Judith Viorst writes as follows.

Ida, the One Who Suffers

Whatever happens to me
Has already happened to Ida, the one who suffers,
Only worse,
And with complications,
And her surgeon said it's a miracle she survived,
And her team of lawyers is suing for half a million,
And her druggist gave a gasp when he read the prescription,
And her husband swore he never saw such courage,
Because (though it may sound like bragging) she's not a complainer,
Which is why the nurse was delighted to carry her bedpan,
And her daughter flew home from the sit-in in order to visit,
And absolute strangers were beginning to give blood donations,
And the man from Prudential even had tears in his eyes,
Because (though it may sound like bragging) everyone loves her,
Which is why both her sisters were phoning on day rates from Dayton,
And her specialist practically forced her to let him make house calls,
And the lady who cleans kept insisting on coming in Sundays,
And the cousins have canceled the Cousins Club annual meeting,
And she's almost embarrassed to mention how many presents
Keep arriving from girlfriends who love her all over the country,
All of them eating their hearts out with worry for Ida,
The one who suffers
The way other people
Enjoy.[5]

What Can a Lady Atlas Do?

Probably each of us has a little Ida or Atlas in us. It is not unusual to carry a knapsack of not-OK feelings about ourselves and resentments against others. However, Lady Atlas and Ida carry a large bundle. Their life scripts not only call for them to be miserable, but also to extract a certain pleasure from their miseries. A Lady Atlas *can* decide to put down her bundle of miseries.

She can:

- Stop feeling sorry for herself.
- Stop encouraging others to feel guilty.
- Stop talking about her miseries.
- Stop concentrating on things that went wrong.
- Stop asking, "Who's to blame for this?"

She can also:

- Start asking more questions like "How can we solve this problem?"
- Start analyzing the problem to see if anything can be done, and then take some action immediately.
- Start talking about strengths rather than weaknesses in herself, others, and situations.
- Start being straightforward about asking for and accepting help.
- Start encouraging other people to feel good rather than guilty.
- Start cultivating a mental garden that has more flowers than weeds.

To start to change her script, Lady Atlas can ask herself:

- What are the problems in my life that I think I have really solved?
- How can I more fully savor my successes?
- What specific steps can I take to straighten out some bad problems in my life now?
- What can I do so that other people feel, "I really like being around you"?

MOTHER HUBBARD GIVES AND GIVES AND GIVES

A Mother Hubbard usually learns her script from her own mother. She is programmed to be a perfect supermother, always taking care of the kids and Dad (whether or not they need it) and devoting herself to "doing" for the family.

Despite all her doing, her husband doesn't pay much attention to how she looks. She often dresses her part by wearing the same old jersey dress year after year or cast-off shirts the kids don't want any more. Since he works long hours, he usually goes to sleep on the couch right after dinner —just like her Dad used to do. She shoos the kids out of the living room, frequently admonishing them, "Now be quiet. Remember, we have to take good care of your father. He works so hard for us." Father rarely speaks for himself.

Having learned the Rescuer role well, Mother Hubbard compulsively cares for everyone's needs but martyrs her own, ultimately feeling victimized. Ringing through her head are messages like: "Do things for others," "Be a good helper," "Stand behind your man," "Make sure no one's hungry." As a result, she often feels uncomfortable if she eats her own dinner before everyone else is satisfied. Even the family dog may get fed before she eats. She plays the familiar games of *I'm Only Trying To Help You, What Would You Do Without Me? See How Hard I've Tried,* and even *Poor Me.* Her *Poor Me*'s include *Ain't It Awful About Me, Harried Housewife,* and *How Could You Do This To Me After All I've Done For You?*

She compulsively structures her time so as to meet the "needs" of others. She bakes cookies for the children's meetings, gives the best birthday parties in the neighborhood, and always serves large and lavish meals whenever there are guests for dinner. She reupholsters the furniture in the family room, takes care of the garden, readily drops everything to drive the kids to the recreation center, and is always available to take a neighbor to the doctor. Even though she tends to be a bit overweight, the family shows her its appreciation by buying her a mixmaster for Mother's Day, a deep-fat cooker for her birthday, and a stove for the Holidays.

If Mother Hubbard has a job, she usually offers to work the Friday after Thanksgiving or to stay late on New Year's eve, and she agrees to take her vacation at the least desirable time each year. She always bakes the cake for office birthday parties. But when a co-worker praises her with, "That is a great birthday cake," Mother Hubbard humbles herself with, "It wasn't anything. It was only a cake mix."

Mother Hubbard often feels guilty and embarrassed when someone tells her she is doing a good job. If a friend compliments her on how well she refinished the old chest, she might quickly point out, "It wasn't in bad condition to begin with or I'd have made a mess of it."

Since Mother Hubbard doesn't accept much recognition for what she does, she seeks satisfactions elsewhere. For example, she not only cooks a lot, but also eats a lot. Her main source of pleasure is opening her cupboard or refrigerator. Sometimes she keeps booze in her cupboard, like Ethyl:

After all I've done around here, all I hear is complaining. "Ethyl this, Ethyl that! Why did you do this? Why don't you stop that?" I'll admit that once in a while I have a little too much sherry, and then I never hear the end of it! Well, what do they expect of me anyway? I spend all day cleaning and cooking and who cares? The kids are always gone. No one's home. It's like running a hotel, with nobody paying.

Sometimes a Mother Hubbard talks a lot—in a one-way monologue. People who spend time with her complain, "She's talking when I walk out of the room, and she's still talking when I step back in. It doesn't seem to make any difference whether I'm there or not."

Mother Hubbard's motto is "Never enough." It's not good enough for her to be competent on the job. She also needs to keep a perfect house, be creative, and act like an all-round superwoman. Give at the office, give at home, give to the neighbors—*give, give, give, give* is Mother Hubbard's life. But her giving is not out of genuine caring. She follows her self-defeating script, sacrificing her own needs and collecting resentment underneath. How disappointing others are! It is little wonder that as she continues to give and give, her cupboard becomes bare.

Women can act out this script many ways—even with their friends.

Vicki gained a reputation among her friends for giving elaborate dinner parties. She specialized in complicated French menus.

After the dinners, her guests frequently offered to help do the dishes and clean up. But Vicki adamantly refused all offers. Later, after all the guests had left and Vicki was still surrounded by an array of glasses and dishes and a kitchen full of dirty pots and pans, she griped to her husband, "You know, you'd think people would realize that we both have to work. But there they go, skipping out of here without so much as lifting a finger. I try my best to be a good hostess, but I only end up with a mess to clean up. Why does everybody take me for granted?"

What Can a Mother Hubbard Do?

A Mother Hubbard who decides to live a more balanced life can:

- Stop acting like Supermother.
- Stop assuming that others cannot ever get along without her.
- Stop using defeating ways to feel satisfied.
- Stop feeling good only when giving.

She can also:

- Start sharing parenting responsibilities with other people.
- Start feeling good about the independence of others.
- Start taking care of her health.
- Start listening to others.
- Start *really* caring about others.

To start to change her script, Mother Hubbard can ask herself:

- What do I do well in addition to mothering?
- What do I really want for myself?

- How can I ask for what I want?
- How can I encourage others to take responsibility for their own welfare?

LITTLE RED RIDING HOOD
REJECTS MORE THAN HER SHARE OF MEN

Little Red Riding Hood's mother allowed her daughter to walk alone through unsafe areas of the woods or tough areas of the city. She also sent her daughter on errands without telling her what she should watch out for and how to be careful. As a result, Little Red Riding Hood's errands frequently took her where there were men who acted like wolves. She was like a "babe in the woods." Later, when Little Red Riding Hood was a teenager, her mother objected only mildly to her hitchhiking.

As a child, Little Red is likely to have been approached sexually by a grandfatherly man (perhaps even her own grandfather). She had trusted the older man, but then felt she couldn't tell on him. Now, as a woman, her life is filled with dirty old wolves and would-be rescuers. She attracts young wolves, but rebuffs them as poor comparisons to the "older man" of her early experiences. She frequently finds herself having to ward off "uncalled for" passes. After all, she was "only stopping by to have a quiet drink" in a bar alone or merely taking a midnight stroll through Times Square.

Even though Little Red Riding Hood looks innocent, she also looks sexy, perhaps in a naive way. Her very naivete is seductive. She plays *Rapo*, communicating sexual availability but then actually rejecting those who nibble at the bait. Other people end up feeling put down and frustrated by her.

Even as an adult, Little Red spends much of her time running errands here and there in the excited manner of a little girl. If Little Red works in an office, she is the one most likely to pull on her red coat and go out for coffee and sandwiches. She usually takes a path where she has to brush off wolves along the way. If in her travels she runs across a problem, she calls for help from a nearby rescuer, but she does little rescuing herself.[6]

Eric Berne describes a Little Red Riding Hood script as having these dynamics:

1. Her mother must have sent her on errands to grandmother's house when she was a little girl.
2. Her grandfather must have played with her sexually during those visits.

3. She must be the one most likely to be chosen to run errands in later life.

4. She must be contemptuous about men her own age and curious about older men.

5. She must have a naive kind of courage, confident that there will always be someone to rescue her if she gets into trouble.[7]

Little Red encourages the men in her life to play *Let's You and Him Fight*. Here is the way one woman acted out this part of her script:

Sacha frequently pleaded with her husband's best friend to be rescued from her identity crisis as a woman. "After 11 years of marriage, Carl still doesn't understand who I really am." Her husband's best friend listened to her maidenly cries of distress and offered an occasional word of gentlemanly advice gleaned from his years of experience. As the relationship evolved from counseling to consoling, Sacha's husband began to get suspicious. She answered his questions with, "You just don't understand me the way Vincent does. I'm confused and I want a separation so I can think it through." Then as Sacha stepped back and watched her husband and his formerly best friend fight over her, she smilingly confided to her neighbor, "Men are all alike. I don't know if I want to have anything to do with either of them!"

A variation on the Little Red Riding Hood script is the Little Pink Riding Hood theme. Like Little Red, Little Pink lacked parental guidance. She is likely to be a "babe in the woods," but her "help others, do your work, and don't complain" message compels her to sit and wait for people to come by who need her help. Although Little Pink has lots of friends, they leave her out in the end. Abandoned once more, she is sad and depressed and feels like an orphan. She plays the part of a waif, sitting sadly and feeling sorry for herself.

She and Little Red tend to clash, as in this fantasy dialogue written by Eric Berne:

"Where are you going?" asked Pink. "I've never seen you around here before."

"I'm taking my grandmother some sandwiches my mother made," replied Red.

"Oh, how nice," said Pink. "I don't have any mother."

"Furthermore," said Red proudly, "when I get to my grandmother's, I'm going to be eaten by a wolf—I think."

"Oh," said Pink. "Well, a sandwich a day keeps the wolf away. And it's a wise child that knows her own wolf when she meets him."

"I don't think those merry quips are funny," said Red. "So good-by."

"How stuck-up can you get?" asked Pink. But Red had already departed. "She has no sense of humor," thought Pink to herself, "but I think she needs help." So Little Pink Riding Hood struck out into the forest to find a hunter who would protect Little Red Riding Hood from the wolf. Eventually she found one, an old friend of hers, and she told him that Little Red Riding Hood was in trouble. She followed him to the door of the hut where Red's grandmother lived and saw everything that happened there. Little Red in bed with the wolf, the wolf trying to eat her, the hunter killing the wolf, and he and Little Red laughing and joking as they cut the wolf open and put stones in his belly. But Red didn't even bother to thank Pink, which made Pink sad. And after it was all over, the hunter was better friends with Red than he had been with Pink, which made Pink even sadder. She was so sad that she began to eat peppy berries every day, and then she couldn't sleep, so she would eat sleepy berries at night. She was still a cute kid and still liked to help people, but sometimes she thought the best thing to do would be to take an overdose of sleepy berries.[8]

In real life, Haughty Red and Sad Pink seldom get along. They don't complement each other or really help each other out. They intuit that they have something in common, but when their paths cross, Red takes advantage of Pink's rescue, whereupon Pink complains and feels sad. If they would give up their scripts, they could become friends.

What Can a Little Red Riding Hood Do?

A Little Red Riding Hood can:

- Stop being ever available for running errands.
- Stop being in the wrong place at the wrong time.
- Stop the quest for younger men to put down.
- Stop the eternal search for the older man who will put excitement back into life.
- Stop running around like a little girl.

She can also:

- Start facing life with the dignity of a woman.

- Start seeing men as individuals.
- Start protecting herself from unsafe situations.
- Start bringing excitement into life on the basis of her own accomplishments.

To start to change her script, Little Red Riding Hood can ask herself:

- How can I be more accepting of men my own age?
- How do I attract men now?
- How can I relate to men without putting them down?
- How can I enjoy my own sexuality more?
- What can I learn to do that I enjoy entirely for myself?

WOMEN FOLLOW STILL OTHER SCRIPTS

In addition to Little Red Riding Hoods and Mother Hubbards, many literary characters are script prototypes for contemporary women.

Rapunzel, who grows her hair waist length in the hopes of attracting and aiding her own Rescuer.

Lady Robin Hood, who works for a welfare agency and feels that she's robbing from the rich and giving to the poor.

Goldilocks, who with a flip of her innocent curls goes into strangers' offices and rips off the supplies and at night goes from bed to bed to find one that "fits just right."

Poor Little Match Girl, who perishes unaided in the flicker of her last match because nobody loves her.

Snow White, who when sent out by a jealous step-mother to perish, surrounds herself with safe, "small" men, each with a flaw. She waits and wishes to be found and rescued.

Wendy, who accepts and mothers a Peter Pan— the man who refuses to grow up and who forever remains a litle boy, but who later abandons Wendy for a younger woman, perhaps her own daughter.

Hera, who spends much of her life's time jealously tracking the escapades of an unfaithful husband, but gets her gratification from the chase and never does anything about it.

> *Europa,* who is seduced by a lot of sweet-smelling bull and is carried away from her homeland without a complaint.

Echo, who is forever destined to live in a cave, never thinking for herself but only echoing what other people say.

> *Little Miss Muffet,* who sits on her tuffet, eating or drinking while waiting for something exciting to jump out at her.

MEN FOLLOW FAIRY-TALE THEMES TOO

All of the fairy-tale script roles described earlier have their male versions.

Cinderfellas, who live woebegone lives while seeking a rescue from rich widows who frequent vacation resorts.

> *Horatio Algers,* who must struggle hard to make it from rags to riches and who need Rescuers along the way.

Sir Atlases, whose shoulders grow weary from carrying the burdens of the world—burdens they dare not unload or problems they dare not solve.

> *Pygmalions,* who like Professor Higgins in *My Fair Lady* must fashion their own perfect women to love—who strive to turn a "sow's ear into a silk purse."

Little Lame Princes, whose masculinity and potency are put down or rejected by the kings and queens in their lives, and so they need the Rescue of a Fairy Godmother—perhaps Mary Jane—which will allow them to fly from their towers and to be turned on to the trees and the grass and the flowers.

Script characters complement each other. Every Beauty needs a Beast. And a Beast may look for Beauty. The woman who plays a Victim role will be attracted to the man who plays Rescuer or Persecutor. The woman who is scripted as the helpmate will feel attracted to the man who has his sights on getting to the top, no matter what. As in the song, some enchanted evening, across a crowded room, these two are likely to find each other—to click, not knowing what really compels them to want to be together.

Movies, television, books, and comics also offer us reflections and reinforcements of heroines and hero types. The scatterbrained lady who wins out over her husband, family, and neighbors is not uncommon. Indeed, a people can often be judged by their heroes and heroines.

You may identify closely with one of the script figures mentioned in this chapter. You may also see bits of yourself or others in many of them. The few examples, whole or combined, provide a basis for you to begin to develop a clearer understanding of *your* specific script.

**STEPS TO
AWARENESS**

Beginning to Identify Your Script

Answering the following questions can help you start the journey to learn more of what your script is about.

Which fairy tale do you identify with the most? Why?

If you identify with parts of several fairy tales, which parts?

What favorite role do you play—Victim, Rescuer, Persecutor? Other?

Do you see yourself playing more than one role? Which ones? In what situations do you switch roles?

What parts do your supporting cast members play?

Are these roles, themes, etc., really what you want to do with your life?

If not, what do you want to change?

Now go back to your fairy tale: Read over the fairy tale you wrote at the beginning of this chapter.

Does it have anything to do with you?

- If so, in what ways?

    What is your character?

    Where is your life leading?

    What role did you play—Victim, Rescuer, or Persecutor?

- Is it like any of the fairy-tale characters mentioned earlier?

- If so, which ones?

If your story did not have anything to do with you:

- Whom did you write about?

- Is this person important to you now?

If you were writing your perfect story, what parts would be different?

- Would you have more thinking, feeling, or doing?

- What would you have to commit yourself to to make more of your "perfect" story come true?

POLARITIES SHOW UP IN SCRIPT CHARACTERS

Most script characters are like Jekyll and Hyde. Their personalities have opposite poles. One way to get in touch with the full range of a script character is to become aware of these polarities. For example, in every mild-mannered Clark Kent lurks a Superman, who can leap tall buildings in a single bound to pull off the superhuman rescue. Both Clark Kent and Superman rescue women, but neither wants to be close to one.

A few possible script polarities are:

- The humble chore girl and the beautiful, mysterious woman at the ball.
- The nagging bitch and the pious savior.
- The overworked family cook and the saintly supermother.
- The naive waif and the sly seductress.
- The saintly looking bank teller who toils for 20 years without a complaint and the woman who retires early on the nickels and dimes she has embezzled.

Even though both extremes may exist in one person, it is common that the individual is in touch with only one. One facet of the script character eludes awareness. For instance, the Mother Hubbard in our example feels put upon, but does not see how she persecutes others with the weekly stew. Do you see any "opposite poles" in your life drama?

An important thing to remember about scripts is that they *can be changed*. Just as a story can be written, it can also be rewritten. To do this well, you need to know what parts of your story are not right for you. In the next chapter you will learn how childhood experiences shape your own personal script. You will also find some suggestions for making the positive changes you decide you want.

Learning to identify script characters and characteristics can be exciting and fun. It also opens up options. The time of your life belongs to you. What do you need to feel and think and do to *really* live "happily ever after"?

4

Mirror,
Mirror,
on the Wall

- How do childhood experiences influence your script?
- In what ways are women trained to focus on their appearance?
- How do groups form collective scripts, and how do these scripts affect individual women?

I see myself through the eyes of others.
I hate waking up wondering what they think of me.
Am I ugly? Am I beautiful?
What shapes do I form in the eyes of their minds?
Oh, God, I hope they like me.
Please let them like what they see.

Dorothy Jongeward

When Jane was a little girl, she decided that she was too homely to be loveable. Her family's pet name for her was "Plain Jane." Her mother and father often stepped back and examined her with hopeless dismay, agreeing that she was the ugly duckling of their brood. When she was a little older, they frequently warned her, "Jane, if you're always so plain-looking, you'll have to have a career."

Without being fully aware why, Jane took her family's opinion and direction seriously. In high school she excelled in math, concentrated on a college prep course, and shunned school dances. With her family's resignation rather than support, she entered college as a civil engineering major. There she filled her days diligently studying, recalling, "I never :llowed a silly social life to interfere with my class work. Anyway, who'd have been interested in me!"

After graduation she began work with a new branch of a small government agency, gradually assuming more responsibility. Now Jane is 42, single, and heads a major research and development program. In spite of her professional accomplishments, however, she finds it difficult to feel good about her career successes.

When she goes home on holidays to visit her family, she still spends much of her time listening to her parents and sisters lament her failure as a woman. To them, Jane's career indicates a failure rather than a success. "To really be successful," Jane shrugs, "I should have been pretty enough to attract a man and not have to work."

Even now, her mother often remarks to Jane's sisters, "It's really too bad about Jane. She's so dedicated to her career. If only some man could have gotten to know her and discovered how nice she really is, the poor thing wouldn't have to be knocking herself out with that job today."

Like Jane, we all make decisions in early childhood. Feeling that she had no choice, Jane structured her life's time—her education, goals, and professional and social lives—to conform to the early messages she had received and the decisions she had made. She had no real data that men would not be attracted to her. Yet she made this assumption and arranged her life accordingly. Even though her colleagues and friends today see Jane as successful, she still suffers nagging feelings of being a failure.

From childhood experiences, Jane decided, "I'm plain" and "Men won't like me." She fulfilled her own prophecy by dedicating her life to a career she did not feel good about and avoiding men, convinced and fearful of their rejection.

WE BASE OUR SCRIPTS ON OUR EARLY DECISIONS

All children receive messages about themselves and others. Yet each child has unique experiences: some joyful or tragic, some protective or brutal, some loving or rejecting. From these messages and experiences, they eventually make decisions about themselves and their world.

Based on their decisions, children adopt psychological positions. These positions may be generalized into: I'm OK or I'm not-OK, and You're OK or You're not-OK (They're OK or They're not-OK). Jane's positions were: I'm not-OK as a woman, Men are OK, Beautiful women are OK. Once having taken such positions, a person manipulates people and situations to reinforce them. Thus a script is written, and the show begins.

The process Jane followed is typical. The formula for her script looks like this:

Early experiences: ↓	"You're plain. You won't attract men. You'll have to work."
Early decisions: ↓	"I'm plain. Men won't like me. I'll have to earn my way."
Psychological positions: ↓	"I'm not-OK. Men are OK. Beautiful women are OK."
Script formation: ↓	Plain Jane.
Script-reinforcing behavior:	Jane avoids men, works hard, but doesn't savor her successes.[1]

Most of us follow this sequence in developing our personal scripts. Becoming aware of this process is the first step to either affirming or changing our scripts.

**STEPS TO
AWARENESS**

Your Early Experiences

To begin to understand how your script evolved, take a few minutes, relax, and think back to your childhood.

- When you were little, what was the *best* thing that anyone ever said or did to you?

- Reexperience this event in your life. Remember and feel now what you felt then.

- When do you feel this way now?

- What was the *worst* thing ever said or done to you?

- Be aware of the pain or anger you felt then.

- How and when do you experience this feeling now?

- What was the best thing said to you because you were a little girl (boy)?

- What did you feel worst about because of being a little girl (boy)?

- Did anyone tell you *who* you were like?

- What were you called when you were a child? Does it have anything to do with your script?

- Did you have a nickname? Is it still used?

- Did anyone ever tell you where you would end up?

- What are you doing *now* that other people told you to do *then*?

- Go back over those things you thought about and listed, asking yourself, "How do these incidents affect my thinking, my feeling, and my doing today?"

- Is this what you want to be thinking, feeling, and doing now?

- If not, what can you do about it?

- Ask yourself, "What am I really willing to do?"

- Now imagine what your experiences would have looked and felt like if they had been perfect.

  See yourself as a child getting what would have met your needs.

  Repeat this fantasy as often as you can. Continue to mentally picture yourself getting what you wanted.

  What is the feeling you experience when you get what you need?

  What could you do to experience this feeling more often now?

Childhood Messages Influence Our Decisions

The messages children receive about themselves and others come from the significant authority figures in their lives. These messages take the form of values, expectations and limitations, approval or disapproval, encouragement or discouragement, and the prompting of proper and improper patterns of behavior. From these messages, children form their first inklings of how they are supposed to live their lives as adults.

Messages mingle in our minds from many perspectives.

- A little girl who *sees:*

  her mother acting helpless
  > may decide that acting helpless is part of being a woman.

  her mother putting down men
  > may contemptuously make fun of the boy next door.

  her father always rejecting her mother's ideas
  > may learn to believe that her own ideas are worthless.

  her mother always postponing important decisions
  > may, as a teenager, herself say, "Oh, I don't know. Let's ask the fellows what they think we should do tonight."

  her father and mother sticking out a hostile or indifferent marriage
  > may feel guilty even considering divorce.

  the members of her family treating one another with mutual respect
  > may easily take turns with her brother babysitting their younger sister.

- Messages are also *heard:*

  What might a little girl decide about herself if someone important to her consistently says, "Good grief, you're just like a girl! If your head weren't attached, you'd lose it!"?

  What might a little girl come to believe if she is frequently teased with, "Men never make passes at girls who wear glasses!"?

  What message might a little girl receive if she overhears her father bragging, "Our department has the cutest chicks in the whole company"?

  What effect might a mother have if her daughter overhears her proudly saying to a neighbor, "This child has never given me a moment's trouble. I wish all my children had been girls!"?

- Messages are also *felt:*

  If a little girl receives smiles or nods of approval for figuring out tough problems, she will probably learn to respect her intelligence.

  If a little girl's parents shrug indifferently when she excitedly bursts through the back door to announce that she has just been picked for the sandlot baseball team, she will probably learn to put down her athletic ability.

Negative Messages and Injunctions. The strongest negative messages people receive are usually communicated at a feeling level. Since the negative part is frequently mixed with a more easily identified positive one, these negative messages are difficult to recognize. After redecision therapy,[2] one woman recognized what had happened in her life. "When my parents kept insisting over and over that they *really did want* a baby girl, part of the message was actually, 'I shouldn't have been me. I should have been a boy!'" Two of the most destructive messages for men or women communicate: "You shouldn't have been born" and "You were born the wrong sex."

Mary and Bob Goulding,[3] in their development of redecision therapy, identify the 12 major negative messages—injunctions—many people receive:

Don't	Don't be a child
Don't be	Don't be a grownup
Don't be you	Don't be important
Don't be sane (or well)	Don't belong
Don't make it	Don't think
Don't be close	Don't feel

Getting in touch with any of these 12 negative injunctions and with other messages is a vital step on the path to personal growth and fulfillment. Many women, especially, face the problem of dealing with the messages: "Don't grow up," "Don't think," and "Don't be important." Other women have reported living by the messages:

Don't enjoy sex	Don't exist
Don't be natural	Don't change
Don't like yourself	Don't be happy

Many injunctions are sent in such a way as to say, "Be something but not something else." For example:

Be emotional
    but don't feel your body.
Be clever
    but don't be intelligent.
Stay alive
    but don't really live.
Be perfect
    but don't achieve excellence.
Be cute
    but don't be beautiful.

Just as messages are sent in various ways, they are also sent about a variety of subjects. Begin to discover the kinds of messages women are likely to receive from the important people around them. As you go through the following exercise, be aware of how childhood messages may be influencing *your* life drama today.

**STEPS TO
AWARENESS**

Childhood Messages

As you read through each of the following questions, think about the comments you heard as a child. You may find it interesting to do this exercise with another person or with a group. Do not be concerned about whether the message was true or false; just ask yourself, "Was it frequently repeated or implied?"

What are the messages you received about:

the importance of your intelligence?

the intelligence of women in general?

your ability to solve problems?

your ability to deal with mechanical things?

your education?

your vocation?

earning money?

marriage?

children?

your relationship to men?

your body?

your ability to excel in sports?

feminine behavior?

masculine behavior?

leadership?

your place in religion?

your spiritual life?

your ability to drive cars, buses, and trucks?

working mothers?

your future duties?

your physical agility and grace?

touching your genitals?

the importance of your appearance?

You probably discovered some new insights about yourself. Now ask:
"How do these messages affect what I'm doing in my life now?"

"How do they affect my relationships with men and with women?"

"What impacts me in a positive way?"

"What impacts me in a negative way?"

"How can I build more of my life around the positive?"

What messages might a *typical* little girl growing up hear? Are they similar to those you received? Are they different? If so, in what ways?

Now ask yourself what a *typical* little boy would be likely to hear about these questions. How are his messages different from a little girl's? From yours? Think about how different messages affect the scripts of most men and women.

OUR SCRIPT DECISIONS CAN BE REDECIDED

In their outstanding work on redecisions, Mary and Bob Goulding point out how our early decisions form the most powerful force in our lives' direction, affecting what we do each day.[4] As infants and young children, each of us picked up all the messages—verbal and nonverbal—and decided on the answer to the question, "What do I have to do to survive around here?" Most of us do not remember the early survival tactics we used. However, through therapy or other avenues to self-discovery, we can get in touch with our early childhood decisions.

One woman going through this process recalled having decided: "I'm going to get hurt if I get close to people." She explained, "This is what I've been doing all my life. I'm easy to get acquainted with and super friendly. But if anyone tries to get too close, I get scared and shut 'em out."

Another woman discovered that as a little girl she had decided: "I'm smart. I can figure it out." She continued, "I didn't realize how important it was for me to be given a chance to tie my own shoes, open my own toy chest, and play games at my own speed. As a result, I've done things all my life that many women are afraid to try."

Here are other script decisions women have shared with us:

- Decisions about themselves:
  I'll never amount to anything.
  I know my place.
  I've got my head on straight.
  I can make it if I try hard enough.
  I can't do anything right.
  I'm not important.
  I don't deserve any better.
  I don't deserve to live.
  I'm as solid as a rock.
  I should be seen but not heard.

- Decisions about others:
  People can't be trusted.
  Someone will always help me.
  Other people have all the answers.
  Men are stupid little boys.
  Women are pushy.
  People should know what I want.

Most people do their best.

People come and then they go.

They don't deserve to live.

As the Gouldings demonstrate, decisions can be redecided. If we make wrong or defeating decisions as children, we can redecide and take a different path as grownups. This process takes place at both the thinking and feeling levels. Intellectual insight into the original decision is important and necessary. But getting in touch with the feeling-level experience is vital for change. This frequently means going back and reexperiencing the first scene in which the decision was made, making the decision explicit, and then redeciding in a way that better fits life today.

One woman going through the redecision process recalled an incident with her father. Part of her dialogue with a counselor went like this:

SYBIL: Sometimes I feel that I don't deserve to live. I want people to like me, but you know how friends are. They just end up leaving you high and dry.

COUNSELOR: When did you feel that way before?

SYBIL: I've always felt that way. Familiarity breeds contempt.

COUNSELOR: Who did you want to be close to when you were little?

SYBIL: (eyes tearing) I wanted my father to love me more than anything.

COUNSELOR: What happened when you wanted your father to love you?

SYBIL: Every time I wanted to be close—wanted to be held or hugged—he pushed me away. (crying) Once I fell off a swing and my knees were bleeding. I ran into the house crying. (sobbing) My mother and father were fighting. I ran to my father, but he pushed me down as he stormed out of the room. "If it weren't for you, I wouldn't have had to get married!"

COUNSELOR: What did you decide when you heard that?

SYBIL: (sobbing heavily) I don't deserve to be here. I've got to really be good if I'm going to be here. (long pause) That's what's been going on. I've filled my days doing and doing and doing. Every day I try to justify my birth. I've got to be the best at everything. I never feel good about any of the things I do. I always believe there's more I should have done. (pause, sobbing quiets some, then speaking loudly) It's not my fault I was born. My father didn't have to get married. I don't have to apologize for being here. It's OK for me to be here. *It's OK!*

The feeling of redecision stayed with Sybil for days. She described it as being on Cloud 9. A weight had been lifted off her. She no longer felt compelled to follow an archaic script issue.

The Issues in Our Scripts

Every person's script deals with three key questions:

1. Who am I as a person? As a woman? As a man?
2. What can I do here? Professionally? Personally? Sexually?
3. And who are all these other people?[5]

Each of us, for better or worse, answers these three questions when still very young. Think about the different life dramas that might emerge from the following sets of assumptions. What would a woman be like today if as a little girl she had decided:

"I'm stupid and ugly."

"I'll never get anywhere."

"You can't trust anyone."

or

"I can figure these things out, and I'm attractive."

"I can do lots of the things I try."

"Most people are pretty fair."

or

"I have the right answers."

"I could do OK if it weren't for this rotten world."

"Men are brutes."

**STEPS TO
AWARENESS**

Your Early Decisions

To begin to see more clearly the connections between events and decisions in *your* early life and the way you may be living today, consider the following questions. (You'll probably find it useful to do this exercise again at different times.)

Close your eyes and let your thoughts go back over your childhood. Then think of one childhood incident that stands out vividly in your memory. Picture in your mind everything you can remember about the event. What did it look like? Feel like? What were the textures? What did it smell like? What were people saying? What did you say? Now that you have zeroed in on the event, ask yourself:

What decisions did I make as a result of this experience? About myself? About others? About how the world is?

Were my decisions about men and women different?

What specific things do I do now that reinforce these early decisions?

When I reexperience this early scene, how do I feel?

When do I feel this way now?

Is this feeling appropriate to my current situations?

Is this doing and feeling the best way to take care of myself today?

If your decisions and feelings are not appropriate for today, what could you change?

What is your plan?

Going through this process with other vivid incidents can give you further insights into your script and the reasons for your behavior today. (If your early life was filled with trauma and recalling old incidents brings you more pain than you think you can handle, seek the help of a qualified professional.)

You may find it useful to develop a dialogue and speak out loud to the people or situations you thought about. Try using Dr. Frederick Perls' unique role-play method.[6] Only three props are necessary: two chairs and a box of Kleenex, just in case. As you role play a part of yourself (or a part of a dream or an ailment or tension), sit in one of the chairs and begin a dialogue with "I." It is helpful to start with what you are feeling. When you seem ready, switch to the other chair and talk back to yourself, responding to what you said while you were in the other chair. Do and say whatever comes to mind. Continue your dialogue until you feel that it has been completed.

Now find a private place. Arrange two places to sit. Imagine that the child you once were is sitting in one chair. Sit in the other and speak to your inner child about this incident. Then be yourself as a child and speak back. Allow an animated dialogue to develop between you. Don't be afraid to talk out loud to yourself. It helps to integrate and clarify old experiences. Continue until you feel that the dialogue has come to a natural finish.

DECISIONS LEAD TO PSYCHOLOGICAL POSITIONS

Based on our early experiences, messages, and decisions, each of us develops a position about ourselves and those around us. These positions can be generalized into:

I'm OK or I'm not-OK

and

You're OK or You're not-OK.

Some people may feel totally "I'm OK" or "I'm not-OK." However, most of us feel OK about some parts of ourselves and not-OK about others. For instance, a person may feel both competent and confident on the job, but feel not-OK in a sexual role.

The classic example of a person who feels OK vocationally but not-OK sexually is recorded in the myth of Cadmus.[7] Although Cadmus was a competent leader who built the city of Thebes, his family life, where his sexual role was important, was plagued with tragedy. All four of his daughters suffered great misfortunes, and his only son met a terrible death in his youth. Grief followed his descendents. The tragic Oedipus was the great-great-grandson of Cadmus.

You may know a modern-day Cadmus who as a business executive skillfully manages a large number of people, but who arrives home each night to an unhappy personal scene. The children may be in trouble with the law or have personal failures in their lives. The spouse may be bored with their relationship. A contemporary Cadmus might feel belittled or even humiliated at home.

In the past, many men developed Cadmus-type scripts. Think about the men you know. How many of them were taught the techniques and importance of fatherhood or the skills of husbanding? How many of them had to *prove* their masculinity?

If two men meet, they are likely to identify themselves by their occupations rather than their sexual roles. In contrast, think about the women you know. Many have been scripted with a strong sense of well-defined future expectations of their sexual roles. They may even identify themselves in terms of these roles—as someone's wife or someone's mother—and ignore their other capacities. Women scripted in this way feel OK only when fulfilling their sexual roles as wives and mothers; they feel not-OK in vocational or other roles which challenge their nonsexual or personal potential.

As a result, a woman learns to negate her own unique potential and to feel uncomfortable using her talents to perform. Like Jane at the beginning of this chapter, she learns that these capacities should be used only if she fails in the "feminine arena." Jane was scripted to never make it as a woman. Even her name was used to reinforce her script. In addition, her nonsexual accomplishments were discounted by her family.

Like Jane, women who achieve vocationally do not always joyfully savor sweet success. Jane's increasing pangs of dissatisfaction are reflected in Matina Horner's research.[8] She found that college women's motives to achieve are distorted by conflicting motives to *avoid success.* She reports that this avoidance is learned in early childhood, as are other ideas about what it means to be feminine. She also found that women who do achieve often experience anxiety and guilt. They unconsciously feel that such success is not feminine.

OUR BEHAVIOR REINFORCES OUR SCRIPTS

After making our decisions and taking our psychological positions, we unconsciously begin to fulfill our own predictions. Our scripts are launched. For example, one little boy was humiliated by his mother and rescued by his father. His mother frequently chided him in front of dinner guests: "You're almost five years old, and you can't even use a knife and fork like a civilized person!" Later, in private, his father would pat him on the back, confiding, "Don't let it get you down, son. We men really have to put up with a lot from women."

The boy finally made the decision: "Women are tyrants and make me feel bad, but men help out when the going gets rough." This decision led him to take different positions about each sex: "Men are OK" and "Women are not-OK."

Once these positions had crystallized in his mind, he felt compelled to act out script-reinforcing behavior. Eventually he married a woman who humiliated him just as his mother had. This in turn justified his evenings out with the boys, who comforted him with, "Ain't it awful living with women!" The cycle had repeated itself.

A girl experiencing a similar situation also decided that women are tyrants and not-OK. In fact, she learned how to act like a not-OK tyrant. As a consequence, her script fits with those of men who have decided against women.

In contrast, a little girl was brutalized by her father and protected by her mother. Her father whipped her across the back of her legs with a leather belt whenever he was annoyed with her. Then her mother consoled her with, "We sure have to put up with a lot to keep a man around." This little girl decided: "Men are beasts who hurt me. They are not-OK. Women are kind. They step in and say 'take it easy.' " This girl eventually chose as a marriage partner a man who brutalized her. (Sometimes women with this type of background choose a milktoast.) In addition, she sought out the solace of other women and spent many mornings at the kaffeeklatsch bemoaning, "Ain't it awful trying to live with men!"

We tend to reinforce our childhood script decisions and positions throughout our lives. The ruts of behavior grow deeper until someone stops to think and chooses to change.

COLLECTIVE SCRIPTS PRESSURE WOMEN

In addition to her personal script, a woman's family, friends, intimates, ethnic group, religious group, and national heritage all press in with prescribed expectations about certain roles and behaviors for her to adopt. Each group has its own set of rules and expectations which the majority of its members adhere to. And each of these collections of people forms a collective script.

The pressure from collective scripts is very much like being caught in a jar. When we are small, we fit and may not even see that there are boundaries around us. As we grow, however, we might hit the edges and bend to fit their limitations. But some of us must burst through to find the fresh air of personal freedom.

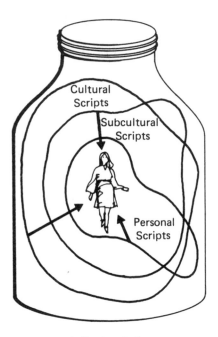

Collective Scripts

The boundaries of the jar—the pressures from collective scripts—tell a woman:

who she is
   her prescribed roles;

where she can go
   her prescribed goals;

what she should do
   her prescribed expectations; and

what she owes others
   her prescribed obligations.

The Tough Woman Script

The cultural scripting of a girl facing the hardships of growing up in an urban ghetto is far different from that of her sister in the suburbs. Rather than the culture pressuring her to be soft, she learns early that she has to be tough. She learns to think and do, but not to feel. Her feelings are shut off. Lola's life reflects the Tough Woman script that often results.

Lola grew up in the decaying central city. Her mother worked hard in a low-paying job and suffered setbacks or periods of unemployment. Her grandmother lived with them and took care of Lola and her baby brother during the day. Grandmother herself was a strong, tough woman. She had survived in the ghetto all these years because of that strength.

Lola received a potent message: "You've got to be tough to survive in this rat race." The rat race for Lola was literal. She had seen her little brother's fingers after they had been bitten by rats.

The men she saw were transient—here today and gone tomorrow. They were not the primary breadwinners, and they brought pain to her own mother. She saw them as eating into the little money available for the family's survival.

Lola got the message: "You've got to make it on your own. Relying on men is only for fools." As a result, she learned to assert herself, to speak her mind. She developed an armored exterior to cope with her life of poor nutrition, plaster falling from the walls, plumbing that didn't work, and schools that didn't meet her needs.

This kind of tough woman knows that she has to get a job. But she may not receive messages about the importance of an education or even understand clearly what kind of an education she needs in order to get a good position. Her motivations are to find work and to earn a buck. Careers are for the rich folks on the other side of town.

Not all tough women are brought up in low-income ghettos. One woman brought up in a wealthy family in which politics was the driving force heard over and over, "Only women with gumption belong in this family. Nothing is more important than the honor of our family name."

Another, whose family belonged to a small religious sect, was prompted with, "You will have to struggle to survive. Show them what you're made of."

Tough women tend to beget tough women.

Conflicting Cultural Pressures

At each level of experience and culture, the pressures on a woman can be either compatible or conflicting. Historically, for instance, black women felt OK about being women. In fact, their sexuality gave them what little power they could exert in a slave community. They learned to feel not-OK *because they were black*. Today, however, collective scripts of the larger culture are likely to judge black women not-OK because of both color and sex—a double jeopardy. Indeed, black women often experience more sex discrimination than they realize. Shirley Chisholm, during her successful campaign for the House of Representatives, observed that overcoming the handicap of being a woman was far more difficult for her than overcoming the handicap of being black.[9]

**STEPS TO
AWARENESS**

Collective Scripts

The groups we belong to influence our scripts in significant ways. List the groups to which you belong, i.e., ethnic group, church group, union, garden club, company, political party, etc. Under each group, list its main ideas or principles.

■ What are the expected roles for women in the group? The roles for men?

■ Which groups have a definite influence on you? Are those groups compatible with one another? If so, how? Or are they in conflict? If so, how?

- How does this affect you now?

Some groups foster a group sense of OK-ness, particularly with people who individually feel not-OK. To accomplish this, they often single out other groups as not-OK by comparison. Thus a group feeling of "We're OK, and They're not-OK" emerges.

- Do any of the groups to which you belong define other groups as not-OK?

- When you think about this, what does it mean?

- How does it affect you as a person?

The Mass Media and Cultural Scripts

Often the mass media startlingly reflect the culture's attitudes and expectations of both women and men. Magazines, television, newspapers, and billboards bombard us with messages:

Women should be thinner, taller, fuller, younger, or blonder.

Men should be broader, taller, richer, stronger, or hairier.

After a barrage of commercials, advertisements, and articles, it is sometimes hard to feel a sense of pride in the real image we see reflected in the mirror. But if we become aware of these pressures from the mass media, we can better understand how they affect our scripts.

Sometimes women like Jane learn to feel that since they do not meet mass-media standards of beauty, their only alternative is to devote their lives to a career. In contrast, women who think of themselves as beautiful may learn to judge this as their only important quality and to develop scripts which exploit their beauty while excluding their full humanness. Such an overemphasis on women who are physically beautiful can be just as destructive as is a contemptuous attitude toward "Plain Janes."

The Beautiful Plastic Woman Script

Other influences in addition to the mass media affect our concept of beauty. Events like beauty pageants are not only beauty contests, but also cultural scripts that pressure, poke, and push millions of women. This type of script convinces women that they are "somebodies"only if they look beautiful. Their size, shape, and appearance are their most important assets. Of course, it helps if they can also sing or dance. Some of these women become plastic dolls—only pretty shells which are hollow inside.

A woman living out such a script strives to meet all the standards the culture dictates for feminine beauty. As a result, she develops a life pattern and identity that hinge totally on her appearance. She may ride high during the years when her skin is soft and supple and her weight easily controlled.

But when her weight begins to shift, her skin dries and wrinkles, and her entrance no longer causes every head in the room to turn, there is literally nothing left for her to do. With the appearance of the first crow's feet around her eyes, her script runs out and gloom settles in. The plastic shell crumbles, revealing the hollow inside.

Eternal bloom is a myth for roses as well as for women. Many women who learn to rely only on their youthful appearance face aging with fears, depression, and frantic efforts to recapture their youthful bloom. To some, even death holds less despair.

The emphasis on appearance inherent in this kind of collective script is especially destructive to non-Caucasian women. They suffer the burden of never being able to fulfill the requirements of the "fairer sex"—fair complexion, silken hair, blue eyes, and fine facial features. Although these criteria may be difficult even for the average blond, blue-eyed woman, they are totally impossible for the woman whose skin is yellow, brown, or black.

Before many black women decided they could be "natural," they suffered an especially severe affront. Grier and Cobbs write:

> One aspect of the black woman's life which attracts little attention from outsiders has to do with her hair. From the time of her birth, the little girl must submit to efforts aimed at changing the appearance of her hair. When she is a babe in arms her hair is brushed and stroked, but in short order the gentle brushing gives way to more vigorous brushing and ultimately combing. Her hair is kinky and combing is painful, but her mother must hold her and force her to submit to it. As far back as her memory will take her, the black woman recalls the painful daily ritual of having her hair combed. It is not insignificant that this painful process is administered in a dispassionate way by the mother. Surely the deadly logic of children would try to explain this phenomenon in some such fashion: "If such pain is administered with such regularity by one who purports to love me, then the end result must be extremely important." And yet, however she might search, the child will never find a reason weighty enough to justify the pain to which she must submit. For, in fact, the combing and plaiting of the hair, in whatever stylish manner the mother may adopt, results in the child's being rendered "acceptable." The combing does not produce a stunningly beautiful child from an ugly one, but simply an acceptably groomed child. For the pain she goes through, she might well expect to be stopped on the street by strangers stunned by the beauty and the transformation wrought by the combing and stylized plaits. Not so. She is simply considered to be of an acceptable appearance.[10]

Beautiful Plastic Women Can Change. A woman with such a script can learn an appreciation for human qualities other than the popular image of feminine beauty. She can learn to recognize and value her own particular kind of physical beauty. In addition, she can decide to *ask for* and *value* other forms of recognition, such as, "You made a good decision." As she learns to invite and accept recognition from others that affirm her talents, intellect, and skills, she becomes more aware of those unique capacities that make each of us a total human. Her repertoire of possibilities expands. She is no longer a hollow shell. She turns on her thinker and accepts that it is OK to grow older. She builds an inner core of confidence. She becomes a *truly* beautiful woman—a beautiful person.

Old Is OK

Mass Media and the Image of Women

To become aware of how the mass media portray women, pick up several women's magazines and page through them. Focus your attention on how the women are portrayed in pictures. Then ask yourself:

What is the image of the ideal woman?

How should she look physically?

What postures and gestures are encouraged?

How are women pictured with other people?
With other women?
With men?
With children?
What kinds of activities are they engaged in?
How many are domestic?
How many are sexy?
How many show competence?

Now, keep track of your television viewing for one night.
How many women were in each program?

Were the women leading or supporting characters?

What dramatic roles did they play—Victim, Rescuer, or Persecutor? Seducer? Clown? Manipulator?

How did other people treat the women? What kinds of remarks did they make to them?

What scripts did these women seem to be following?

Did the women seem to be affected by collective scripts? If so, how?

What did the commercials seem to say about women?

SCRIPTS CAN BE CHANGED

When a woman becomes aware of the negative or destructive elements in the messages she has been programmed to follow, she realizes that she has options. If she chooses, she begins to examine these messages for what they are: ideas recorded in her brain most likely before her eighth year. She no longer limits her growth to bend to the boundaries set by collective pressures. Instead, she recognizes that *many of life's miseries are optional.*

Just as a little girl can make early decisions that affect the blueprint of her life, a woman can make a *redecision* to change her life's direction in a positive way. She can help the little girl inside her choose to be a winner. Women with insight can learn to write their own "happy endings"—happy endings that in reality might actually come true.

5

Someone Touched Me

- How are women and their scripts affected by the lifelong need for touch and recognition?

- How do people collect negative and positive feelings, and how are these feelings like trading stamps?

- What are the ways that women "cash in" their collections of feelings on themselves and others?

Lord, I keep thinking
about that seventeen-year-old girl
who told me her mother
hadn't hugged her
since she was in the
seventh grade—
What makes people
hold their hugs
back?
Is there someone
who's waiting
for a hug
from me?

Robert Raines[1]

Everybody needs hugs. Hugs are usually a happy form of touch, and infants need touch even to survive. Something in the touch of others stimulates a baby's growth chemistry and sets it in motion. Babies who are not held and touched by others will either not grow at a normal physical and emotional pace[2] or will give up on life altogether. Touch is a biological and emotional necessity. How we go about getting or avoiding touch and other forms of recognition plays a significant part in the development of our scripts.

STROKES RELATE TO OUR SCRIPTS

Eric Berne calls *any* form of positive or negative recognition a "stroke."[3] A stroke could be an affectionate embrace, a slap in the face, a nod across a crowded room, or a contemptuous gesture with a finger. A stroke is a positive or negative way of conveying "I know you are there." Such recognition is necessary for life and for either a sense of well-being or of just being alive. The need for strokes is so urgent that children soon figure out that even negative strokes feel better than none.

Here are the dynamics of stroking:

- The absence of strokes can kill—physically and psychologically.

- Negative strokes are better than none at all, but can cause psychological handicaps.

- Strokes that seem positive but that are for inappropriate behavior usually damage the personality.

■ However, positive strokes that are genuine and appropriate stimulate both mental and physical growth. They nourish the human spirit.

Strokes in Childhood

Since we all need strokes to survive, as children we all learn our unique pattern of getting and giving them. This pattern forms the major links in the chain of script-reinforcing behavior. Later in life we seek, over and over again, the same kinds of strokes we grew used to as children. After all, these strokes—good or bad—kept us alive.

Little boys and little girls regularly receive approval for quite different things. If we stroke a little girl for being clever rather than intelligent, she learns to hide her brains—especially to avoid looking smarter than men.

If we stroke a little girl for being passive, she is likely to increase her passive behavior and suppress her natural need to be expressive and assertive.

If we stroke her for being obedient, she is likely to feel comfortable with compliant, obedient behavior.

If we stroke her for being a tomboy, weird, or not like the other girls, she may learn to seek strokes that set her apart from other, "more typical" women.

If we stroke her for always being sweet and clean, she may well grow up thinking that she and other little girls are indeed sugar and spice and everything nice. And on the flip side of this, she may learn to expect different actions from men, because "boys are made of snakes and snails and puppy-dog tails." Thus although she expects to receive strokes for her own purity and goodness, she gives negative strokes to men because they are nasty and dirty. As one such woman put it with a haughty tilt of her head, "I wouldn't stoop to equality with men."

STEPS TO
AWARENESS

Strokes for Boys and Girls

Contrast the kinds of strokes *commonly* received by a girl or a boy in these situations:

Situation	*Strokes for a girl*	*Strokes for a boy*
Coming home with a black eye.		
Making scrambled eggs with cheese.		

Reading poetry.

Rolling in the mud.

Dancing ballet.

Playing "tea party."

Teetering on a high fence.

Building a tree house.

Teasing a cat.

Primping before a mirror.

Running away from home.

Cuddling a baby doll.

Now think back and recall the kinds of strokes you received (or think you would have received) in these situations.

Getting in touch with your own stroking pattern can generate a high payoff. You can discover more of your script, and you can change those patterns that may be unhealthy for you today. But first you need to become aware of the unique ways in which you give and get strokes.

**STEPS TO
AWARENESS**

Your Childhood Stroking Patterns

List the things that you got negative strokes for when you were little.

List the things that you got positive strokes for when you were little.

Now go back and decide whether these strokes were a positive or a negative force in shaping your life or whether they didn't make any difference. Mark each item on your list with a plus (positive force), minus (negative force), or zero (didn't make any difference).

In the spaces below, list three significant authority figures for you when you were a child. List the kinds of negative and positive strokes you got from these people.

Sources of strokes	Negative strokes	Positive strokes
1.		
2.		
3.		

Now go back and decide whether each kind of stroke was a constructive or a destructive force in shaping your life or whether it did not make any difference. Mark each item with a plus, minus, or zero.

Now ask yourself:

- "Who gives me the same kinds of strokes today?"

- "What do I do to get them?"

- "Do these strokes feel good or bad to me now?"

- "Are they helpful or harmful in my life today?"

Your Stroking Patterns Today

Looking at your life now, think about the various sources that you have available to you for strokes (i.e., friends, co-workers, family members, teachers, religious leaders). Write in the kinds of negative and positive strokes that you get from each of these sources.

People who stroke you	Negatively	Positively

After you have studied your present sources of strokes, ask yourself, "What can I do to get more positive strokes from these people?"

Now list the people who get strokes from you. What kinds of strokes do you give them?

People you stroke	Negatively	Positively

After studying your stroke patterns, ask yourself to whom and how you could give more positive strokes.

Now think about all the ways in which you either endorse yourself or put yourself down.

List the things you do to put yourself down.

List the things you do to endorse yourself.

SOME STROKES SNEAK UP ON US LATER

Some strokes *appear* positive but actually have insidious repercussions. They feel good in childhood but later on lead us to do the wrong thing at the wrong time. Such strokes give approval for inappropriate behavior. For example, a little girl may be continually praised for being "quiet and polite." Later, as a mother, she may live up to being "seen and not heard" by failing to speak out for better education for her own children. Originally this stroke sounded positive. Yet because it trimmed down her area of choice, it ultimately had a negative effect.

Here are some strokes that sneaked up on women we know:

"With looks like hers, she'll never have to lift a finger."

"We're sure lucky she's ugly. Think of all the worries we won't have when she's 16."

"She looks so fragile. She'll always have to have someone take care of her."

"Thank goodness you are a girl. Think of all the money for education we'll save."

"You're the cutest little trick on the block."

Women praised for always playing a helpmate, rescuing role can easily end up as real victims. One such woman opened the door to a strange man, unthinkingly falling for the story: "A child has been hit by a car. I must use your phone!" Another woman was conned into moving toward a parked car: "Ma'am, will you please come and give me directions to Central Station?"

Positive-feeling strokes for submission can contribute to tragic encounters. Attackers find submissive women easier prey than their spunkier sisters. To further complicate the problem, women may not move assertively to protect themselves physically. Such tactics as scratching, screaming, or gouging someone's eyes who intends them bodily harm and humiliation may seem out of their possibilities.

The strokes some women receive later impair their contact with the full spectrum of their feelings. For example, tenderness, laughter, shyness, guilt, inadequacy, and martyrdom are commonly approved of in women. Anger is not. Yet in many situations, anger or indignation is the most authentic response.

But since many women have learned to *internalize* their anger, they may withdraw and not deal directly with their feelings. Internalized anger brings on depression and self-deprecation. These women adopt an I'm not-OK and You're OK posture. In the extreme, this posture leads to death. In fact, women commit suicide more frequently than they do murder. Only 10% of all violent crimes are committed by women.

Women who learn to hide their assertiveness, to silence their feelings of aggression, internalize their anger and save resentment. This resentment can either silently seethe inside and be displaced or be "cashed in" in insidious ways. Not an uncommon example is the woman who encourages her husband to drink too much and eat too many fats and carbohydrates or who pushes him to achieve more and more until he finally wears himself out. She "gets even" while outwardly appearing to be the perfect wife.

Women who are cut off from their anger lack skills in resolving it. Each time someone steps on them, they collect more bad feelings. They hurt themselves, setting in motion a vicious, self-destructive cycle rather than dealing with anger in an open, healthy way.

Becoming aware and changing usually form an emotional progression. If a woman who operates from the I'm not-OK and You're OK position gains insight into why she feels that way, she might switch to the I'm OK and You're Not-OK position. Her heretofore concealed anger bursts forth, most frequently as blaming. Parents, men, society, government—all become the target. Enough truth lies in each of these areas to fan the flames.

Once she has vented, and if she continues to grow, this woman eventually moves to the I'm OK and You're OK position. Rather than placing blame, she focuses her energies on problem solving and productive change. For example, one woman bitterly angry about not being admitted to medical school eventually ended up working to see that women and their possibilities were better represented in school books. She also campaigns for equal opportunities for education.

What do *you* do with your anger?

Your Sneaky Strokes and Anger

Think about the good-feeling strokes you received as a child. Did any of these sneak up on you later? If so, how?

- What can you do about this now?

What do you do with your anger?

- Is this productive for you?

- If not, what could you do instead to vent anger without hurting anybody, including yourself? (For example, you may decide to find a private place where you can yell and pound your fists on a pile of pillows, smash a ball or pillow against a wall, or kick an old cushion.)

Racket Feelings

The kinds of strokes women *learn* to accept and seek from their collective scripts and authority figures will eventually be associated with a collection of "favorite" feelings—not favorite in the sense of being good, but favorite in the sense of being "favored" over other feelings. You probably know people who, no matter what happens, get mad. Their angry feelings surface almost immediately.

Such feelings are called "racket feelings" because of the dishonest ways in which people set up and interpret situations to go after them. A racket feeling is one that a person habitually turns on, no matter what the situation.[4] This type of feeling is learned in childhood in response to difficult or unrealistic situations. It is an early substitute for a feeling that was not acceptable. "You shouldn't feel that way! Shame on you for getting so upset. You're not mad, you're just tired." Today, however, these old feelings are not realistically related to the current situation. They are not healthy, authentic feelings. We indulge ourselves when we repeat those old feelings.

Yet once we become used to a feeling, we tend, without awareness, to go out of our way to find people and situations which provide a ready source for feeling that way again. We repeat ourselves. We keep our world the way we knew it and maintain our own status quo.

Each of us has a notion about what kinds of feelings certain transactions have to offer. Some people and some situations offer guilt feelings. Others offer anger. Still others offer feelings of depression.

One woman discovered her bad-feeling racket when she came in touch with a definite pattern. She finally realized that whenever things seemed too happy, she phoned her mother-in-law, who did not like her. Her good mood soon changed to depression: "What a racket! I really set myself up to be depressed. I know I want to get along with my mother-in-law to keep peace in the family, but I don't have to go out of my way to feel bad."

Another woman discovered that she made promises with "good intentions" which she rarely kept. When other people responded with annoyance or disappointment, she felt inadequate: "No matter what I do, it is never right." It took quite a bit of soul-searching for her to admit that she lied or made false promises in order to feel bad about her own abilities. This came to light when she was on the verge of a most successful business venture with another woman. The prospects of being supersuccessful pushed her to go after her bad feelings harder than ever. But it also exposed her racket so that she could deal with it.

Other women have discovered their own rackets:

"Never balancing the checkbook right keeps him calling me a 'dumb cluck.'"

"Always blaming others make me feel pure and self-righteous."

"Having 'good intentions' keeps my guilt going."

"Seeking out situations I fail in gives me a guarantee for feeling insecure and inferior."

"Not being clear and not letting people know my standards allows me to be angry.

WE CAN TRADE IN BAD FEELINGS

Our collection of recurring feelings is our *psychological trading stamp collection*. It is like collecting trading stamps with purchases so that we can later redeem them for a prize. If we go after our racket feelings and hoard them, we add to our *gray stamp collection*. If we go after positive, authentic strokes, ones that are honest and feel good, we add to our *gold stamp collection*.

We save up our feelings and store them inside us—often in tense muscles, ulcered stomachs, swollen joints, or tight sphincters. Then at the "right" time, we cash in our holdings for a psychological prize. It is just like getting a toaster at the stamp redemption store! Have you ever been "fed up to here" and then allowed yourself to blow up at an innocent person? If so, you were redeeming your psychological trading stamp collection. You probably felt justified in doing so, too.

Different people save up different amounts of feelings before redeeming them. We each learn our own style, but generally the bigger the collection, the bigger the prize.

Whatever the size, the prize for cashing in gray stamps usually involves justification without guilt for unusual behavior.

- One woman saved blue depression stamps until she had two or three pages. Then she cashed them in for a "good cry."

- Another woman saved anger stamps until she had four or five books. She then cashed these in on a week-long rage at all the people she supervised on her job.

- One woman suffered in silence while collecting 20 years of little hurts. Cashing in her drawers of stamps for a guilt-free divorce, she explained, "After all, look at what I've put up with for all these years."

- Another woman collected stupid feelings all of her married life and cashed them in for a divorce which left her almost penniless and with no vocational skills. This was a seriously stupid position for a 46-year-old woman with no income, no job, and no income prospects.

- Still another woman saved and saved her feelings of depression until she had boxes and boxes of emotion-filled stamp books. Then she cashed them in for a guilt-free overdose of sleeping pills.

Your Stamp Collection

Do you express your feelings and your resentments as things occur, or do you save them up and then unload them in bundles?

Begin to get in touch with how you cash in negative feelings. Do you blow up, sulk, get depressed, or what?

How do these feelings and patterns relate to your script?

If you find that you are hoarding resentments and bad feelings and then unloading them in bunches, develop a plan for handling situations as they occur. Outline your plan. Check out how it works. Then redesign it if you can improve it. Reward yourself for what works.

If you have something that needs to be expressed but find it hard to do so, try: "I have some unfinished business I need to talk over with you. Here's what's happening to me. I . . . ."

Also, try expressing your resentment to an empty chair. Sitting in one chair, face the other and develop a dialogue. It may help to start, "I resent. . . ." Say whatever is on your mind. Shout if you feel like it. If you have the urge to switch chairs and talk back to yourself, do so.

To whom do you seem to be talking?

Continue until you feel finished. Then, if you have any good feelings about this person, state them out loud.

WE CAN COLLECT GOOD FEELINGS

Life begins to feel better when we give up our negative collections and learn to collect more of the good feelings associated with gold stamps.

- One woman who collected many good feelings about herself cashed them in for a Saturday's basking in the sun's warmth at the park. "Why not? I deserve it."

- Another cashed them in for a trip to visit with favorite friends. "It feels good to be with old friends."

- Another woman became a doctoral candidate. "I've got the brains to do it," she said, and rewarded herself.

- Still another opened an art gallery. "I've got the talent. Why not display it?"

What are the ways you can collect and cash in more gold stamps?

The Stroke Economy

Claude Steiner proposes the idea of a stroke-deficient economy.[5] This emotionally sterile environment develops if we teach children to follow one or more of these rules:

Don't give strokes.

Don't share your good feelings or enthusiasms. Don't go around saying nice things to people.

Don't accept strokes.

Don't savor a good feeling. If someone gives you a compliment, put yourself down immediately or give it right back to that person.

Don't reject strokes.

If someone gives you a stroke you don't want, like a kiss on the lips from an estranged relative, just stand there and take it.

Don't give yourself strokes.

Don't tell anyone—even yourself—if you have done something you really like.

Don't ask for strokes.

Don't ask for what you need. Unless others spontaneously give you what you want, it isn't worth anything.

These bad habits can be broken.

Expanding Your Positive Stroke Sources

Just as we get used to giving and getting certain strokes, we may also get used to getting them from a few limited sources. For example, many little girls learn early in life that the best strokes must come from boys. Sometimes this means competing with other girls for boys' attention. Julie realizes that this constant competition with other women began with her "more attractive" sister:

When I was a teenager, my mother frequently chided me, "Your sister always has more orchids in the refrigerator than you do." It was years before I figured out the implications of what I was learning. It was just one of the ways I learned to feel that my worth was determined by what a man thought of me. Having orchids wasn't enough. They had to be boy-bought orchids. It wouldn't have been OK for me to go out and buy flowers for myself. The orchids represented my competing with other women for a scarce commodity—men. And now that I think about it, it was a woman, my mother, who encouraged me to compete with my own sister! Today, even though I know it doesn't make sense, I find that when I go to a party, I first look around the room at the other women. I'm still sizing up my competition. It's still more "orchids in the refrigerator."

There are many ways to expand your sources of strokes. Expanding your number of relationships almost guarantees it. Increasing the number of good things you say to yourself in your own head does it. Another way is to broaden the base for interesting contacts. Studying new subjects adds ideas and energy and increases your capacity to relate to other people.

High-Intensity Strokes Through Intimacy

In addition to expanding your sources of strokes, you can add energy to your life by increasing the amount of high-intensity strokes. Strokes from an initimate encounter may last a lifetime, whereas those from a ritualistic "Hi, how are you?" may last only a few minutes.

Hearing "You're someone special to me" from a person you respect and care about stays with you incomparably longer than has a ritualistic peck on the cheek. In fact, you may go back and revisit the good feelings over and over.

Here is how some women describe these high-intensity feelings:

"Knowing you're really in tune with each other."

"Sharing pain and happiness all at the same time."

"The joy of her knowing I'm not perfect and still accepting me."

"Feeling warm and toastie all over."

"Squeezing hands as our daughter says, 'I do.' "

"Fun, crazy, high-school feelings all rolled up in one."

"Believing for the moment that there's nothing else in the world except us."

"Suddenly alive—alive to what's in me and alive to what's out there— like energy bubbling up and spilling over the brim."

"Silently enjoying the wind on our faces, the sounds of the night in our ears."

"Like standing at the top of the Empire State Building with someone I love and knowing that New York and the world are ours."

"Just holding hands and caring about each other."

These are the ways some women have described intimacy—the knowing and being known that adds meaning to life, sparkle to existence, and color to the ordinary. Intimacy is the being accepted as I am for what I am —not for what I look like, not for whom I know, and not for what I earn.

Intimacy is the moments of open contact with another person that bring a new dimension to life. It is the light that can suddenly burst forth from game-free personal contact. It is mutually giving and receiving without exploitation. Intimacy is habit-forming. Many women tell us over and over that once they allow themselves to get strokes through intimacy, life is never the same.

Once we have experienced it with one person, our capacity for authenticity with others expands. This note following an evening studded with moments of openness testifies to the contagion.

"I felt so invigorated after the time together, so lively, so with it that I could have broken down concrete walls. And I feel so close and in touch with the people around me and so much in tune with their needs and their hopes."

Just like the drop of a pebble in a pool, energy and awareness ripple outward. Strokes through intimacy last and they energize.

As you look for ways to expand your sources of strokes, think about these questions:

Are the strokes I want good for me?

Will I be hurt in any way by them?

Will anyone else be hurt by my getting them?

Am I burdening anybody with my stroke demands?

Does the person I want them from care about me?

Is there someone who really gives the strokes I want?

Do I give enough good strokes to others so that some come back my way?

In addition to limiting their sources of strokes, some women may learn to expect a *particular kind* of stroke. Such a woman may want a hug, a "you really did that well," or a "you look pretty in that" from someone who does not give it. Again, she is frustrated.

Insisting on getting a particular kind of stroke from only one person is similar to liking Crunchy-Snap breakfast cereal, going into one grocery store looking for Crunchy-Snap in the cereal section, seeing an empty shelf, and then standing there demanding Crunchy-Snap while banging a fist on the empty shelf.

Just as there are many stores for breakfast cereals, there are many people who have something to offer. If you ask for what you want but do not get it, think about your situation. You may want to find a new stroke source. There are more than 200 million people in the United States. Each has unique interests, capabilities, and stroking patterns.

Margaret thought through this problem in her life.

I used to feel that because we were best friends in school and still live near each other, we had to see each other all the time. But whenever I see Fran, I end up depressed and frustrated. I know she's not going to take my advice, no matter how many times she asks, so I've decided to look for a new friend—someone I'll feel good being with.

Just because you have learned to get and give particular kinds of strokes in a certain way does not mean you cannot change. If you discover a stroking pattern that is no longer good for you, you can deliberately create a new pattern, one that makes more sense for your life today.

- Know what you are getting.
- Know what you want.
- And go more frequently where you will get what is good for you.

LEARN TO ASK FOR WHAT YOU WANT

Many of us do not know how to ask for what we want. Unfortunately, some of us believe in the magic of crystal balls. But other people are not likely to have crystal balls. Unless we let others know our needs and wants, they are put in the awkward position of having to outguess us. One woman held this notion and kept herself unhappy by believing, "If I have to tell someone what I want, what they do for me isn't worthwhile."

When we begin to think better of ourselves and take care of ourselves, we learn ways of telling others what we want. Our stroke hungers reduce when we work on a "free-stroke economy." [6] We can establish this by talking over what we want with others and agreeing to listen to and give each other recognition. Asking for what you want may sound like:

"I need to know how you feel about what happened last night."

"Do you think I'm working well with our customers?"

"I'd really like you to sit next to me."

"How do you like my new casserole?"

"What is your opinion of my tennis game?"

"Send me a card on my birthday, and I'll send one on yours."

"I'd like a hug."

"Would you feel OK about critiquing my presentation?"

"I really feel bad when I don't celebrate a promotion. Would you like to celebrate my new job with me?"

"How do I look in this?"

"I'd like your shoulder to cry on."

As you think about your life, is there someone you are expecting to read your mind?

STEPS TO
AWARENESS

Putting Down or Building Up

Do you put yourself down about any of these areas? If so, how?

Your intelligence?

Your ability to be sociable?

Your sexuality?

Your body?

Your talents?

Your skills?

Your spiritual life?

Your ability to earn money?

Now looking back at the list, what positive things are you doing in all of these areas?
- Think of something in each area that you feel good about, that you do well, that you feel proud of, that gives you warm feelings, that endorses you.

Who in your life do you want to endorse you more?
- Close your eyes and imagine what it would be like if it were how you wanted it. Imagine this scene frequently.
- What do you need to do or say to get this validation brought into your life? Imagine yourself doing or saying what you need to.
- After practicing this, step out and try it.

How do you endorse yourself?
- List six things about yourself that are really good.

What are three things you can do to bring more good-feeling strokes into your life?

As we become more aware of how strokes affect script development, we can begin to see more clearly the different paths women and men are set on. They may follow these paths even though they are unproductive or hurtful.

Strokes that equate femininity with low achievement and subordination encourage racket feelings that hurt. Once a woman discovers her racket feelings, she can work to minimize this hurt. When we give up racket feelings, we automatically give up many of our games. Part of the reason for playing games is to collect and to give bad feelings.

Each day as you contact people, take a few minutes to sharpen your observations of the types and patterns of life-sustaining recognition that go on in your life. What do you see? Positive? Negative? Touching or non-touching? Appropriate or inappropriate? As you continue to discover the differences in strokes women and men get and go after, ask yourself, "Who says it must be so?"

Women coming in touch with their gray stamp collections and any negative script-reinforcing behaviors can step back, take a look, and make new decisions. In terms of thinking, feeling, and doing, they can develop genuine, honest feelings. Women deserve to feel good about themselves.

Women who have the bad habit of putting themselves down or hiding in the background can learn to accept themselves, love themselves, be proud of themselves, and without apologies, feel good. Women who like themselves are free to like other women and free to like men. They are also free to let others like them back. Good strokes make the world go around. They help women to be winners.

6

The Watchful Inner Eye

- How can you gain more appreciation for the diversity of your personality and those of other people?

- In what ways can you encourage positive change by using the Parent, Adult, and Child structure of personality?

- How have significant people affected your behavior?

- Why and how have some women learned to deny their wholeness—to feel OK only in certain sexual roles?

Talking, talking, talking,
  All those people in my head;
Pushing me and pulling
  Till my stomach turns to lead.

Sometimes they support me,
  Sometimes they put me down.
Sometimes they fight among themselves,
  As if I weren't around.

Sometimes they give me good advice,
  Sometimes they run me ragged,
Sometimes I grin down deep inside
  Sometimes my nerves feel jagged.

How do I control them all?
  How do I say "no"?
I'd better get to know them—
  Since it's really all my show.

Dorothy Jongeward

People are talking in our heads all the time. Where does all the talking come from? What do the people say? How do we feel in response?

Our brains record what our senses experience. All this dialogue and imagery in our heads forms significant parts of our personality. Learning to understand the sources of our thoughts, feelings, and opinions helps us understand who we actually are. This growth means coming in touch with how we use our psychic energies, what stimulates our feelings, and what motivates our actions.

Sharon shares how this process worked in relation to her sexual response.

Sharon had never had an orgasm. "When Wally and I married, I remember believing that I'd hear rockets bursting and bells ringing. Right now I'd settle for a small firecracker. On our wedding night I remember thinking, 'I've waited all these years for this?' "

Recently, much to her surprise, Sharon read that many women really enjoy sexual relations. In fact, some even claimed to be sexually aggressive. Sharon hadn't talked to anyone about this problem before, but now she sought professional help.

During one session she told the therapist that her mother had frequently warned her, "Sex is really ugly, but it's the duty of every good wife." As a result, Sharon reported, she now "submitted" to sexual relations, feeling she had to. The whole experience seemed nasty.

In addition to her feeling of duty, Sharon also felt panicky. When her husband approached her, she grew scared and wanted to run away. During a later session, she talked about a frightening childhood experience. She was walking home from a friend's house when a man suddenly appeared out of the bushes and chased her. He overtook her and exposed himself. But when a car came by, he fled down an alley. Sharon discovered that she was reliving with her husband now the same old feelings of fright that she had felt then. "It's like an instant replay of a bad movie."

Sharon took a step toward solving her problem when she became aware of the reality that she had three parts to her personality. One part was what she had absorbed from her parent figures, including her mother. Rather than experiencing sexual intercourse and its full breadth of feelings for herself, Sharon was unknowingly copying her mother's attitudes, which she had learned from Sharon's grandmother. Three generations of women had repeated, "We women have a terrible cross to bear."

A second part of herself was what she had learned in childhood. Without being aware of it, Sharon brought a frightening childhood incident to her marriage bed. She relived a panic she had felt at age five.

The third part of Sharon's personality was her rational thinking. In spite of her mother's influence and her childhood experience, which were both negative, Sharon could function rationally. She gathered and updated her information, became aware of her problem, and made a decision to do something about it. She followed through on her decision by getting professional help.

Sharon used her increased awareness to push open the doors to more choices. She discovered that she did not have to stay stuck with the problem. It could be solved. Her past did not have to dictate her present. She could learn to enjoy her body and her sensuous feelings. Understanding herself was the first step.

WE ALL HAVE THREE MAIN SOURCES OF THINKING, FEELING, AND DOING

Eric Berne made a landmark contribution to understanding human behavior when he identified the three main parts of personality (structural analysis).[1] He termed these parts the Parent ego state, Adult ego state, and Child ego state.* Berne defines each ego state, or state of mind, as "a consistent pattern of feeling and experience directly related to a corresponding consistent pattern of behavior."[2]

His approach is practical. You can actually see and hear people operating from these different parts of themselves.

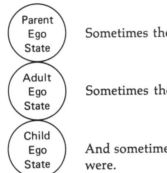 Sometimes they act like their parent figures.

Sometimes they are rational and reasonable adults.

And sometimes they act and feel like the children they once were.

One woman responded from all three levels when her widowed mother moved in with another man.

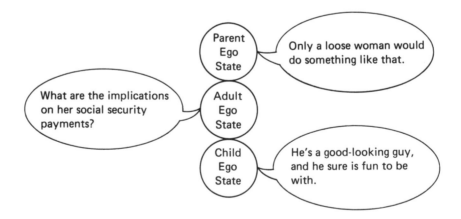

---

* When capitalized, the words Parent, Adult, and Child refer to ego states. When not, they refer to actual people.

The Parent Ego State

If our parents were inconsistent, we are likely to be inconsistent. If our parents were warm and loving, we are likely to be warm and loving. If our parents were overprotective, judgmental, or scolding, we are likely to be and do those same things.

All of us, in childhood, absorb the personalities of others into our own. Usually without knowing it, we pick up other people's postures, gestures, habits, ideas, and expressions. This collection of attitudes, feelings, and behaviors copied from any and all significant parent figures becomes the Parent. We record these ways of seeing and doing things in our brains and nervous tissue; in later life they become almost automatic responses. For example, we are likely to give the same kinds of negative or positive strokes to women that we saw our parents give to the women in their lives. Or we may withhold strokes from women the way they did. If our parents downgraded women or put them on pedestals, we will probably do the same and be unaware of it.

Understanding the Parent ego state is particularly important to women, since people usually think of women as the nurturers, the bearers of life, and the preservers of life. But because we *learn* how to parent, women who choose motherhood gain much from understanding this ego state.

The Adult Ego State

Thinking independently, rationally, and objectively is characteristic of the Adult ego state. We use this part of our personality to test out current reality, estimate the probable consequences of certain actions, and make decisions on the basis of facts rather than opinions. Looking objectively at the facts can help us decide if women do indeed belong on pedestals, in the gutter, or some place else.

If you want to change something about your life, your Adult can help. Your Adult can gather information about your inner Parent and Child. For example, if a woman examines her Parent ego state and decides that

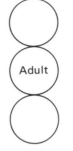

her attitudes about femininity are self-defeating, she can use her Adult to look at those attitudes, think them over, and choose different ones for herself.

The amounts and kinds of strokes given a woman for her intelligence, independent thinking, and decision making greatly affect the quality and development of her Adult ego state. If her Adult is put down or ignored, her "thinker" may not function as frequently or as well as it could. In contrast to many men, relatively few women are generously stroked for being straightforwardly intelligent and talented—for using their Adults.

The Child Ego State

In addition to our Parent and Adult, each of us has a little child inside—that part of us right now which is still the little person we once were. Acting from the Child doesn't mean "acting childish." Rather, it means that no matter how old we are, each of us sometimes feels and behaves today like we once did as children.

Each child experiences the outside world, responds to it, and copes with it with feelings, thoughts, and behavior. A woman who feels smart or dumb, beautiful or ugly, confident or inadequate—just as she did as a little girl—is experiencing her Child. A woman who tries to get what she wants from men in the same way that she got what she wanted from her father when she was three years old is also using her Child ego state. *A person's sense of worth or worthlessness lies in the Child ego state.*

**STEPS TO
AWARENESS**

Who Is Talking?

Each of the following situations has three possible responses. Which ego state
do you think each response comes from?

1. Clara has just decided to attend a seminar about equal employment opportunity for women, and an acquaintance jeers, "Oh, so you're going to
   burn some bras, huh!"

   - "Well, you ought to go to some of those meetings yourself. You wouldn't
     be making inane comments like that if you did!" _____
   - "Do you think I shouldn't go? I don't want to make anybody mad." _____
   - "What is your understanding of the term 'women's lib'?" _____

2. Some friends have just eaten a delicious dinner at Michael and Helen's
   home, and Michael mentions how much he enjoyed doing the cooking.

   - "Well, my wife wouldn't even let me near the kitchen. I'd just burn some-
     thing or get everything all messed up. I can't even boil water." _____
   - "Where did you learn how to cook?" _____
   - "And do you wear rosewater behind your ears too?" _____

3. The picture of the newly selected woman corporate director of planning has
   just appeared in the company magazine.

   - "I'll bet her children aren't getting all the mothering they need!" _____
   - "If only I had her looks, I could have had a nice job too." _____
   - "I'm going to find out her work background. There may be some good
     ideas I can pick up." _____

4. A secretary wears very tight pants to work.

   - "Wow, look at that." _____
   - "I wonder why the new secretary chose to wear that to the office?" _____
   - "Tight pants should not be allowed in this office!" _____

THE PARENT SETS THE RULES

The Parent holds all the traditions—the collective scripts—that have been
passed down from generation to generation. In the recesses of our minds
often lie the remnants of attitudes about women held by our ancestors.

Aristotle (384–322 B.C.) described women as "female by virtue of a certain incapacity. . . . [They] are weaker and cooler by nature than . . . males

and we must regard the female character as a kind of natural defectiveness."[3]

St. Thomas Aquinas (1223–1274) believed women to be ". . . defective and accidental . . . a male gone awry . . . the result of some weakness in the [father's] generative power . . . or of some external factor, like a south wind, which is damp."[4]

Martin Luther (1483–1546) said, "If a woman grows weary and at last dies from childbearing, it matters not. Let her only die from bearing, she is there to do it."[5]

Sigmund Freud (1856–1939) considered women as insufficient and defective. He believed that a woman's psychosexual life is shaped by her having been "deprived" of a penis and that she suffers from envy, insincerity, secretiveness, and an underdeveloped sense of justice and honor. These inadequacies render her incapable of the "higher human tasks." Rather, her destiny is determined by her beauty, charm, and sweetness.[6]

Whatever the rules are and for however far back they reach, the Parent sets them. These rules consist of shoulds, oughts, and musts.

"Do what you want."

"Don't bother me."

"Do what I say, not what I do."

"Figure it out for yourself, you have a good head."

Such Parent rules about women's role and femininity are often strongly held and loudly expressed, but they are rarely examined. Yet an examination of these definitions is a key step in a person's becoming autonomous. Here are a few of the "shoulds" that women have shared with us. Perhaps you have heard some like these.

"Girls are born to be helpmates."

"A woman isn't truly feminine until she holds her first baby."

"She's a good woman. She never complains about her suffering."

"Girls should sit pretty and keep their knees together."

"A *really* feminine woman dresses like a woman."

"Fooling around is OK for men, but a decent woman wouldn't do it."

"You're a girl. I expect you to be special."

"There's nothing worse than an aggressive woman."

"Smart girls are smart enough not to show it—smart like a fox."

"A lady never uses profanity."

"I expect you to do more with your life than I did."

"A woman should stick by her man, no matter what."

"Women should watch out for men. They're all alike."

"Nice girls don't get dirty."

"Women should keep out of a man's world."

"What can you expect? She's only a woman."

"Would *you* want someone with premenstrual tension in the White House?"

**STEPS TO
AWARENESS**

Your Parent Messages About Femininity and Masculinity

Begin to get in touch with your Parent messages about femininity and masculinity. You may want to share what you recall with other people.

List some messages you learned as a child about what it means to be feminine.

What are some messages you learned about what it means to be masculine?

What are some characteristics of a healthy adult?

How do your three lists compare? What are the implications for women? For men? For you?

To learn more about your Parent programming, complete the following thoughts in the way an important parent figure in your life would.

Women should: *Men should:*

Every woman wants: | *Every man wants:*

Every woman needs: | *Every man needs:*

- How does *your* Parent influence your opinions and feelings now?

- What parts of your Parent are constructive? What adds to your winning streak? What does not?

Parent Tapes

Living with the Parent messages in our heads is almost like living in a room full of videotape recorders. Each recorder's start button is ready to be activated by the slightest jar. Some tapes get turned on frequently. Others remain unplayed until the right situation comes along and the buttons get pushed.

Some Parent messages are supportive and encouraging. We draw on these helpful tapes when we feel "down." They may teach us to care about other people—to move away from our own self-centeredness when someone else needs help. They can serve as a constructive, ever-ready rule book for everyday activities. They can give us guidelines for nurturing and rearing children. But it all depends on what we learned from our actual parent figures.

Some women heard messages like:

"You can do it."

"Don't be afraid to try."

"You figure things out faster than anybody else I know."

"Take good care of your body. Your health is important."

"Temper your risks with reasonable caution."

"You're your own best friend. Treat yourself well."

"You're a neat person."

Others have negative messages that are inaccurate, irrelevant, and unrealistic. The results can be destructive:

A woman with an I.Q. of 160 works hard to make sure she does not look too smart.

A woman spends time and energy pulling the strings—manipulating people from behind the scenes to make sure she is not labeled an "aggressive woman."

A talented, creative woman sits passively and submissively, her hands folded in her lap, in an attempt to live up to her Parent ideas of being "a real lady."

Parent Actions

We use our Parent in two ways. A person actually doing what her or his parent figures did is *acting from* the Parent. This person is copying parent figures. A person whose behavior changes to conform to or defy parental messages is *responding to* the inner Parent. The person listens to the inner Parent tapes and responds—most frequently from the Child.

The following women *act like* their parent figures. Do any of them seem familiar to you?

- A wife nags her husband about spending too much time watching football on TV, just as her mother had nagged her father for sitting around on Sunday afternoons.

- A woman admonishes her boss, "Now you better take the time for a good, nutritious lunch if you expect to keep up your strength," just as her favorite aunt had often admonished her.

- A mother comforts her small daughter at the death of her dog, just as her grandfather had long ago done for her.

- A mother rocks and soothes a sick child, just as her father had many times rocked and soothed her.

- A woman scolds her friend for getting a low test grade in college, just as she had been scolded for "frittering time away and not paying attention to your studies."

Now let us look at some people who are acting *toward* women from their Parent ego states.

- A neighbor with furrowed brows and hands on hips critically watches two ten-year-old girls playing football in the vacant lot.
- A bridge partner ridicules a woman with, "Why are you worried about investing for retirement for yourself? You have a good man taking care of you."
- A manager reports at a staff meeting, "The girls in *our* office don't want to be bosses. They're happy where they are."
- A husband insists, "You won't catch me doing housework. What are you trying to do to me? My dad would turn over in his grave!"
- A friend saying, "You shouldn't take that part-time job. No one can take care of the children like you can."

Parent Voices

When we hear our Parent voices in our heads, our inner Child is likely to sit up and take notice. A sharp "Watch out!" may keep us from stepping in front of a car. If a little girl gets Parent strokes for being obedient, her inner Child is likely to obey. Little girls who obey get more goodies. However, some rebel and fight back—very unfeminine! Some pout—maybe because they're girls. Some feel stuck and paralyzed. And some get stubborn, stall, and put things off. An inner Parent-Child conversation looks something like this:

1. C = Wow, this math is easy.
2. P = Don't outshine the boys, honey, or they won't like you.
3. C = Yeah, I'd better cool it. George thinks I'm cute.
4. P = You're a good girl. You really know how to play it smart.

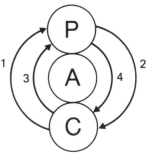

Inner Dialogue

Each of the following women is probably *responding to* Parent voices from her inner Child:

- A woman about to let herself go hears in her head, "Nice girls don't do 'that,' " and tightens up.

- A woman puts on clean underthings before she goes shopping, because "What would people think if you were in an accident and had on dirty underwear?"

- A woman makes her bed before leaving her hotel room, because "You should never leave your room a mess. 'Messy is as messy does.' " (Or maybe she leaves it in a terrible mess, rebelling against her mother's admonition.)

- A woman feels uneasy because the raise will make her salary higher than her husband's; she's heard, "Never outdo your man."

- A middle-aged housewife feels guilty about taking a space in an over-crowded community college class, because "Education is most important for young men."

- A woman cringes when she tries on patent leather shoes, because "If you wear patent leather shoes, the boys will see your panties!"

- A marketing manager disregards a letter of application for sales representative from a woman, because "Women can't travel."

- A working woman feels guilty when her husband does the grocery shopping or cooking, because "You shouldn't degrade a man with woman's work."

- A woman refuses to do any grocery shopping at all, rebelling against "You're the oldest. You take the list to the store."

- A woman protects herself from pregnancy, because "Children fare better if you really want them."

- A woman writes a book because she has been encouraged with, "You have a way with words. Use it."

STEPS TO
AWARENESS

Hearing Your Parent Voices

How did the Parent messages mentioned fit the ones you learned? Did any sound familiar?

Which other messages came to your mind?

What are the Parent rules in your head?

Do you want to shut off any Parent tapes? Turn up the volume on any?

If so, what can you do more of? Less of?

Parent Games

Just as we copy our parent figures' facial expressions, voice tones, opinions, values, and so forth, we also learn to play their games. We go through the dialogue and motions, often unaware of what we are really doing.

Uproar is a common family game. The first round is usually a put-down or a nonverbal act which shows annoyance. Then the players go through a dialogue of attack and defense. Eventually they collect so many negative feelings that they physically go their separate ways. One player usually shouts down the other, and they storm away, slamming doors behind them. They thus avoid intimacy or the risk of closeness. For example, a couple just finished with *Uproar* will not likely be ready for loving sexual contact. Here is how one couple played their parents' favorite game of *Uproar*.

Mary Lou grew up in a quarrelsome household. Dinner-table conversations were usually arguments. Accusations and counteraccusations flew across the table, and little attention was given to the food. Many dinners ended with one of her parent's slamming down a napkin or a fork and storming from the room. Mary Lou vowed that when she grew up, there'r be no fighting over her dinner table.

But Mary Lou had learned the game of Uproar *well. As a grownup, she did not fight at the table; instead, she and her husband often sat over their food in silent, seething anger. As she put it, "I had trouble figuring out what we were really doing, but one night it came through very clear. We were eating silently and had shot a few sharp glances at each other across the table. Suddenly, Todd heaved a sigh and stood up. Throwing his napkin on his plate, he stomped off to his den. The slam of the door pierced the silence. I thought, 'Good grief, that's just what my dad used to do.' It's the same film with different sound track. I realized for the first time Todd and I were playing* Uproar, *just like Mom and Dad. We had the same ending—isolation from each other for the rest of the evening. We later had to learn that it's OK to get close. In fact, it feels good. We both need time for each other and time to ourselves without playing games to get either. Actually, now that I think about it, it was funny. Imagine what a movie of us would have looked like."*

To begin to come into contact with your family games, think back over dialogue and actions that happened over and over again. Games tend to be repetitive. We do the same things and say the same things again and again. If the repetitious act ends with someone feeling bad, it is probably a game.

HOW CAN YOU DEAL WITH YOUR PARENT EGO STATE?

When we first incorporated our parent figures, we were very young. At the time it was a natural thing for us to do. We looked around at the models available to us and copied them. Some of what we incorporated then may still be very useful, some may be hurtful or downright destructive, and some may be outdated and outmoded.

Most parents do their best to be good parents. But some don't know how. Our parents had pain, problems, and frustrations of their own. Sometimes we distort our parents through the eyes of the children we once were, expecting them to be gods. We can either carry these gods on our backs, forever resenting what they did or did not do; or, we can accept them as people and forgive them for what they did not know or felt they could not do. Hate and guilt can give way to understanding.

Understanding Your Parent Figures

Who are your two most important parent figures?

Thinking about each in turn, get in touch with their ego states. Raise these questions:

What were *their* parents like?

How did this affect their Parent ego states?

What kind of education did they have?

Were they good at solving problems?

What did they do for fun?

How did they feel about themselves inside?

Now take a fantasy journey. Imagine that you are overhearing your parents talking. Your mother has just learned that she is pregnant with you. How does she feel? What does she do? How does she tell your father?

What is your father's reaction?

What happens between them?

What are they both thinking, feeling, and doing?

How do you feel about this?

Blaming parents for our negative or self-destructive messages no longer helps. Instead, we must recognize, "This is part of me. I act this way. This is *my* personality. Maybe I got those ideas from a real person. But now it's my responsibility to be more selective about what I choose to listen to in my own head. It's now *my* problem, not anybody else's."

Sometimes negative Parent messages can be turned to advantage. Rather than trying to get rid of them, alter them. Turn them around. Reinterpret them. Give them a new slant. Talk to them.

Jeanine's message was: "Never have fun 'til the work is done." She responded to this message by working all the time. Much of the time she was harried, trying to take on more and more work in order to please the Parent tape in her head. The way she had interpreted the message was: "Never have fun. Always work."

When Jeanine came in touch with how she had chosen to respond to this message, she was able to alter it. Each day she outlined what actually had to be done rather than what she only felt had to be done. When she looked at her days objectively, she found that she did a lot of "busy" work and volunteered to take on a lot of extra work, just to stay working.

She decided to turn her message to her benefit. She figured out exactly when her work would be done and what she would then do for play. After doing this for a while, Jeanine discovered that not all work was joyless, and she began to feel like more of her work was play. Eventually she brought a better balance into her life.

The following diagram helped Jeanine to organize this balance:[7]

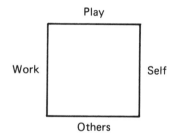

Play

Work   Self

Others

Jeanine began to recognize that her life needed a balance of work, play, time for herself, and time for others. Before, she had felt that only work had a place in her life, and her diagram looked like this one:

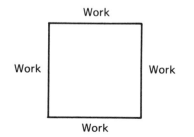

Work

Work   Work

Work

By deciding that there was a time when the work *was done*, she came to feel very OK about using the rest of her time for other things.

Along the way, Jeanine put her message (her Parent) in an empty chair and talked to it (first from her Child and then from her Adult). She switched back and forth, portraying her own conflicting ego states. Her voice grew louder and louder.

as Child: You're on my back all the time. Work, work, work. That's all I do!

as Parent: Who are you to complain. You don't have sense enough to do it right.

as Child: Do it right! I have clean kids, a clean house, help out in every organization around town. Damn it, I can do it right. Why don't you ever tell me I've done it right?

as Parent: My foot, you do it right. You'd have time to sit outside half the day if you'd just get organized. Why should I have to tell you?

as Child
and Adult: I know what I have to do. I can organize it for myself. *I can organize my work for myself.* **You don't have to tell me when it's right. I can decide.**

Jeanine looked up and said, "That's why I work all the time. I never know if I've done it right. I never know when something's done. I've been waiting for someone to tell me it's done and it's all right!"

The Parent message in Eileen's head was different. She always felt guilty about the way she kept her house. She was surprised at what she found out when she put the old message ("You should keep your house cleaner") in an empty chair and talked to it.

One Saturday night my husband was watching TV, and I was waxing the kitchen floor and feeling frustrated. I decided I had to do something different. So I put two chairs together and talked to my feelings. Chair 1 was my feelings; Chair 2 was my message. I sounded like this:

1: *I don't want to be working.*

2: *This house is filthy. You should get busy and keep your house cleaner.*

1: *But I'm tired. I work all week. My husband works all week.*

2: *What do you mean, "tired"? You shouldn't feel tired cleaning house. You don't even have any children. Think about women who have children and still manage to keep their homes clean.*

1: **That doesn't make any sense. It doesn't matter if I have children or not. I'm hiring a a housekeeper.**

Eileen leaned back and looked up. "Wow, you mean I've been carrying around that load of guilt just because I don't have any children?"

You may want to put a bothersome Parent message in an empty chair and talk to it, be it. You may be surprised at what you find out.

**STEPS TO
AWARENESS**

Your Parent Ego State

To get an even more complete picture of your Parent ego state, ask yourself the following questions.

How do I use my Parent in negative—critical, judgmental or prejudicial—ways?

What happens to my relationships as a result of these behaviors?

What are five ways I can nurture and protect other people in healthy ways?

Do these things more often. Why not? It feels good.

Weeding Out Your Parent Garden

Think of your Parent ego state as if it were a flower garden. Most parents do the best they know how; so in our gardens there are likely to be many kinds of flowers, fruits, and vegetables that please us and nurture us. There are also likely to be many kinds of weeds and pests. Your Parent probably has a mixture of both.

Part of the reason for understanding what your Parent is all about is to help you to weed out your mental Parent garden. Allow the food from the soil, like your psychic energy, to feed the roots of healthy, beautiful things. Do not let the weeds sap up all the nourishment and energy.

EACH WOMAN IS MOTHER, WOMAN, AND GIRL

The world would be a sorry place without the Parent ego state. Who of us has not been injured, humiliated, or ill and panicked at the thought that there would be no one there to help? It is the Parent ego state that in many ways allows us to put our own needs aside and bring our energies fully to another person.

Since this process seems to be *learned*, the preservation of a healthy Parent ego state is not only important to individuals, but also is the crux of a caring society. When the Parent ego state becomes twisted, cruel, and indifferent, individuals and groups of people will feel the pain.

Parenting is caring. It is giving a darn about others. It is setting limits when the situation calls for it. It is more than helping youngsters become mannerly. It is helping others of any age express and understand their feelings.

It is arms to hold you when you feel bad.

It is a tender touch, a sympathetic smile.

Someone is out there.

Someone cares.

Someone will help you with it.

Someone will bring you what you need.

Many women have Parent tapes which dictate what they should do and be in terms of traditional female roles. Some of these messages are no longer appropriate to the kind of lives today's women are likely to live.

You deserve to be a happy, productive person. But any "garbage" in your old programming is a stumbling block. Learning where the garbage is and throwing it out can help you or a woman in your life become even more of a winner as a woman.

7

Sugar
and
Spice

- In what ways can you better understand the feeling level of your personality?
- What is the source of your creativity and intuition?
- How can you find out more about your expressiveness and the ways you cope?

I want to laugh
I want to cry
I am aggressive
I am shy
I feel strong
I feel weak
I feel confident
I feel meek
I look pretty
I look bad
I feel happy
I feel sad
I am love
I am hate
I act crazy
I act straight
I feel soft
I feel tough
I feel sexy
I feel rough
Many emotions amidst each day
together with reason are what guide my way
Susan Polis Schutz[1]

Our gut-level feelings are likely to come from our Inner Child. When you think, feel, or act the way you did when you were young, you are acting from your Child ego state. This does not mean *childish*, but *childlike*— much like the little girl or boy you once were. Since your experiences as a youngster were unique, so is your Child ego state. In fact, no two Child ego states are exactly alike.

STEPS TO AWARENESS

Seeing Your Child

One way to recall some of your childhood feelings and experiences is to look through old photo albums.

- Get the family albums out and reacquaint yourself with the Child in you.

- What do you see that is positive in your life today?

- Are you building on this as much as you can?

Now close your eyes and picture yourself as a child. Go back to a time when you were really having fun or a time when you felt very special. Get in touch with what you were doing, what it looked like, where you were, and how you felt. Relive this experience for a few minutes.

- Do you ever have these same feelings now?

- If so, when? Where? With whom?

- If not, would you like to?

- If so, what can you do to arrange it?

When were you the happiest as a child?

- What were the circumstances?

- Does this have anything to do with what you enjoyed now?

List five things other people would have said about you as a child.

1.

2.

3.

4.

5.

Would these things describe you in any way today? If so, how?

Which of these things do you see as positive and which as negative?

PEOPLE ACCEPT ONLY PART OF THE
NATURAL CHILD IN WOMEN

On a sunny, clear day, Gwen and her two children cut through the park on their way to the store. In a sudden burst of energy she yielded to the excitement of spring appearing. She twirled herself around while singing "Oh, What a Beautiful Morning" at the top of her voice. Both her children flushed with embarrassment and groaned, "Oh, Mother." Their groans brought Gwen's impromptu dance to a sudden halt.

Gwen's impulse to run and sing came from her Natural Child—one of the three parts of her Child ego state. Her Natural Child, along with her Little Professor and Adapted Child, form her unique Child ego state. The three parts of the Child can be thought of like this:

Adapted Child: trained thoughts and actions under outside influence

Little Professor: primitive ability to figure things out

Natural Child: inborn impulses and expressiveness

"Whee," "wow," "super" characterize the Natural Child. The uncensored impulses that every infant is born with lie here. These natural ways of behaving come as standard equipment and can always be expressed, no matter how old a person is. Your Natural Child is the affectionate, fun-loving, sensuous, selfish, curious, fiesty, playful part of you.

Since little girls are often cuddled and touched more than little boys are, some girls express certain feelings more easily. They can be affectionate—cry, giggle, and stomp their feet—more openly than boys. As a consequence, we tend to accept these parts of the Natural Child more readily in women than we do in men.

These women show their Natural Child in many ways:

- One woman who now enjoys kneading bread once made mud pies and even ate the better ones.
- One woman who now enjoys sunbathing once enjoyed pulling off her clothes and running nude through the warm air at the water's edge.
- One woman who now always demands her own way once was yielded to with few restrictions because she was so cute.
- One woman who now loves to have the wind blowing through her hair remembers the excitement of the wind as her father ice skated with her on his shoulders—the only times he touched her.

The Natural Child shows when a woman:

Slams the door because she did not get the promotion.

Sticks out her tongue when her boss turns away.

Bralessly enjoys the fuzzy feel of a sweater.

Joyously downs an ice cream cone.

Enjoys the skin of another person next to hers.

Saves the biggest piece of cake for herself.

Expressiveness springs from the Natural Child. Yet typically women learn to feel that the way they look is more important than self-expression. Here are some ways the Natural Child gets stifled and then adapts:

"Don't get dirty";

"Don't touch that nasty lizard"; and

"Don't touch yourself"
cool down natural feelings of curiosity and sensuousness.

"Don't play football";

"Don't wrestle. It's not feminine"; and

"Don't you two roll in the dirt"
temper the urge to playfully touch.

"Keep quiet";

"Do what you're told"; and

"If you ask one more time, I'll hit you in the mouth"
kill the tendency to speak up for what is wanted.

Your Natural Child and Your Imagination

If you feel that your Natural Child is too often squelched, use your imagination to start to change. Think of something fun that you would really like to do.

- Now close your eyes and picture yourself getting ready to do what you want to do.
- What would you wear (or not wear)?

- See yourself going where you need to go.

- Fantasize that you are doing what you want to do.

- Take this fantasy trip several times.

- Now bring your fantasy to reality. Choose a time to do what you have imagined yourself doing. Be sure to fantasize only what would be good for you. (We all have fantasies that are best to stay that way—just fantasies!)

WOMEN GET MOST OF THE CREDIT FOR THE LITTLE PROFESSOR

"Eureka" characterizes the Little Professor. Intuition, manipulation, and creativity are other marks of the Little Professor. This part of the Child ego state represents unschooled wisdom—that sense for figuring things out on the basis of subliminal information and the need to cope. Here is how one little girl cleverly used her Little Professor.

Traveling on a bus late at night, a two-year-old girl sat on her father's lap. Weary and sleepy travelers coming home after a long holiday weekend filled each seat of the bus. The little girl was far from weary, however. She bounced up and down, happily exploring different parts of the seats and the floor. Her father first cautioned her softly, "Be quiet." She heeded his caution for almost a minute, then began bouncing up and down again. Scolding her a little bit louder and shaking his finger, he

cautioned her, "Be quiet or I'll spank you!" With this stern warning,
she remained quiet—for almost five minutes. But soon she started bounc-
ing up and down again. This time her father grabbed her solidly by her
shoulders, shook his finger in her face, and threatened. "I'm going to
spank you right now!" With both hands she gently pulled her father's
shaking finger toward her. Holding it to her lips, she planted a kiss. Dad's
anger appeared to melt away. And with a grin he mumbled, "Isn't
that just like a girl."

Without benefit of formal study, this toddler had figured out that this
was not the time for open rebellion. But she did not want to give in. So she
did what was exactly right to get on the good side of old dad.

Feminine Intuition

When a little girl, like the toddler on the bus, cleverly figures out how to
get her own way, she is smilingly credited with "woman's intuition." In
the face of power, underdogs use their intuition and sharpen their wits to
cope. Ashley Montagu writes:

> Women have to keep their eye on the main chance; they have to be
> on their guard; they must always have their antennae extended, with-
> out appearing to do so, so that they may operate on the correct wave
> length and pick up the proper signals without anyone noticing, as it
> were. All this makes for a certain artificiality. Elegantly decorated, such
> artificiality is not displeasing to men, even when they are able to dis-
> tinguish it as such, any more than the artificially deformed feet of
> Chinese women were displeasing to the perpetrators of such deformi-
> ties, for it was considered beautiful to have feet that peeped beneath
> the skirts or trousers of the women like little mice. The artificialities of
> the women of Western civilization possess an elegance of a different
> kind, for they represent a contrived confession of inferiority on the
> part of the female. It is a form of feminine wooing of the male.[2]

The belief in woman's intuition holds firm, even though there is no
research evidence to prove that intuitive skills are sexually based. Our
cultural scripts, however, ascribe the use of intuition predominantly to
women. Such beliefs encourage many women to rely on their ability to
psyche things out at the expense of not bothering about factual data. In
contrast, if intuition is thought of as "feminine," many men will just deal
with what facts they have and not consider their hunches about voice
tones, body language, and all those things that tickle the sixth sense.

The healthy adult of either sex needs the ability to think things through factually, teamed with a sensitivity to hunches. The feminine label on intuition does a disservice to both men and women.

Feminine Manipulation

Little girls frequently learn how to get their way by manipulating others without asserting physical strength. They may hear, "Never talk to your father about that until he's had a chance to have a drink. You know he's always tired when he gets home from work." Or, "Don't worry about asking Dad about going to the beach for the weekend. We'll plant the seed, and in a couple of days he'll think it's his idea." Tears, wiggles, and flashing eyes may all be part of a successful act at age 2, 3, 4, or 40.

This part of the Little Professor acts out a game of "Let's Pretend." "Let's fool Dad. Dad's delicate. You have to be smart enough to make him believe that he thinks things up on his own." Honesty is unbecoming to a woman.

As a consequence of these types of Little Professor manipulations, a grown woman may still be pretending with her man. She may fake a sexual response in order not to disturb his fragile masculinity. She still may go after what she wants with tears, wiggles, or flashing eyes.

For example, one three-year-old girl's tears, which originally came in response to real pain, may become a learned tool with which to manipulate the big people who hold the power over her. Later, as a woman, she uses this same technique on a male boss confronting her about tardiness.

However, it is unfortunate if a woman manipulates others to assert herself and gain power. If people do not see through these "feminine wiles," they may unwisely believe that they are being admired or helped, as in this story.

Once a shipwrecked man and woman were swept up on a deserted island. Though strangers, they clung together in their desperate situation. Finally, she looked up at him and said, "Whenever even two people are together, someone needs to take charge. Because you're the man, I think you should be in charge." He put his arm around her, nodding in agreement.

Feminine Creativity

Traditionally, creativity has had sexual spheres. Women can spruce up the nest, make clothes, and arrange flowers. Serious creativity, however, such as art, music, and literature, has been in the male domain. In the past, a few women who "made it" in the arts took on masculine names in order to be taken seriously.

The two most famous cases attended the publications of *Jane Eyre* by Currer Bell in 1847 and *Adam Bede* by George Eliot in 1859. The shock that Currer Bell (Charlotte Brontë) was a woman rocked the literary world. "Most significantly, many critics bluntly admitted that they thought the book was a masterpiece if written by a man, shocking or disgusting if written by a woman."[3]

That George Eliot might be female was so unthinkable that an imposter with the name was able to bask in the glory of literary limelight until Marian Evans was forced to reveal her identity. The instant success of *Adam Bede* soon came under fire by critics. Those who had previously lauded the powerful mind of George Eliot turned to criticizing a disturbing, unladylike coarseness which appeared here and there.[4]

Even Louisa May Alcott wrote under an assumed name—A. M. Barnard—until *Little Women*. Hiding her feminine identity, she "was able to let down her literary hair and distill her passion for dramatics as well as her intense feminist anger at a world in which a woman was expected to polish her master's muddy boots."[5]

As a consequence of traditional scripting about significant creativity, a woman might still ignore or dabble in her area of talent. She may even feel guilty if she invests time developing and expressing it. Yet we tend to expect creative men not only to produce, but also to have a woman backing them up.

STEPS TO
AWARENESS

Your Little Professor

Go back in your mind's eye to being a little girl (or a little boy).

- How did you get what you wanted from people?

You may find it helpful to recall a specific incident and remember what you actually did and said.

- Did you do different things with men and women?

■ Do you do any of these things today?

■ If so, how productive or unproductive are they?

MANY WOMEN EXPRESS TOO MUCH ADAPTED CHILD

"Yes, ma'am" and "yes, sir" characterize the Adapted Child. It is this part of the Child that is trained. It develops under the influence of significant authority figures, collective scripts, and early life experience.

Many of a child's natural impulses need to be tempered to fit the demands of living in a larger group. Appropriate adaptations civilize children, helping them become aware of the needs and rights of other people. It is the Adapted Child that is socialized. Through this part of the personality, we learn to live with others, perhaps saying "please" or "thank you" or taking turns. Children who learn to consider others do not grab the last biscuit on the plate, do not spit on the floor, and refrain from picking their noses at the dinner table. Such graciousness greases the wheels of sociability.

Unfortunately, not all adaptations which children receive are rational, appropriate, and geared toward safety and sensitivity. Many adaptations are irrational, inappropriate, and unnecessarily inhibiting. Little girls often receive rewards for compliance—for being obedient. Yet too much compliance squelches their self-expression.

Even though traditionally women are thought of as feeling and emotional, this is not so with their sensuousness. In some women, sexual sensuousness is so suppressed that even in the aura of permission in marriage, they never reach the golden ring of orgasm. Years of protecting young women from unwanted pregnancy by threats and admonitions rather than through data and choices have ingrained in many women feelings of fear, confusion, or revulsion toward their own sexual responsiveness.

Sex clinics, books on female sexual response, arguments about clitoral versus vaginal orgasm, and articles and experts telling women "they can" are proliferating. They all attest to the extent of the problem and to an increased willingness to do something about it. In contrast, many young men are "supposed" to make sexual conquests, no matter how fearful they might really feel inside. As one young man confessed, "I didn't date for two years, because I thought I had to make love every time and I didn't know how."

Sexuality and Sexual Expression

For much of history, male homosexuality was accepted as a high mode of companionship. Men and the virtues of strength, daring, and prowess were celebrated. Even St. Thomas Aquinas saw women as being defective, but he conceded that they were necessary for procreation. And in more modern times, Professor Higgins sings, "Why can't a woman be more like a man?" The sexuality of women has a history of being discounted.

These attitudes were rejected when in the Christian era, the church attempted to raise the status of both marriage and male-female relationships. To complicate the matter, the practice of worshipping virgins grew in popularity. St. Ambrose resolved this conflict by arguing that marriages were after all acceptable, for otherwise virgins could not be born.

Eventually homosexuality among men became a taboo. However, the practice of men working together, playing together, roughing it together, with women meeting their everyday needs has continued. Currently, many members of the homophile community—both female and male homosexuals—seek full rights and protection under the law.

Infants do not seem to be born with a sexual preference. Sexual preference appears to be an adaptation. Collective scripts, early experience with members of the same sex and the opposite sex—all influence a child's decisions. These decisions later affect the persons sexual preference, fears, and expression—be they toward the opposite sex, the same sex, both, or neither.

At 23 Pamela shared, "I looked at my mother and decided that wasn't for me. She gave her whole life to a husband, house, and three kids. She was like a rug. I wouldn't take on that kind of life for anyone. I don't hate men, but men aren't ready to live with women on an equal basis. Life with another woman is more satisfying."

At age 37 Mary still felt the impact of her father. "My father beat me, humiliated me, and used me sexually before I was six years old. I hated him and did my best to keep out of his way. I don't know if this has anything to do with my being lesbian or not, but I've always felt more comfortable with women."[6]

Common Adaptations

A litle girl may distort her self-concept by learning to:

- Reject her sex.
- Feel dumb.
- Hold a contempt for her body.

- Act helpless rather than use her own resources.
- Always subordinate her own needs.
- Squelch her natural expressiveness.
- Sit in submissive silence.
- Act sexy but be sexless.
- Feel inferior and in general not-OK.

Specific adaptations will be explored much more fully in Chapter 8.

Inner Conflicts in the Child

Some of our deepest inner conflict occurs between the wants of the Natural Child (NC) and the trained Adapted Child (AC). As these two factions argue inside our heads, we may feel unable to move or to solve the problem. Such conflict results in feelings of turmoil or of being stuck—of being at an impasse.

Carolyn's dialogue between these two parts of herself sounded like this:

NC: I want to fly. I want to get in a plane and soar over the mountains.

AC: That's stupid. How could you ever learn to fly?

NC: I could learn if I really want to.

AC: Oh, yeah! Who says? You'd be a stupid woman driver in the sky just like you feel on the ground—a stupid woman driver.

NC: I drive a car OK even if part of me feels shaky about it.

AC: Sure I shake you up when I start acting like a know-it-all. I step on you. I keep you down, down on the ground where you belong.

NC: I don't have to feel bad about driving anything. You don't have to hold me back. **I can fly. I can learn to fly. I don't have to feel stupid about wanting to fly!**

AC: Maybe that would be exciting, but what would happen to me?

NC: It is exciting! Enjoy it.

AC: You sound as if you could really do it.

NC: **That's right. I can really do it.**

Carolyn's warring parts of her Child finally came to an agreement. She strengthened the part of her that wanted to learn something new. She weakened the part that held her back with irrational feelings of stupidity and fear.

141

**STEPS TO
AWARENESS**

Your Adaptations

Begin to understand the unique ways you adapted. Think about the following questions.

- What did you get approval for when you were a small child?
    Was it when you "acted" feminine? Masculine?
    When you were perfect?
    When you pleased someone?
    When you tried hard?
    When you were strong, or stoic?
    When you were hurrying to catch up?
    When you couldn't figure things out?
    When . . . ?
- Do you still feel and act in the same ways as you did in childhood?

- Do you see any implications of this for your life today?

- Do you still cope with problems in the same ways?

- Do you still expect strokes in the same ways?

- What do you see as positive?

Think back and recall three major ways you adapted. Looking at how you responded in specific situations will probably help you.

1.

2.

3.

■ How do these adaptations show now?

■ Are they helpful, or do they get in the way?

■ If they get in the way, talk them over with yourself. Project a parent figure onto an empty chair. Be yourself as a child and sit across from your imaginary parent. Begin a dialogue. Switch back and forth being both parts of yourself. Bring your conversation to a feeling of conclusion. To gain this feeling of closure, you may need to hold the conversation more than once.

If you have inner conflict between what you want to do and what you are trained to do, get a conversation going between your Natural Child and your Adapted Child.

WE ADAPT TO PLAY GAMES

In the beginning children are straight. However, many soon learn coping techniques that are crooked. Psychological games are one of the results. Those games which lie deepest in our psyches are played from our adaptations as children. Based on our early decisions, we play these games to keep our world and the people in it predictable—even though it hurts.

We reinforce the decisions we have made through the eyes and feelings of a child—even though these may be distorted.

We reinforce the positions we have taken about ourselves and others —although our experiences may have had tight boundaries.

We collect and hand out the kinds of feelings we grew used to—rational or not.

We act out scenes that form the scenario of the meaning and purpose we weave into the pattern of our life's direction—whether it fits us or not.

We further our scripts.

Games are transactions with a hidden agenda. We are saying and doing one thing while something else goes on underneath. That something else reinforces a sense of not-OKness and strengthens our racket feelings.

For example, Penny learned to get negative strokes from her father. When she married, she played *Kick Me* and *Stupid* with her husband to keep alive the actions and dialogues that were familiar to her. Her husband had had a long-suffering mother, so he knew well how to play his complementary hand, the game of *Now I've Got You*. In one instance they acted it out like this.

Penny nagged Art about getting a physical. When he finally said he could manage it three weeks from Tuesday, she promised to make the appointment.

Three weeks from Tuesday, she was puzzled when he didn't go to work. "Well, I arranged to take the day off for my physical." "Oh, no!" she exclaimed, "I forgot to make the appointment. How dumb. How could I have done such a dumb thing?"

"You mean I've taken a day off and don't have an appointment! Damn it. You know the old man will have a fit if he finds out. Every time I rely on you, you always . . ." etc.

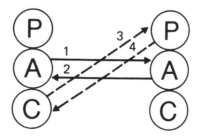

Plausible level: Adult to Adult (lines 1 and 2)

1. "You need an appointment. I'll make it."
2. "All right."

Ulterior (hidden) level: Child to Parent and Parent to Child (lines 3 and 4)

3. "I'm a bad girl who can't do anything right."

4. "You sure as hell are! Just like my mother."

You can learn to play two kinds of Child-motivated psychological games. They can be acted out in endless variations on themes.

1. Games played to put yourself down or to feel self-pity. These include such games as:

   Kick Me—provoking someone else to bawl you out, be exasperated with you, or at a more intense level, assault you.

   Stupid—doing something dumb that erks someone else enough to call you stupid, to punish you, or maybe to make you wear a dunce cap or send you to jail.

   Schlemiel—doing something clumsy but apologizing so profusely that someone else takes pity and forgives you: "Love me no matter what I do."

   Poor Me—investing time in self-pity or self-depreciation. This game can be played in a variety of ways, such as *Why Does This Always Happen To Me?, See How Hard I Try?,* and *Ain't It Awful?*

   Alcoholic—committing slow suicide.

2. Games played to put others down, trip them up, or catch them in the act. These include:

   Blemish—nitpicking, piercing the Achilles heel. *Now I've Got You, You S.O.B.*—waiting for someone to make a mistake (or setting the person up to make a mistake), then pouncing on the person about it.

   See What You Made Me Do!—blaming others for your own mistakes.

   If It Weren't For You—blaming others for your own lack of achievement or competence.

   I'm Only Trying To Help You—giving people ineffective help they may neither want nor need; then when they come back to you because it doesn't work, both you and they end up feeling put down.

Sweatshirt Messages and Games

We often use our Little Professor to figure out who plays our games. The Little Professor tunes in to the vibes others radiate. The process is much like intuiting a message from an imaginary sweatshirt. We pick up such a message from a person's facial expression, posture, clothing, voice tone, and other types of body language.

Sometimes we are unaware of the hidden meaning or pretense our sweatshirt messages send out. For example, Adele dressed in sexy, provocative clothes, but complained that men were "always making disgusting passes." She was unknowingly sending the message, "I'm Available."

If the overt, surface message is responded to, the sweatshirt wearer switches messages, and someone ends up feeling hurt. This is the essence of the psychological game of *Rapo*, which Little Red Riding Hood in Chapter 3 plays. When *Rapo* is played sexually, one partner baits the other with a seductive come-on. If the other partner takes the bait, she or he gets put down. This is the payoff; one person feels triumphant, and the other feels kicked. It proves one more time, "Men are no good." This is likely to have been the decision of a little girl who had experiences with men who treated her in inappropriate sexual ways.

Social *Rapo* is similar, but without the sexual undertones. One person sends the sweatshirt message "Let's Be Friends." If the invitation is taken, the message becomes "You've Got No Business Making Demands On Me!"

In addition to "I'm Available," women have shared these other common sweatshirt messages.

"I'm Helpless." A Victim does this by looking up through lashes, forcing a tear, spreading heels with toes pointing in, tilting head, dropping shoulders, raising the voice, and whining.

"I'm Fierce." A Persecutor does this by firming the jaw, rearing back shoulders, putting hands on hips, glaring, looking down the nose, lowering the voice, and spreading feet.

"I'm Always Here to Help." A Rescuer does this by maintaining smile lines and crow's feet, being ever ready in the right place at the right time, looking "motherly," speaking soothingly, looking interested, but not listening.

Do you pick up these or other messages from anyone you know? What kind do you send?

People with particular messages attract each other. For example, an "I'm Helpless" attracts a "Lean on Me." "I'm Fierce" attracts a "Please Don't Kick Me." "I'm Always Here to Help" appeals to "How Could I Be So Stupid." Learning to recognize sweatshirt messages helps you also recognize what games are being played.

Your Child Games

Think about some of your repetitive transactions.[7]

- What keeps happening over and over again?

- What happens first?

- Then what happens?

- Where does it lead?

- How does it end?

- Who ends up feeling bad?

- What could you do differently?

More on Getting to Know Your Child

Discovering and understanding the uniqueness of your Child—both the positive and negative elements—opens the door to personal growth. The deep roots of many of the problems women want to solve lie in the Child.

The Child discovers and learns and relearns through experience more than through information. For this reason we are including some additional Steps to Awareness for you to learn and choose from.

Discovering Your Childgram

Look at your Child ego state as if your Child energy were divided into three parts.[8] The amount of *time* you spend in each one is an indicator of how you spend your Child energy.

Natural	Little	Adapted
Child	Professor	Child

Would *your* Childgram look like this?

Natural	Little	Adapted
Child	Professor	Child

Or this?

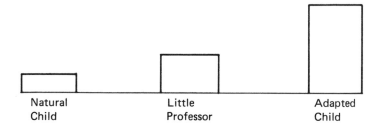

Natural	Little	Adapted
Child	Professor	Child

What is yours?

Natural Child	Little Professor	Adapted Child

Are you satisfied with this?
If not, what are three things you could do about it?

1.

2.

3.

Fun with Your Child

What in the world are you most curious about?

If you had x-ray vision, what would you like to see through?

Imagine that a silver-winged fairy has mysteriously appeared in front of you and announces that you have just been given one magic wish. What would you wish for?

What do your answers tell you about your Child ego state?

Your Childhood Play

When you were small, who were your playmates?

Did you play by yourself a lot?

Were there certain people you could not play with? Why couldn't you play with them? Do you avoid those kinds of people now?

When could you play? After all the work was done? After a hard day? Anytime? Never?

Picking Playmates

You can use your Little Professor in positive ways. Picking people to play with is one. Usually when we really like being with someone, it is because we like the Child in that person.

- Who do you have the most fun with?

- Can you figure out why?

- Can you find these qualities in other people?

- What does this person seem to bring out in you?

- Can you be this way with more people?

Think about the following situations and ask yourself: What kind of Child would I most like in another person in each situation?

On a picnic	To take a trip with
At a party	Going to dinner
On a backpacking trip	Visiting a museum
On the job	To study with
To build something with	In bed

- Do you see any pattern about the people you like being with?

- Do you have enough people in your life with whom you have fun? If not, what can you do about it?

Do you believe other people think you are fun to be with? Where do you guess you would be on their lists?

Now ask yourself, "How do I want *my* Child to be in those situations?

What people, situations, and behavior of mine would bring me the most happiness?

Fun Is OK

Women get more strokes for being childlike—for being helpless, weak, dependent, cute, or decorative—than they do for being direct, assertive, and intelligent. On the happy side, this leads more of us to accept women as feeling creatures. However, their thinking is discredited, and an unhealthy passivity often results.

Many women adapt to feel that they are winners only if they lose. This literally might mean losing a tennis match or a chess game in order to appear to be a "winner of a woman." Such adaptations can suppress talent and hinder actualizing and living to one's full potential. Even Mother Hubbard might be lauded "the perfect mother" because she so willingly, even if unnecessarily, sacrifices herself at the altar of ingratitude. Isn't that what women are for?

Negative, unrealistic adaptations cause an emotional and physical energy drain. Continuing to invest energies in archaic problems is like driving through life with one foot on the gas pedal and one foot on the brake. As a result, a significant number of women feel not-OK about their minds, their bodies, and their spirits.

Understanding your Child helps you to understand your feelings. Having your head and heart together makes you whole. What you do holds more purpose, more meaning.

Your Child is the expressive, charming part of you. It is the part that speaks up, has fun, and makes something new. It is the part that learns to be polite and to get along with others. Do something good for your Child every day. You deserve it, and others around you will be happier, too.

8

Losing to Win

- In what ways do women adapt to early influences?
- How can these adaptations later affect women's lives?
- How can you get in touch with your own Adapted Child?

Pretty little face,
Cute little figure,
Stand back boys,
Till I get a little bigger!

When her parents had guests, Carol would enter the room, cup her chin in her two little hands, sway her body back and forth, and chant this chant. It always won smiles from her entire family. Carol glowed with her sense of pleasing them.

Carol's father frequently gave her playful swats whenever she wiggled seductively, tilted her head, and looked up at him wide-eyed. He smilingly cautioned her not to try to use her "unfair feminine wiles" on him. But he often beamed and bragged to other family members, "Why this kid is only three years old, and she already knows every feminine trick in the book."

When she was 26, Carol landed a promising job with a manufacturing company and did well. Her success was not unnoticed. An officer of the company asked her to develop a program to facilitate moving high-potential women up the ladder.

Carol threw herself into this task and developed a good program. However, none of the male managers she presented it to either took the program or her seriously. Discouraged, she sought out advice from a work colleague and close friend. Her friend advised, "I don't know if you're aware of this, Carol, but when you talk before a group of men, you somehow act 'cute.' You tilt your head and stand in a way that looks provocative. Maybe they're confused between the words you say and what they see."

As Carol thought this over carefully, she became keenly aware of her body posture. She reflected, "You know, I was doing just that when I was four years old. It never occurred to me that I was doing it now."

With this awareness, Carol improved her presentations, and her program eventually became a success within the company. She also learned something else about herself—that although she was provocative to men, she had no really close male friends. She realized, "I'm still telling them 'I'm a pretty little girl, but stand back boys 'till I get a little bigger.' I think at 26 I'm grown up enough to get to know some men a little better."

Getting in touch with the ways you adapted and the ways many women in general adapt can help you like it did Carol, to define more clearly what might need to be reevaluated. With understanding and commitment, negative adaptations can be changed so that your life and relationships enjoy the enrichment of reality.

WE ADAPT FOR REASONS

When we first learn to adapt our impulses, we have reasons for doing so. We must cope with the power of big people. We believe them. We want them to love us. We want their smiles. We will do it; we will do it for them.

Some of what we decide to do enhances us. Helpful adaptations prod us from the core of our own self-centeredness. Appropriate adaptations help us grow in concerned caring about other people. They help us to understand—understand what it is like to be in someone else's skin. They sharpen and refine our social skills.

Our Ups and Downs

Life deals us a mixture of joyful, sad, funny, and tragic experiences, and we respond to what flows our way. Sometimes it seems that there is nothing we can do about our down times—our bad moods—and we are stuck at a gray impasse. This may be true. But sometimes it is not.

We can put a high priority on our health and nutrition. We can respond to a dismal day with a crackling fire in the fireplace or happy music on the stereo. We can make choices even in the most constricted situations.

Victor Frankl's ability to choose his response while in a concentration camp attests to this possibility. His report in *Man's Search for Meaning* shows that our ability to decide always confronts us.

Practically everybody feels guilty some of the time, or wants to please other people some of the time, or on occasion wants to do things perfectly. A key question is, "What am I doing out of reasonable choice and what am I doing because I feel compelled to, even when it does not make sense for me today?" For example, wanting to please *everybody* is an adaptation, a driving force which may unravel your uniqueness. But deciding to please somebody at a special time or to be more pleasant to be around is an act of choice.

Our feelings are affected by our early decisions. Getting to know how you adapted is one of the most fruitful grounds for learning to understand and better direct your good and bad feelings.

Adaptations geared to your safety, health, and social integrity are necessary and purposeful. However, our goal for the next section is to focus your attention on inappropriate adaptations and to assist you in sorting out what needs to be thought over and what needs to be changed.

FEELINGS OF INFERIORITY OFTEN GROW
OUT OF ADAPTATIONS

Negative adaptations drain our energy. This personal energy crisis signals a number of self-defeating feelings and behaviors. Later we hang on to these feelings like the proverbial security blanket. Even though it is tattered and dirty, we do not want to give it up. We know it. It may be uncomfortable, but at least it is predictable.

Old, adapted feelings that people cling to run a gambit too wide to explore fully. However, in the next few pages we describe a few we have lived or that other women have revealed to us.

Feeling Unfeminine

The distressed cry of, "But I just don't feel feminine," can be heard from women who are beautiful or ugly, young or old, fat or thin, tall or short, married or single, mothers or nonmothers, employed or unemployed. From this we can easily conclude that most women base their feelings of being "feminine" more on personal experience and early decision rather than on objective observation.

Consequently, what one woman chooses to feel feminine about may not mean a thing to another. As one woman says "I know I can balance a checkbook, but it sure doesn't make me feel feminine. So I collect all the bills, and Archie takes care of such things." Another complains, "I feel really feminine only when I'm baking for my family and the whole house smells of bread and cookies." Another reflects, "I really feel feminine when I'm making love and especially when the throbs of orgasm come."

Many women link feeling feminine with feeling clean. For them, if cleanliness is not next to godliness, it is certainly next to femininity. Such fanatic preoccupation with cleanliness may range from keeping an antiseptic house to maintaining compulsive personal hygiene. Such a woman may feel compelled to clean house before the cleaning person comes on Tuesday. In an effort to keep her female organs spring clean, this woman may even unnecessarily douche away the very bacteria that keep her body healthy. Attitudes like this are shadows of the past, going back centuries to when women were not allowed in temples during their menstrual flow.

The multimillion dollar feminine-hygiene industry survives on the assumption that "femaleness is dirty." One executive summarized the strategy as, "How do women stink? Let us count the ways." As a consequence, women invest their time, energy, and money in products that are at best unnecessary and at worst physically harmful.

Parent-programmed definitions of femininity often are not based on Adult reality. The Adult reality is that **a human being with female sexual organs is feminine** and that these sexual organs are not innately dirty. On the contrary, they do a superb job of cleansing themselves.

For many women, however, there appears to be no correlation between their *feelings* of femininity and the *facts* of femininity. Consequently, some women drain their energies trying to prove what a physician certified moments after their birth.

A woman's *feelings* about her femininity—her response to her Parent programming—lie in her Child ego state. These Child feelings often confuse a woman's sexual identity with her personal identity. For example, the woman who plays dumb with numbers in order to feel feminine may unknowingly restrict her educational expectations and vocational choices. Her sense of femininity thus shuts off her development as a person.

Helping women of all ages feel OK about themselves as human beings as well as about their sexuality enriches the lives of both men and women.

**STEPS TO
AWARENESS**

How You Feel About Yourself

Right now go and get your bathrobe and slippers, or bring out the things in your underwear drawer. Look at them. Study them. Feel them. Smell them.

- What do they tell you about yourself?

- Do they say anything about what you think you are worth?

- What do they reveal about your feelings toward being the sex you are?

- Do they in any way show how you take care of yourself?

Feeling Ugly

It is a rare woman who appreciates her body for whatever it is. How many women do you know who pull off their clothes at night, stand before a mirror, and proclaim, "Wow, I like my body!" It is far more likely to be an "Ain't it awful?" session, with the woman passing time bemoaning that some parts are too big, too small, in the wrong place, or do not deserve to be there at all.

The proliferation of articles on diets and appearance pitched at women reflects a continuing anxiety about physical appearance. The Beautiful Plastic Woman script, coupled with childhood patterns of stroking girls primarily for their looks, intensifies this pervasive anxiety.

Strokes for appearance are not in themselves destructive. The danger comes if these are the most important strokes a young girl receives and if they become the only kind she later values. For example, five-year-old Margie just finished building a four-foot tower out of an erector set. However, her accomplishment was greeted with a condescending, "My, aren't you a cute, sweet girl to make such a nice, little thing." Later, as a woman, her script runs out when she feels that her physical beauty runs out. How long can she stay "cute" and "sweet"?

Some feelings of ugliness are responses to direct verbal put-downs. Some women heard:

"Poor little Janet, she will never turn the boys' heads like her sister Margaret did."

"How tragic for a girl to be born with such a big nose."

"It's a shame you're going to be so tall. You'll have so few men to choose from."

"Hey, piano legs!"

"Look at string bean!"

"What a tub of lard!"

"She's such an ugly duckling. Poor thing."

"Her face would stop a clock."

Sometimes the roots for feelings of ugliness or of being unfeminine lie in a woman's having been born the "wrong sex." A woman whose parents rejected her sexuality likely rejects her own. Her femininity is an ugly mistake. Some of these women heard as children:

"Your daddy was just furious! He wanted his first-born to be a son."

"If only you had been a boy."

"Now there's no one to carry on the family name."

"After three girls, we were so disappointed when you arrived."

Feelings of ugliness are reinforced not only by the Parent, but also by collective scripts that reach back in history to a time when first-born female children were buried alive or otherwise disposed of in humiliation.

To counteract any feelings of ugliness you may have, take some time to get in touch with your sensuousness.

STEPS TO
AWARENESS

Appreciating Your Body and Your Femininity (or Masculinity)

Pick a time and place when you can have quietness and privacy. Remove your clothing and begin to become more aware of your body. Stand in front of a mirror and study yourself for a few minutes. Look for textures, hues, shapes, and designs. Get acquainted with your body. Learn to recognize your uniqueness.

- Now run your hands over your skin, again being aware of shapes and textures. You might like to use a body lotion. (If you have Parent messages against touching your body, you may find that massaging with a medicated lotion will help to appease the inner criticisms.) Be aware of the pleasant feelings of your skin. Be aware of the good feelings and sensuousness in different parts of your body. If you have never done this before, it can be useful to do the exercise every day for a week. Then repeat it occasionally to remind yourself of your body's good feelings.

- Now lie down in a comfortable position. Close your eyes and focus your awareness on the feelings of each part of your body. Moving from the top of your head to the tips of your toes, concentrate on all sensations— temperature, air movement, tingles, dullness, pressure, fullness, contractions, and so forth. Be aware if you skip any parts of your body. If you do, go back and include them.

- If you meditate or pray, begin including your appreciation of your body and your sensuousness.

Continuing to unify your mind, body, and spirit moves you closer to being a balanced and whole person. People who love their own bodies are likely to find that this makes it easier for others to do the same. Accept that bodies of all kinds and shapes are OK.

Bodies Are OK

Feeling Stupid

Many women still adapt by acting stupid rather than by using their inborn intelligence. Such playacting hampers a woman's ability to make independent or joint decisions, to earn money, to be effective at home or at work, and to contribute as a full citizen in a democracy.

If a woman learns to feel stupid, she consistently trusts the judgments of others over her own. This occurs even though she knows that other people have limited information or biased viewpoints. One such woman felt that all decision-making belonged to men—particularly to her husband. When this woman was a child, her mother looked puzzled when a decision had to be made and with a confused expression said, "Gee, I just don't know. I'll have to wait to ask your father." Today, as an adult, this woman may have problems when she buys a new winter coat, car, or house.

A woman may use a number of ways to show that she has learned this adaptation. She may feel that she cannot achieve, may lack self-confidence, or may fear going to school. She may also have difficulty even considering getting out of an unhealthy relationship, especially if her family, friends, or religious group disapprove.

Adaptations that women are not intelligent also appear in the organizational scripts of banks, loan companies, gas companies, and department stores. Most have just begun giving loans and credit card accounts to women on the same basis they do to men. The change reflects the reality that most women will at some time in their lives need to be responsible for handling money.

A woman who adapts to feel stupid about money may at some time in her life find herself in the same unfortunate financial plight as hundreds of elderly women who are easily bilked out of their life's savings. A woman victimized this way is likely to explain in her bewilderment, "But that nice man said he just wanted to help me."

If a woman adapted to feel stupid works outside the home, she will need frequent attention from her supervisor and continual feedback that she is doing the job correctly. She may perform sophisticated laboratory tests and yet feel inadequate. She collects stupid stamps. She has a hard time judging her abilities accurately; consequently, any criticism of her work—real or imagined—can trigger a flood of tears. She thus puts herself in a double bind, reinforcing her not-OK position. This is a no-win situation. If she does a good job, she doesn't know it; if she does a poor job, she is criticized.

One woman recognized her adaptation when she noticed that she repeatedly made remarks like, "How could I have done such a stupid thing"; "That made me feel so dumb"; "I could kill myself for not asking about that before now." She also discovered that she was really angry at other people and blamed them for making her feel stupid. "Now it's such a relief to know that I am smart and to feel good about it. If I don't feel I measure up to other people, it's not their fault—and it's not my fault, either."

Needing to Please Everyone

Another common adaptation is being a pleaser. Most little girls are expected to comply with rules, regulations, and socially controlled behavior far more rigidly than boys are. For example, boys who throw rocks at street lights might be excused with, "Boys will be boys." In contrast, most people would be shocked to see girls destroying property. When women kill, maim, or torture, it somehow seems worse.

People who learn compliance as a primary method of coping, as do many women, often must please other people in order to feel OK. "Appease everyone" becomes a driving script force.

Such a woman may unquestioningly yield to others. She yields to a salesperson who says, "You must buy the latest model"; to a supervisor who tells her, "This clerk's job is made for you"; or to a boy in the back seat of a car at the drive-in who declares, "You're the only girl I've ever felt this way about." As a consequence, she might find it hard to do such things as return faulty merchandise to a department store, ask for a deserved raise, turn down dinner invitations from boring people, or say no when that is what she really wants.

A woman who is a pleaser wants *everyone* to like her. In fact, she feels uncomfortable if she thinks anyone dislikes her. Judith Viorst explores this feeling in her poem.

The First Full-Fledged Family Reunion

The first full-fledged family reunion
Was held at the seashore
With 9 pounds of sturgeon
7 pounds of corned beef
1 nephew who got the highest mark on an intelligence test ever recorded in Hillside, New Jersey
4 aunts in pain taking pills
1 cousin in analysis taking notes
1 sister-in-law who makes a cherry cheese cake a person would be happy to pay to eat
5 uncles to whom what happened in the stock market shouldn't happen to their worst enemy
1 niece who is running away from home the minute the orthodontist removes her braces
1 cousin you wouldn't believe it to look at him only likes fellows

1 nephew involved with a person of a different racial persuasion which his parents are taking very well
1 brother-in-law with a house so big you could get lost and carpeting so thick you could suffocate and a mortgage so high you could go bankrupt
1 uncle whose wife is a saint to put up with him
1 cousin who has made such a name for himself he was almost Barbra Streisand's obstetrician
1 cousin who has made such a name for himself he was almost Jacob Javits' CPA
1 cousin don't ask what he does for a living
1 niece it wouldn't surprise anyone if next year she's playing at Carnegie Hall
1 nephew it wouldn't surprise anyone if next year he's sentenced to Leavenworth
2 aunts who go to the same butcher as Philip Roth's mother
And me wanting approval from all of them.[1]

Picture a woman like this at a party. She knows that 29 of the 30 guests like her, but *she feels* that one does not. Because she has convinced herself that she needs total approval, she finds herself worrying and fretting about that one person. She fails to really enjoy any of the 29 others!

A woman like this who has chosen to be a homemaker can spend her entire day keeping house, baking, cooking, and sewing. Like Mother Hubbard, she may do more than is necessary, expected, or even wanted of her. Later that evening she snaps back at a complaint from her husband with, "I was only trying to help you and make things easier by tidying up your work bench."

A woman who tries to please everybody ends up being nobody herself. As she scrambles for this impossible goal, her energies drain. She anxiously molds herself to fit what she thinks everybody else wants her to be. She fails to use her capacity to objectively evaluate when to accept and when to reject what other people think of her. She pays the price by not forming and expressing her own opinions, ideas, and uniqueness—by not being herself.

A woman who carries the burden of a strong "please *everybody*" adaptation is likely also to have a strong feeling of "please me." As a result, other people never quite live up to her expectations. Without understanding why, her birthdays and other gift-giving holidays always fall short of her expectations. She often allows a mood of sadness to overshadow whatever efforts might have been made in her behalf. No matter what others do, it is never enough. In fact, "never enough" becomes her motto. Whatever she does is never enough. Whatever is done for her is never enough.

**STEPS TO
AWARENESS**

Trying to Please Everyone

If this adaptation is a concern for you, think through the following questions. Picture a person you feel uncomfortable around because you feel you do not please that person.

- What is it that the person does not like about you?

- What evidence do you have that this is true?

- What information does this person have about you?

- What difference would it make if the person did like you?

- What do you need to do for the person to like you? Is it worth it to you?

- What is the worst thing you can imagine happening to you if this person *never* likes you?

- What would happen if you concentrated on other people rather than putting your energy into this person?

Now think about what you expect from others.

- Do people frequently fail to live up to your expectations?

- Is this a recurring pattern? If so, figure out if you do anything to bring it about. (One possibility is doing things for people that they have not asked for and may not even want you to do.)

- What is one thing you do now that would be better for you to stop doing?

- What can you do instead to take better care of yourself?

Possessiveness and Jealousy

Ownership is sometimes part of the expectations in a close relationship such as marriage. A little girl may learn to believe that when she marries or has a steady boyfriend she literally owns part of that person. If anyone else shows interest in what she owns, she becomes jealous.

Collective scripts often reinforce the idea of ownership. In fact, the marriage vows themselves can convey the idea that people "belong" to each other. The possessiveness and consequent jealousy that result from such attitudes place a heavy burden on some intimate relationships. Many people, whether or not they are aware of it, resent the feeling that they "belong" to someone else. This can be a trespass against their autonomy. To really have another person, one must let that person go.

A woman can also learn that she *should* "belong" to someone else. As a result, she ends up feeling more like an object than a person and, without understanding why, collects resentment.

Jealously more often reflects feelings of suspicion than of love. Also, a woman's jealousy can be a cover-up for her own feelings of guilt if she has any desire for someone outside of the relationship she is committed to. She thinks: "Because I have these feelings, I assume that you are having the same feelings, and that makes me mad."

Acts of possessiveness are likely to induce the very behavior that stimulates the jealousy. Jealousy reflects a flaw in ourselves, a feeling that "someone else is better than I."

STEPS TO
AWARENESS

Your Projections

Many of us see our own feelings, behaviors, and desires in other people (projection). Think of something you feel jealous of or dislike in another person.

- What do you accuse this person of feeling, doing, or wanting to do?

- Do *you* feel or do or want to do any of these things?

- Are you recognizing yourself in someone else? Whenever you accuse someone else of something you don't like, recall, "It takes one to know one."

- Do you also see likeable traits in others, traits that might well be yours?

- Think about it.

Striving for Perfection

Young girls learn this adaptation by getting approval only when they spend a great deal of time trying to do things perfectly. For example, Paula received a pat on the back from her mother only after making and remaking her bed to get the bedspread fringe six inches from the floor around the entire edge. When Paula's bed was finally "perfect," her mother would nod approvingly, "Now wasn't that worth all your trouble?"

Today, Paula spends much of her time on the job working at things until they are *just right*, rather than doing the *right things*. She has a hard time deciding when a job is done well enough. Consequently, she often misses deadlines and may find it hard to set priorities. Paula's early training taught her that leveling the bedspread fringe was just as important as taking a needed medication. Paula's acting out these adaptations often causes both her and her employer to end the day in frustration.

Ruth learned perfectionism in a different way. She experiences the dangling carrot. Just when she thinks she has done something right, she discovers that she could have done it better. Mother says, "The table you set looks lovely. But don't you think the pink napkins would go better with the plates than the ones you chose?" And Father may say, "Your piano piece really sounds great. Just think how good it would sound if you practiced four hours a day instead of only two."

Like a carrot on a string, the point at which something will be finished perfectly keeps skipping elusively ahead of wherever Ruth is at any moment. No matter how much she does or how well she does it, she never feels that she has finished the task. "No matter how hard I try, it's never good enough," she complains.

Now, when Ruth prepares a meal for guests, she apologizes, "It would have been better if the roast hadn't been well done." When she finishes sewing a dress, she complains, "It certainly would have been better if I had used smaller buttons." "It would have been better if . . ." is the theme of much of what Ruth does and says.

Lydia was another woman who grew up with this scripting. However, she decided that the pain of trying to be perfect was too much, and instead she risked the uncertainty of change.

Lydia was in her thirties when she finally realized that she would never be able to live up to the perfectionist standards she had learned as a little girl. Even as an adult, her relationship with her father was still characterized by his reacting to almost everything she did with such comments as: "Your dinner was delicious, but I'd have enjoyed it more if it had been served a little earlier"; "Yes, your house looks beautiful, but don't you think such modern furniture is a little too stark to be cozy?" and "Yes, I did enjoy your Christmas gift; however, it isn't the brand I usually use."

Lydia gradually became aware of what was going on. She decided that she should write her father, who now lived 2000 miles away, and tell him of her decision to stop trying to please him at any cost. She wrote that although she still loved him dearly, she had decided that attempting to meet his exacting standards was spoiling their relationship and that it wasn't a constructive path for her to follow. She particularly was not going to try to be perfect anymore. In a hurry to have him read the letter, but not having any regular stamps in the house, she quickly licked and pasted on a special delivery stamp and dropped the letter in the mailbox.

The following week she received his reply. It motivated her to also decide that she could change even though her father didn't. His letter read: "Dear Lydia, I'm delighted that you are thinking through some things in your life. However, I just happened to notice that you used a special delivery stamp on the envelope. You know, you could have saved money if you had used the right stamp!"

Women whose happiness depends on other people changing often have a long, cold wait.

Early Parent messages are not the only source of messages about perfection. The mass media often intensify any perfectionist feelings of an anxious woman. Advertisements nag: "Have you served your family the same meal more than once this month?"; "Are you getting all your laundry sunshine clean?"; "Do your friends wrinkle their noses when they walk into your house?"

Even though most women today have a choice about the "duties" of making the butter, weaving cloth, tending fires, or bringing in the crops, the demands on a homemaker have expanded to fill many newly emptied hours. It is no longer enough to merely provide food for the family. Today's homemaker is cajoled to: "Be a perfect mother, wife, lover, homemaker, career woman, interior decorator, nurse, chauffeur, and veterinarian. And in your spare time, keep up to date on world events so that you are a more interesting conversationalist at the parties you give."

Just think of the growing number of products to clean areas only recently identified as demanding care—spray to use when turning the mattress each week, cleaner for the dirtiest spot on your electric can opener, liquid to dissolve those troublesome rings. What gnawing sources of phony guilt!

Phony guilt often runs hand in hand with painful compulsions to perfection.

Guilt because she does not have a career.

Guilt because she has too many children.

Guilt because she has no children.

Guilt because she does not like to entertain.

Guilt because she spends too much time in superficial relationships.

Guilt because she should be more like someone else.

Guilt because she is the wrong sex.

Guilt because she is not petite.

Guilt because she is too small to be strong.

Guilt because she does not like to cook.

Guilt because she overfeeds her family.

Guilt because she wants to be alone.

Guilt because she does not have enough friends.

Guilt, guilt, guilt, and pain; the pain pushes her to perform with more perfection. And so the expectations spiral ever outward to fill the time available—be it 4 hours or 40.

But the pangs of the perfectionist's unused capacities are still there. The not-OK feelings of never measuring up are still there. So she doubles her efforts to fill her time—sometimes expanding her work to fill whatever time there is available.

Dealing with Perfectionism

If you think that an adaptation of trying to be perfect is getting in your way now, here are some steps you can take.

- Listen to the message you hear in your head when you feel that you must be perfect. What specifically is it? Is it something like, "You should have done better" or "That's nice, but not good enough"?

- Now exaggerate your message and your response to it. For example, if you feel that you cannot stand the sight of dust, walk around your living room or your office, exaggerate your contempt for dust, say out loud how awful you feel about dirt in the room, look in every crevice, and run your finger across table tops, lamps, and door casings.

- Pick one object and begin to clean it thoroughly. As you are cleaning it, talk out loud about how you feel when you get in and clean out every last speck of the dirt.

- As you talk out loud and listen to your comments, become aware of what you are feeling. Sit back for a moment and close your eyes. Ask yourself, "When have I had this feeling before? What other feelings went with it? When I felt this way, what happened or what did I get? How appropriate is this to my life now?"

Another way to tackle your perfectionism is to ask yourself:

- What happens if I do this 100% rather than 80%? Is it worth it to me?

- What is the worst thing that can possibly happen if I do not do this perfectly?

■ What will happen if I don't do this at all?

Begin to think about your compulsive feeling of perfectionism in terms of your own personal value system. Ask yourself, "What are the things that I really want to give my time to? What are the things I give my time to now that really do not matter that much?"

Continue to clarify for yourself what you honestly value. Begin to structure more of your time with what is important to you today.

Passivity

Many little girls overadapt the assertiveness characteristic of the Natural Child. Little girls who learn to be seen and not heard, who learn that what they have to say is not important, who learn that they will be ridiculed if they speak up, who learn to be wallflowers, who learn to wait until everyone else has had a turn or is satisfied—these little girls are likely to develop passivity patterns.[2] Like women scripted exclusively into the helpmate role, their vulnerability may make them easy prey for pain.

Sitting and not speaking, waiting and not doing, holding and not expressing—all result in a piling up of inner resentment. These temporarily displaced resentments later come out in irrational spurts against people and things. One way to avoid this and to tackle passivity is to more frequently ask directly for what you want. Anne learned to do this.

When Anne got in touch with how this adaptation was keeping her from enjoying life and the people in her life, she started doing things differently. She used to say things like, "Yesterday was my birthday, and nobody did anything." Now, rather than expecting other people to know what she wanted, she started expressing her wants directly. She started telling people that she really enjoyed birthday celebrations. She now does this before her birthday, rather than the day after. "Birthdays are so much fun now. I've celebrated mine six times this year already!"

Confronting Passivity

Here are some questions to help you decide if passivity gets in your way.

- Do you frequently wish you had done or said something *after* the event?

- Are you frequently disappointed about people who do not do what you want them to?

- Do you often say things like, "They should have known I . . ."

- Do you spend a lot more time and energy responding to what others do and say than you spend initiating things on your own?

- Do you get attention for being compliant and passive?

- Do you frequently look for others to solve your problems or tell you what to do?

If you decide you want to be more assertive, pick a recurring situation in which you think you are now too passive. Which of these techniques would be good for you?

- Think of someone you know who would handle the situation very well. Now vividly imagine yourself handling your situation the way this person would. Replay this scene in your mind several times a day. Tailor it to fit your unique needs. Look for an occasion to handle the situation in a new way. Set a specific goal for moving your imagery into reality. Perhaps once a day or once a week would be a good timetable. Reward yourself with something you want that is good for you when you use your new idea.

- How can you learn more from people who handle similar situations assertively?

- How can you ask more directly for what you want?

■ Who in your life is pleased when you are being more direct and taking care of yourself? Who can you add to your life who would appreciate your new directness? How can you arrange to brag to them when you have handled a situation well? Taking this step will reinforce your new learning and increase your ease in repeating it.

As a general rule, when you are in a situation in which you feel you are being too passive, ask yourself, "What is it that I want?" Figure how you can let others know what your wants are. Now bring your doing into better balance with your thinking and feeling by acting on your decisions.

Passivity, perfectionism, or feeling unfeminine, stupid, or ugly are only a few of the adaptations common to women. Yet they significantly affect the way many women feel about themselves, get their strokes, structure their time, relate to others, and fulfill their scripts.

**STEPS TO
AWARENESS**

Your Adaptations

Thinking through the various kinds of adaptations that were mentioned here, begin to get in touch with your own unique ones.

Did you identify with any of the adaptations mentioned in this chapter?

■ If so, which one (or ones) seems the most prevalent in your life drama?

■ Jot down all of the ways in which each of these adaptations may affect your life drama in a negative way.

■ Now consider each of these negative aspects and figure out what you could do that would be different from your old, programmed response.

■ Develop a plan of action for your personal work on each negative adaptation.

Now select one adaptation that you think is particularly destructive. Give it priority to work on.

- Using the Gestalt technique of role playing, sit in a chair and project this adaptation onto an empty chair directly across from you.
- Talk to your adaptation, stating your feelings, thoughts, and opinions about it. Then switch and be your adaptation. You might say, for example:

  "I am perfection. I push you to . . ." and then continue with whatever comes to your mind. Switch back and forth to see if you can bring both insight and closure to this problem. You may need to repeat this role play several times. Or you may gain considerable insight the first time.

WE ARE RESPONSIBLE FOR OUR FEELINGS

A common myth is that we have no control over our feelings. All of the adaptations mentioned here, as well as many others, can serve as an unaware motivation for some women to justify indulging themselves in their bad racket feelings. If we use rackets to reexperience old feelings, we can get caught up in depression or anger and take no personal responsibility. It is as if an outside force is "making me feel that way."

"Jim makes me angry when he scolds me like I'm a child."

"Sally depresses me when she talks about her troubles."

"My children make me feel stifled."

"Harold makes me feel dumb every time I try to talk to him."

"That professor makes me feel guilty about being two minutes late to class."

"My boss makes me feel sick to my stomach."

These feelings are like flashbacks to the coping techniques of a child. They are the old defenses that were used as armor for self-protection, for survival. Now they are used to blame others for making us feel bad.

See how the meaning changes when we take responsibility for choosing our own way to feel.

"I make myself angry when Jim scolds me like I'm a child."

"I make myself depressed when Sally talks about her troubles."

"I make myself feel stifled because of my children."

"I make myself feel dumb every time I try to talk to Harold."

"I make myself feel guilty about being two minutes late to class."

"I make myself feel sick to my stomach because of my boss."

Confronting our feeling rackets even more directly, we might try saying:

"I choose to be angry when Jim scolds me like I'm a child."

"I choose to be depressed when Sally talks about her troubles."

"I choose to feel stifled because of my children."

"I choose to feel dumb every time I try to talk to Harold."

"I choose to feel guilty about being two minutes late to class."

"I choose to feel sick to my stomach because of my boss."

Learning to take responsibility for your own feelings opens up an array of options that might otherwise elude you. Why not choose to feel good about more things? Why not increase the time you invest in good moods? You can sustain more of your highs.

These two women illustrate the meaning of taking personal responsibility. Eleanor Roosevelt is reported to have said, "No one can make you feel inferior without your consent." And as 17-year-old Jill put it, "If a worm is in your apple, it gives you no excuse to 'eat worms.' "

Negative adaptations interfere with a person's ability to think clearly and to learn the skills of talking straight. These skills can be developed and practiced. Each of us can become more whole.

Not
for
Parents
Only

- In what ways does the Parent ego state affect parenting?
- How does the Child ego state affect parenting?
- How can you show more love and nurturing toward yourself?

There was an old woman who lived in a shoe,
She had so many children she didn't know what
*   to do;*
She gave them some broth without any bread;
She whipped them all soundly and put them to bed.[1]

The old woman in the shoe is not alone. Countless other parents feel at one time or another they do not know what to do. And countless attempt to gain control in the only ways they know how. Few situations point so vividly to the need for understanding our own ego states as does the circumstance of being a parent. This understanding, combined with strategies to meet the needs of all of our ego states, helps clear the way for better parenting of children and of ourselves. This chapter points out significant helps and hindrances to achieving this goal.

IS THERE A MATERNAL INSTINCT?

"You should know what to do with this crying baby. After all, you're a woman!" How many new mothers have heard that? Joyce was a victim of this false belief.

I had never been around a baby and even though I was pregnant, I really didn't have the slightest notion what to do with one. When I was in the hospital with my first-born, I believed that my instincts would surely come to my rescue. In fact, I remember thinking that there was a window shade in my brain. Once I had my baby, I thought, the shade would go up, and I would know what to do.

As I lay in my bed, it gradually dawned on me that there was no window shade going up. A terrible panic hit me.

Three weeks at home with a new baby totally exhausted me. We had to hire a nurse, and I went away to a hospital, diagnosed as suffering from "battle fatigue."

I know now that if I'm going to be a parent, I need to learn how. There's no magic moment when you can say, "You are now a qualified mother. You passed the test by giving birth. Now progress to 'Go.'" How it would have helped me and my young son if I had caught on to this a little sooner.

The label of "maternal instincts" discourages many like Joyce from learning how to improve their parenting skills. The "maternal" label also offers little incentive for fathers to be more involved in parenting. This belief continues in spite of the large number of children who are battered by their parents each year. If parenting were instinctive, how could the battering take place? Harlow's studies prove that even lower primates, Rhesus monkeys, have to learn to parent.[2]

Despite the lack of evidence of "maternal instincts" in people, many well-intentioned persons—mothers, fathers, judges, juries, and even those in helping professions—continue to casually and confidently extoll its virtues. Relying on the notion of "maternal instincts" hurts everyone. Building on the concept of educating people to be better parents helps all around—mothers, fathers, children, and our society at large.

THERE ARE NEW STRESSES IN PARENTING

In most places in the world today, several adults live in the same household. Until recently, this was also true in the United States. Studies show that children who are reared by many caring adults seem to develop more stable personalities.[3] The extended family offers children the opportunity to be protected by and to learn from many grown-ups in their lives.

In contrast, children who are brought up in the nuclear family—mom, dad, and the offspring—have fewer models. It appears that the more models children have, the more opportunity they have to expand their repertoire of Parent ego state behaviors. In some cases the nuclear family contributes to an underdeveloped Parent ego state and increases the possibility for not-OK feelings in the Child. The nuclear family also places an unprecedented stress on persons who parent, since the whole burden of childrearing falls on the shoulders of one or two people.

Women In Isolation

Mothers who are alone with their children and who feel trapped and isolated face frustration. Their own inner Child longs for fun and freedom. They may also yearn for the strokes that come from contact with other adults. Such women may begin to harbor feelings of resentment against their own children. Lisa expresses her ambivalence.

Mark and I thought that his transfer would be an adventure. Well, it has been, for him and for the children. But I'd pack up everything tomorrow if I had a chance to go back where we came from.

Mark and I both grew up in a large city. We both went to college there, and I worked for a couple of years after we were married. After Susie was born, my mother stayed with her every morning while I worked at my old job on a part-time basis. Mark and I had many friends, and life was fun. Then this transfer came along, and we thought, "Sure, let's move to the suburbs; the children can have more space and we can be on our own."

I feel guilty even complaining about it. Mark works hard to give us everything we need. But I'd like to get away just once in a while. I feel so stuck here, and there aren't any part-time jobs for me. I'm in the house all day with a three- and a four-year-old. Mark's met lots of people at work whom he likes, and the children love exploring in the woods in back of the house, but I'm miserable. I miss the excitement of the city. I miss my family and friends. And I miss fixing myself up and working for at least a few hours a day.

Mark keeps saying, "Honey, just wait until we've been here a little longer. People warm up slowly in this part of the world. You'll love it as soon as you get into things. I know we can't afford babysitters right now, but that will change." He's probably right, but it will take so long. I'm only 27. I hate this feeling of being trapped.

The number of people on the move increases every year. This feeling of rootlessness that frequently follows relocating spreads. Often, women with small children feel the isolation most keenly. Many wrestle with the feeling of ambivalence that grow out of the constant demands of parenting. Children feel the isolation too, since fathers may be away a large share of the time. From both frustrated mothers and frequently absent fathers, children often find themselves consistently segregated with other children their own age and with few meaningful adult contacts.

The Single Parent

As a result of divorce, separation, or the death or injury of fathers, more and more women face rearing children alone. In 1975 there were 8,612,000 families with a single head—7,127,000 women, 1,485,000 men. For women, this was an increase of 21.1% since 1970; for men, an increase of only 3.3%.[4]

Rearing children without help works well for some, but for others it can be a lonely task.[5] A single parent may feel stuck and unable to get away from the children. Finances may be tight. Children may need to approve of new friends and lovers. Children may also miss the benefits of having both male and female models. Even if single parenting is done skillfully, there are few immediate rewards for competence.

SOME PARENTS BRUTALIZE THEIR CHILDREN

When a woman becomes a mother, the needs of her offspring sometimes conflict with those of her own inner Child—especially if she is a reluctant mother. On call 24 hours a day, she may find it difficult to fulfill her own wishes for fun, dependency, and affection.

Part of being a capable parent is the ability to postpone immediate gratification and to focus on the dependency needs of an infant. When this happens, the parent's Parent ego state takes pride in doing a good job. On the other hand, the parent's dissatisfied, unhappy Child ego state may show itself through pouting, self-pity, irritability, depression, and in extreme cases, brutality. Claude Steiner points out that destructive messages from the Child ego state of the parent may result in tragedy.[6] For example:

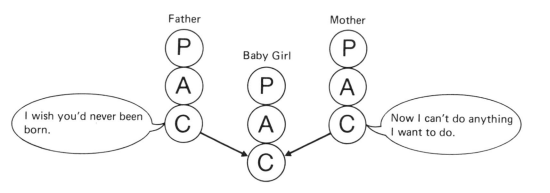

The intensity of parental dissatisfaction ranges from feelings of being trapped to ones of desperation. For some parents, problems loom to dramatic and even cruel proportions. Sara's unbelievable actions show this stress.

I don't know how I could have done such a horrible thing. But I just felt that I couldn't take the baby's screaming any more.

I got pregnant when I was a senior in high school. When the baby was born, I felt that my whole life was over. Now I spend day and night taking care of a screaming kid. And I don't even know how.

The baby has colic and cries night after night. One night she just went on and on. I was so exhausted! I put some water on the stove to make coffee to keep me awake. When the baby started screaming again, I just went to pieces. All I could think of was, "I gotta make it stop crying." I grabbed the kettle and poured the water on the baby, but she kept on screaming. A neighbor drove me and the baby to the hospital. That night the newspaper headlined, "Five-Month-Old-Infant Scalded by Mother." I couldn't believe that that story was about me!

But I couldn't stand listening to the crying any more. I just can't seem to help myself. I didn't know that being a mother would be like this. I'm alone most of the time, and I have to do everything for the baby. I didn't mean to hurt her.

Hardly a day goes by in any city without a headline similar to Sara's. In 1973 alone, there were more than 60,000 cases (up 30% over a decade) reported in the United States of babies being beaten, strangled, burned, or otherwise harmed.[7] *Authorities estimate that twice as many cases go unreported.*[8]

Parents who abuse and batter their children are likely to have been abused themselves as children. Battered children are also likely to be by-products of youthful marriages, illegitimacies, and unwanted births—all of which often relate to not-OK feelings of personal frustration in the Child ego state. Planned Parenthood cites this startling research:[9]

> Unwanted children do not fare well in life. A Swedish study of 120 children born to women denied therapeutic abortion shows the unwanted children are worse off in every respect in comparison to the control group over a 21-year period. Among unwanted children, antisocial and criminal behavior, public dependence, and psychiatric illness were twice as prevalent. The impulse to violence is high among those who were denied a mother's love and who experienced little humanity at the hands of others.

> Each day two thousand unwanted children are born in America, a disproportionate number of them to the poor—two thousand lives that begin with defeat and often end in disaster. Each year, thirty million unwanted children are born in the world and exact staggering penalties from families and society. Desperate women limit births by the only means they know. A third of all pregnancies end in abortion, many of them self-induced.[10]

Of course, not all unwanted children suffer neglect or abuse. But the problem of unwanted children remains. Parent programming can add to the pressures to have children. Messages such as *"When you have children . . ."* rather than *"If you have children . . ."* assume that all women should have children. As a consequence, some women have children by compulsion rather than by choice. To complicate matters, there may be messages against putting unwanted children up for adoption.

Parents who feel driven to brutalize their children are not alone. Most welcome help and the support of others.[11] If you have ever acted on this urge in a destructive way, seek outside help. Call a county hospital and ask for a referral. Go to a priest, rabbi, or clergyman. Call your local Mental Health Association or Social Welfare Department. Everyone, including yourself, will benefit.

SOME PARENTS OVERPROTECT THEIR CHILDREN

Some children face the opposite of being neglected or brutalized. In a sense, they are wanted almost too much.

Prolonged or overprotective parenting fosters undue dependency and inhibits children's emotional growth. Such illegitimate parenting often occurs when women feel good about themselves *only* in the role of mother. These women, who have little life of their own, continue to play the role of mother even though their children have long since reached adulthood. This emphasis encourages women to build their entire lives around a role that many will be actively involved in for only part of their lives or that some will never experience.

Grown children who hear, "You haven't written for two weeks"; "Why don't you call more?"; "You mean you're not coming home again this weekend?" feel the painful pinch of this type of programming. At a deep level, too much mothering encourages guilt in children, who feel somehow responsible for their mothers' lonely hours. Such guilt only drives the two generations farther apart. Rebecca struggled with this problem.

Some people say that I worry too much about my son, but honestly, what do they expect? He's been everything to me since his father died ten years ago. The baby is 23 now and lives on his own in one of those fancy, young people's buildings. And he can afford it. He's got a good job, a real good job. I'm so proud of him, I don't know what to do.

Sometimes, when I call him up, I can hear over the phone that he's got friends over. He's so short with me on the phone, he's almost rude. After all, he'll spend all evening with them, and you'd think he could spare me five minutes once a day. But then, I guess I understand. He's got to be on his own now. But I notice that he's not so independent when it comes time to do the laundry or fix a seam. Then he's only too happy to come running over, saying, "Hey, Mom, would you mind . . . ?" But I'm glad he does that. It gives me a chance to see him and talk to him for a moment, and of course I don't mind doing things for him.

Sometimes I'll sit here at night and wonder what on earth I'll do when he gets married and has a family. Then he'll spend all his time with them. And that's the way it should be, I guess. But where will I fit in? I guess instead of seeing him once a week, I'll see him once a month. He is a big boy now. But I do miss him.

Although mothering may be one of the most important things a woman chooses to do, it no longer fills a lifetime for most women. Retirement comes all too early, since good parenting usually means working oneself out of a job.

Women who parent well and whose children are grown can seek needed and appreciated outlets for their skills and talents. For example, some children's hospitals have "Parent Banks" for neglected or battered children. Young mothers often need help with new babies. Some school children need special attention. Foster grandparents are happy additions to many homes. These are legitimate ways to continue parenting.

**STEPS TO
AWARENESS**

Your Parent Ego State

To get an even more complete picture of your Parent ego state, consider the following questions:

- If you have children, how do you copy your parent figures with them?

  Is this behavior productive or unproductive?

  What do you want to change?

- Think of five ways you can nurture and protect children and adults in healthy ways.

  Do these things more often. Why not? It feels good to both of you.

HOW CAN PARENTING BE IMPROVED?

Parents of both sexes can explore ways of allowing their children to learn from a variety of people. This may mean permitting children to spend more time in the park, more time with other family members, more time with supervised groups of children, or more time living with other parents and children. In an environment with more caring adults, children receive less discounting, negative strokes, neglect, and brutality. This helps minimize the development of not-OK feelings in the Child.

People can vividly see their own Parent ego states when they are around children—particularly their own. To avoid programming children negatively, it is important for parents to get in touch with their own Parent messages.

Men and women can examine their Parent ego states and decide whether or not these behaviors are what they want to pass on to another generation. If they decide no, they can find many ways to improve parenting techniques by putting the Adult to work. They can read.[12] They can model after others that are doing a good job. They can take courses in parenting.[13] They can seek professional help. Good parenting *can* be learned.

The rewards of being a mother are many. How good most mothers would feel to hear from a daughter the following words from Susan Polis Schutz:

Thanks, Mom
Since I had a mother
whose many interests
kept her excited and occupied

Since I had a mother
who interacted with so many people
that she had a real feeling for the world

Since I had a mother
who always was strong
through any period of suffering

Since I had a mother
who was a complete person
I always had a model
to look up to
and that made it easier
for me to develop into
an independent woman.[14]

Parenting Is OK

Fathers Can Mother, Too

It is certainly true that children need parenting. Parenting, however, is not always mothering. With the obvious exception of breast-feeding, most of an infant's needs can be met by either sex. Both women and men can:

- cuddle, hold, feed, and comfort infants;
- set rational limits for safety and health;
- invest time in listening;
- invest time in showing how;
- examine their own Parent behaviors to determine whether these should be programmed into their own children;
- seek information and help about parenting and work together to preserve the health, welfare, and dignity of growing human beings;
- learn to recognize the needs of their own Child ego states and work out mutually satisfying ways to see that these needs are met.

People who follow these principles are bound to be good parents. Effective parenting, in turn, develops healthy Parent ego states.

Parenting Ourselves

Good parenting is important not only to children, but also to adults. This is true for both men and women and at all ages—9 months, 9 years, 49, or 90.

There are times in the lives of each of us when we need the nourishing and nurturing touch and concern of another person. There are times when we need to allow ourselves to reach out to help one another.

But perhaps one of the most important things to learn about parenting and the Parent and Child ego states is that we can be our own best friends or our own worst enemies. Part of becoming our own best friends is taking better care of ourselves as a healthy, concerned parent might take care of us. For instance, it is paramount that new mothers, who are often physically tired themselves, sharpen their awareness of *their own needs* and develop ways to keep *their own Child* ego states healthy and happy in legitimate ways.

In an effort to keep up with the household chores and laundry, busy mothers may fail to take care of themselves. For example, they might take on all of the home-care responsibilities simply because they are physically at home. They use the time when baby is napping to do the ironing, mop the floors, or clean the oven, believing that this is the best time to get things done.

Although this may work out fine for some women, others make better use of their time by taking a nap themselves, meditating, putting their feet up to rest and read, or taking a sun bath or leisurely bubble bath. They in some way meet their *own* needs for satisfactions. Feeling good about oneself helps avoid the depression that sometimes follows birth. It also frees more energy to take good care of children.

Other members of the family can often assume a share of household responsibilities, child care, shopping, and planning. It is far more important for an infant to have a rested and happy parent than to have perfectly sanitized floors and ironed sheets.

If you have discovered any negative or destructive Parent tapes in yourself, you can replace them with new behaviors—ones that reflect a concern about you, ones that say, "I care about me." Healthy Parent tapes help you to care for and about infants, and they also are needed to help you take a positive attitude toward yourself. They should encourage you to take good care of *your* health, *your* welfare, *your* comfort, and *your* happiness. They should also support you in undertaking new endeavors, in facing new horizons, and in taking reasonable risks.

Turn on your positive Parent tapes more often. Listen to them. Follow them. Embellish them. Pass them on to others.

**STEPS TO
AWARENESS**

Parenting Yourself

In what ways do you take care of yourself *now* that are like the ways your parents took care of you when you were a child? For example, what did they do when you were sick or hurt? What did they do when you made a mistake or were embarrassed?

- Which of these behaviors are negative?

- Which are positive?

- How can you build more on the positive?

Take a close look at how you care for yourself.
  - What do you do under stress?

  - When did you have your last physical?

  - Do you have any "habits" that are ruining your health?

  - What could you do to be healthier and happier?

  - Which of these things are you doing now?

  - Which of these could you do more of?

  - List at least three ways you can take better care of yourself.

YOU ARE WORTH LOVING

Parenting has always had its stress. Until recently many parents watched their children suffer with disease, and many bore the pain of burying them. Although this is less likely to happen today, new stresses confront contemporary parents. To be more effective in parenting others, it is important to be aware of what these changes mean to people. You *can* learn parenting techniques to match today's new needs.

Part of good parenting includes parenting yourself in healthy, concerned, and productive ways. When you learn to really love yourself, you parent yourself well. You learn to love your neighbor *as* yourself rather than instead of yourself. You allow the Child in you to be expressive, curious, joyful, sensuous. You temper those self-centered, possessive aspects of your inner Child with an attitude of goodwill toward others. Making the world a better place starts with taking better care of yourself.

10

The Capable Woman

- What can you do to
  sharpen your awareness
  of your unique Parent,
  Adult, and Child
  ego states?
- In what ways can your
  Adult intervene for new
  decisions and change?
- How can you move
  toward autonomy?

Who can find a capable wife?
Her worth is far beyond coral.
Her husband's whole trust is in her,
   and children are not lacking.
She repays him with good, not evil,
   all her life long.
She chooses wool and flax
   and toils at her work.
Like a ship laden with merchandise,
   she brings home food from far off.
She rises while it is still night
   and sets meat before her household.
After careful thought she buys a field
   and plants a vineyard out of her earnings.
She sets about her duties with vigour
   and braces herself for the work.
She sees that her business goes well,
   and never puts out the lamp at night.
She holds the distaff in her hand,
   and her fingers grasp the spindle.
She is open-handed to the wretched
   and generous to the poor.
She has no fear for her household when it snows,
   for they are wrapped in two cloaks.
She makes her own coverings,
   and clothing of fine linen and purple.
Her husband is well known in the city gate
   when he takes his seat with the elders of the land.
She weaves linen and sells it,
   and supplies merchants with their sashes.
She is clothed in dignity and power
   and can afford to laugh at tomorrow.
When she opens her mouth, it is to speak wisely,
   and loyalty is the theme of her teaching.
She keeps her eye on the doings of her household
   and does not eat the bread of idleness.
Her sons with one accord call her happy;
   her husband too, and he sings her praises:
"Many a woman shows how capable she is;
   but you excel them all."
Charm is a delusion and beauty fleeting;
   it is the God-fearing woman who is honoured.
Extol her for the fruit of all her toil,
   and let her labours bring her honour in the city gate.

Proverbs 31
The Bible
New England Version

This "capable wife" had many adult tasks. Buying a field, selling to merchants, seeing her business going well, planting a vineyard—all require thoughtful intelligence, a good Adult. Her achievements and their rewards go back many centuries.

A woman using her Adult gathers new information, thinks things through, decides to experience or to postpone gratification, and tests out current reality. It is characteristic of the Adult to be logical, rational, and open to new information.

To put her Adult ego state to good use, a woman needs to learn how to recognize it. There are many clues to Adult functioning.

THE ADULT CAN BE RECOGNIZED

Certain voice tones, words, postures, and gestures are signs of the Adult:

Looking directly forward with head level;

Being alert;

Using a calm, steady voice;

Making eye contact;

Listening attentively;

Keeping an open posture—no clenched hands or arms crossed over chest;

Using such words as, "why," "what," "how," "probably," "discover," "the facts," or "here's how I see the problem."

Asking straight questions and gathering information also signal the use of the Adult. Some Adult questions are:

"What do you think?"

"How do you feel?"

"What is the problem?"

"How can we solve the problem?"

"Why was I passed up for a promotion to maintenance worker?"

"Do you have suggestions for improving this report?"

"I don't know if I'm right or not, but I feel you've avoided me this week."

"What are our alternatives?"

"Why do you think so?"

"Is something wrong?"

"Where can I get information on the classes for self-defense?"

The *way* something is said gives the clue as to the real message. Voice tones often are better indicators of ego states than words are. Think of the different ways this simple question can be asked:

An accusing, "Would you go to a woman doctor?"

A straight, "Would you go to a woman doctor?"

A frightened, "Would you go to a woman doctor?"

Even though everyone has an Adult and can gather information and make decisions, the quality of the Adult depends on many things. That quality varies with the strokes a child receives for being or not being intelligent, the abundance or lack of experiences and education, and the ability to use the communication symbols of the group, such as reading, writing, and dealing with numbers.

For example, a little girl who begins to believe that education is not important to her because she is only a woman learns a pattern of discounting her Adult. She views her independent-thinking processes as insignificant. As a result, she may not educate herself for a vocation that suits her real potential and that gives her satisfaction.

**STEPS TO
AWARENESS**

Adult Functioning

This exercise can help you gain a clearer profile of how you operate from your Adult ego state right now.

On the following continua, check where you rate your Adult functioning. If you have a close and trusted friend, perhaps you can get another opinion.

Openness to considering various sides of an issue:

Can't be bothered	Completely objective

Problem-solving abilities:

Very inept	Very skillful

Decision-making abilities:

Completely ineffective	Completely effective

Following through on decisions:

_____
Careless   Thorough

Success in changing bad habits:

_____
Without   Very
success   successful

Being competent in a particular field:

_____
Totally   Completely
without skill   competent

- What area did you find you excelled in?

- Why do you think this happened?

- Overall, are you satisfied with how you rated yourself?

- If not, what seems wrong?

- What can you do about it?

- What is your plan?

■ Outline three positive steps you can take to gain more personal satisfaction.

Arrange three chairs in a triangle. Imagine your intelligence on one of the chairs. Talk to your brains from the other two chairs—one your Parent and one your Child. Be a significant parent figure and tell your brains what your opinion is of them. Be the child you once were and tell your brains what you feel about them. Be your brains and respond. Move from chair to chair, acting out each part, until you feel you have finished the dialogue.

WOMEN'S INTELLECTUAL CAPABILITIES ARE OFTEN DISCOUNTED

Strokes give recognition, even though some of that recognition may be negative. Discounts, however, do not. A discount is a lack of attention, a lack of affirmation which hurts both emotionally and physically.

Problem Solving and Discounts

For centuries the problems of women in general have been ignored. Even today, many women and men discount the problem-solving abilities of women. Jacqui Lee Schiff points out that discounts happen in four different ways:[1]

1. The problem itself is not seen—is ignored, is discounted. "What in the heck are women hollering about? They've got everything their own way now."

2. The significance of the problem is not taken seriously—is discounted. "Women don't have it so bad. Think of all the men who are working their tails off for them."

3. The solvability of the problem is ignored—is discounted. "That's just the way it's always been done, and nothing's going to change."

4. The person's ability to do anything about solving the problem is demeaned—is discounted. "There's nothing *we* can do about it. The system is against us."

Even Freud pondered, "What is it that women want, anyway?"

Sometimes women are discounted by not being encouraged to perform Adult tasks. Early in life a little girl's abilities may be ignored and her cuteness stroked positively.

A businessman walking down a busy city street was stopped by two seven-year old youngsters. A girl and a boy were both selling candy bars for their third-grade class. The businessman stopped his hurried stride and bought a candy bar from each of the children. To the boy he said, "Young man, it looks as if you're doing a good job." Turning to the little girl, he patted her on her head and commented, "My, don't you look cute today."

This incident, combined with the thousands of others a little girl may experience, would scarcely encourage her to value her "meet and deal" ability. She would not be likely to go home and say, "You know, I was really good at selling today. I sold 27 candy bars." No one would be surprised at her logic if she decided that the best way for her to get approval and strokes was by being cute rather than by accomplishing.

Sometimes our senses are dulled to the real meaning of what we are saying or not saying. For example, if two men are talking about one man's wife, the first man might compliment the other with, "Your wife is certainly a beautiful girl." However, it would be unusual to hear one man say to another, "Jim, your wife has a brilliant mind. I envy you." Indeed, some husbands might be embarrassed to hear such a compliment, having learned to feel more comfortable with, "Your wife is a great cook and hostess. How lucky you are to have someone who entertains your clients so well." Here again, the woman is getting recognition for her Parent nurturing abilities or her Child qualities exclusively. She is deprived of strokes for her Adult problem-solving and logical thinking abilities.

STEPS TO AWARENESS

Different Strokes for Different Ego States

Here is a way to test whether your Adult is discounted or if it receives sufficient positive strokes. Write down the last six compliments you received. Decide whether they were strokes for your Parent, Adult, or Child.

Compliments   *Ego state stroked*

1. _____   _____

2. _____   _____

3. _____   _____

4. _____   _____

5. _____   _____

6. _____   _____

- What did you discover?

- Which ego state received the most strokes?

- Are these strokes for appropriate behaviors?

- Which ego state gets the least strokes?

- Are you satisfied with this?

- If not, what can you do to change the kinds of strokes you receive?

Write down specific strokes (not necessarily compliments) you have received over the last two days.

Which of your ego states received them?

What kind of strokes would you like for your Adult?

What are some ways you can get them?

The Adult Doing Its Thing

The power of change lies in the Adult. Through her Adult a woman can decide:

- *If* she wants to change;
- *What* she wants to change;
- *What steps* she needs to take to accomplish this change;
- *When* she is going to take those steps.

By activating and using her Adult, a woman can learn to make decisions, solve problems, talk straight, and apply the process of Adult intervention.

MANY WOMEN NEED PRACTICE IN TALKING STRAIGHT

Although all women have the capacity to be direct, many have not taken the opportunity to practice this skill. Talking straight is not always easy. In fact, a woman who is straightforward and direct may be considered blunt and unfeminine. If she is not straightforward and direct, she is accused of "thinking like a woman." She is caught in a double bind; she is damned if she thinks like a woman and damned if she does not—a game of *Corner.*

At the close of a management seminar led by Dorothy, a participant told her that he had gained many good ideas from the program. He ended with, "It was really great, Dorothy. You think just like a man." She had heard "think like a man" comments a number of times and had always accepted them as well intentioned. This time, however, she decided to affirm what was constructive and, in addition, to point out the mixed message. She responded, "Thank you, Malcolm. You said that with the tenderness of a woman." They both laughed, and Malcolm went away a little wiser.

As a result of choice, divorce, death, or longevity, more women face life alone. As a consequence, their ability to make their own decisions increases in importance. These changing circumstances of women provide them with new opportunities for making Adult statements that might sound like these:

"If I'm going to get the job I want, I'll have to go back to school."

"My husband and I have decided not to have children. I don't think I'd like being a mother."

"My husband and I believe that we'd be good parents. We've decided we want to have two or three children."

"Do you give the same loan terms to divorced women as to divorced men?"

"What is your thinking behind counseling my daughter not to major in chemical engineering?"

"I have decided not to continue assuming that I should do all the cooking and housework when we both work full time."

"I've decided that it's best for the kids and for me if I stay home while they're young."

"Would you consider letting two women work half time to fill one full-time job?"

"I feel better about myself and do better with the kids if I have a job."

"I'd like to work to help set up a neighborhood child-care center."

"Let's *ask* Sally if she wants to take a job transfer to Chicago and not assume that she wouldn't move for a better job."

"I want to have sex with you, but I've forgotten to take my birth control pill. Is there anything we can do about that?"

Talking straight means:

- Separating constructive and nonconstructive feedback;
- Being open and honest, with no ulterior purposes;
- Making thoughtful observations about what is actually happening now;
- Learning to raise the right questions to bring about change.

The following examples portray some Adult statements and questions that might come from women changing their scripts. Think of what it might look like and sound like if some of the fairy-tale characters decided to talk straight.

A Cinderella might say:

- "What kinds of things do I need to do in order to get a promotion next year?"
- "Rather than going out for a few drinks again this Friday night, I'm organizing an equal-rights-for-women meeting."

A Beautiful Plastic Woman might say:

- "I'm glad you like my legs, and what do you think of the idea I just recommended?"
- "Sure, I'd love to go on a backpacking trip. I enjoy being out of doors and roughing it."

A Little Red Riding Hood might say:

- "Rather than taking a walk in Central Park this evening, I think I'll wait until tomorrow morning."
- "I would enjoy spending the evening with you, but if you are looking for a bed partner, you may be happier with another date."

A Beauty and the Beast might say:

- "Rather than my defending Bill, I think it would be best for you to talk with him directly."
- "Jim, when you've stopped gambling, I'll be happy to talk about getting together again."

A Mother Hubbard might say:

- "Even though I've been on the cleaning committee for the last four parties, I'm turning this request down."
- "I'm going to spend some time just for myself every day."

EACH OF US IS CAPABLE OF THINKING FOR OURSELVES

Problem solving and positive change are made possible when you use your Adult. Here is how some people put their Adults to work to solve their problems.

Maria and Jose's Housekeeping Problem

Both Jose and Maria were professionals and had demanding, full-time jobs. Though they lived in a small apartment, there were still many chores to do. Before their marriage they had agreed that they would not assume traditional roles, but they soon found that Maria was doing the shopping, making arrangements for the laundry, and cooking the meals. She had collected so much resentment that one night she felt justified in blowing up. "Things have to change, or else!" she told Jose.

Jose was at first astonished by her attitude, but then agreed that Maria should not automatically be responsible for the household chores and that he should not automatically be responsible for the car and the financial decisions. They talked the problem over and made a decision.

How They Solved It. They wrote down all the chores that had to be done, even such things as emptying the garbage, watering the plants, and dusting. Then they took turns choosing the chores they would most like to do. They flipped a coin to determine who would have the first choice. After they had gone through the list once, they found that there were several things that they both felt lukewarm about but would not mind doing. So they flipped a coin again and took turns choosing the tasks they would prefer doing.

But there were still some chores remaining—ones that neither Jose nor Maria wanted to do. They wrote each of these items on a slip of paper and put the slips into a hat, agreeing to accept whatever chore they drew out of the hat. Then at the end of the month, they could trade these least desirable chores.

Jose and Maria agreed to sit down and talk again after doing their chores for three months. If they wanted to make changes, they would either trade or draw from the hat again. Both felt satisfied that neither was taking advantage of the other and that they were both carrying their load.

Janice's Problem of Pressure to Get a Job

Janice loved homemaking and community work more than anything else she had ever done. She had had some paid work experience after two years of college, but preferred being home full time. However, she felt pushed and dissatisfied with herself because she was not aspiring to more. She also felt that the new pressures on women meant that something was wrong with her if she did not seek paid employment.

How She Solved It. Janice began an objective evaluation of her situation. Whether to stay home or not boiled down to economics. Could she afford to stay home? She investigated her husband's retirement, disability, and medical plans to find out what her financial situation would be if he became disabled or died. She visited her local Social Security office and gathered information about her possible status as an unemployed widow. She looked over the family's debts and investments and checked out various funeral and burial costs.

On the basis of all this information, she decided that indeed she could stay home. However, she needed to periodically monitor her financial position, plan for the unpredictable, and prepare for living on a fixed, relatively low income in her old age. Financial planning became one of her new interests. She felt good about her decision, but was aware of the vigilance it required.

Betty Lou and Monroe's Divorce Problem

Betty Lou had worked to put Monroe through law school. After he established a good practice and began to move in "prominent" circles, she no longer fit into his social life. Monroe asked for a divorce.

He felt a deep sense of guilt, but stood by his decision. Betty Lou felt angry because her only skill was that of a high school graduate's typing.

How They Solved It. Betty Lou and Monroe eventually arrived at a mutually satisfying solution. Monroe set aside money for Betty Lou to complete a bachelor's degree. She had a guaranteed education. He had his guilt relieved.

In each of these problem areas, people used their Adult ego states to gain a wider perspective and to arrive at a satisfying solution.

STEPS TO
AWARENESS

Getting a Clearer Picture of the Problem

You can use the following process to look at *all* the elements in a situation when you are solving problems and making decisions.

Pick a specific problem you want to solve, conflict you want to resolve, or decision you want to make. Think of a title for your choice and then summarize the issue in 25 words or less.

Title:

The problem in brief:

Brainstorm as rapidly as you can, writing down all of your thoughts, feelings, and opinions about this problem. Write down your ideas without stopping to evaluate them. As other ideas occur to you, include them.

Look back over the list and mark each item Parent, Adult, or Child, depending on how each of *your* ego states seems to be involved. For example, if you feel down, your Child is probably involved. If the item is factual, it is probably your Adult. If it is opinion, supportive, or a "shouldism," it is probably your Parent. One item may involve more than one ego state.

Now make another list of what you would think and feel *if* the problem were solved.

Again, mark each item Parent, Adult, or Child.
When you compare the lists, what do you see happening?

Does your first list:
- Contain several Parent and Child items but only a few Adult items?
- Show mostly Adult and Parent involvement but few Child goodies?
- Leave any ego state out?
- Show that one ego state seems to dominate the others?

Does your second list of probable elements when the problem is solved contain:

- A mixture of Parent, Adult, and Child involvement?
- Anything for your Child?
- Anything for the Child that would *not* be OK with your Parent? (For example, if you wanted to lose 25 pounds, would looking more attractive, perhaps more sexually attractive, displease your Parent?)
- A conflict between your Parent and Child? (If there are conflicts, you may want to use the Gestalt two-chair dialogue technique to work toward resolution.)

What does this information reveal to you about your problem-solving and decision-making capabilities and blocks?

What can you do to make the solution equally attractive to all three of your ego states?

Setting a Goal

Once you have defined a problem and have gained insight into the effects your ego states have on solving it, set out a goal you want to accomplish. This would be your long-term goal. Since it is impossible to climb a huge mountain in one leap, setting minigoals helps. It is like tackling the mountain 100 yards at a time. Break down into smaller elements what needs to be different. Then decide what needs to be different by specific points in time.

Minigoals

This is what
will be different in:

1 day   _____

1 week   _____

1 month   _____

3 months   _____

6 months   _____

1 year   _____

Main goal

This is the
end result I want   _____

Making a Decision

If you are currently grappling with a decision, look at it from a fresh point of view.

- What would your two most important Parent figures want you to do?

- What are the facts involved?

- What are your hunches about what you should do?

- If you make a change, will you feel better, have more fun, be able to be creative, make more money, have more time off, or what?

After you have studied your responses, ask yourself:

- Which ego state is in charge?
- Which ego state is being left out?

Is there a possible decision that would please all three of your ego states to some degree and in constructive ways?

Clara used this process of making a decision as she grappled with criticism about her life-style. She had heard many times that "real" women were married. It hurt to examine the inner pain she felt because she had decided to remain single. Her symptoms were guilt and depression.

Clara, who is 28, attractive, and popular, had just returned from a four-day holiday weekend with her parents, her two brothers, and their wives and children. After spending much of the time defending her single life-style and explaining that she really is happy, she went home, depressed, to her stylish apartment. Her inner dialogue looks like this:

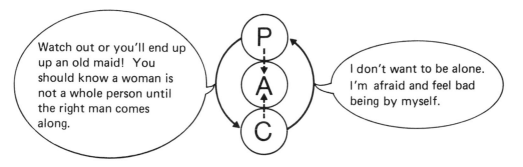

Awareness of Parent and Child

After she came in touch with this dialogue, Clara's Adult began to intervene.

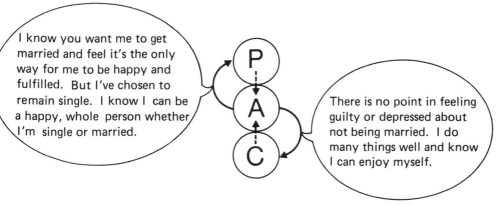

Adult Intervention

After this intervention, she reached a different decision.

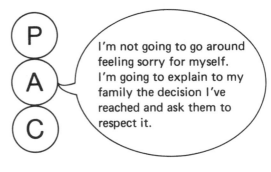

New Decision

Another woman going through the decision process was Sylvia. She was missing out on much of what was happening around her.

Sylvia had just sat through a solid hour listening to jokes, but she couldn't remember one punch line. She tried hard to listen, but the more she strained and told herself she had to listen, the harder it was for her to remember what she heard. Her energies went into trying, not doing. In the end she didn't hear much.

The Parent-Child messages yelling back and forth inside her head drowned out what was actually happening on the outside. Her internal dialogue looks like this:

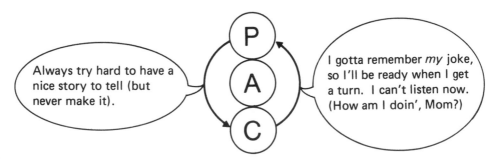

Awareness of Parent and Child

After becoming aware of her internal Parent-Child dialogue, Clara's Adult stepped in. Now her dialogue looked like this:

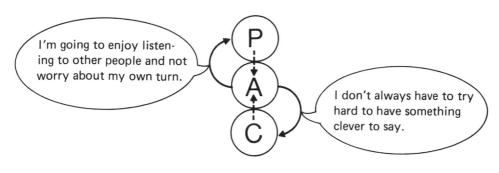

Adult Awareness

Amanda became aware of a strong "Be Perfect" message as a driving force in her script.

It is the afternoon before Amanda's committee meeting. The chairperson calls with an urgent request: "We need an update on the fund-raising campaign. Since Lee's sick, I'm counting on you to give the report. Now, I know you like to do everything perfectly, but we're very short on time." Amanda's inner dialogue looks like this:

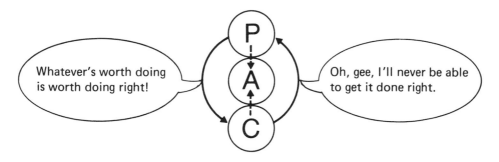

Awareness of Parent and Child

After she became aware of this inner dialogue, Amanda's Adult took over.

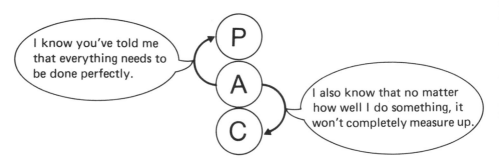

Adult Intervention

Amanda's Adult intervention enabled her to think through a new decision which eventually changed what she did.

Decision Based on Awareness

Frances had a different type of problem. She struggled with fat.

Frances was enjoying the food at her friend's dinner party, but was beginning to feel uncomfortable. She had already gained back a few of the 20 pounds she had worked so hard to shed. The voices in her head went through a dialogue like this:

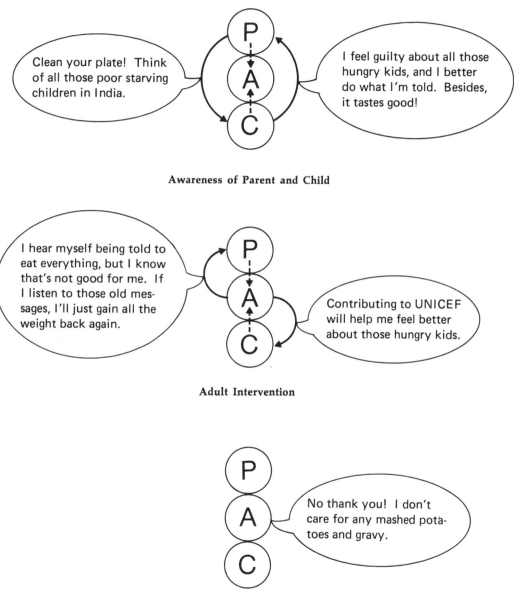

Awareness of Parent and Child

Adult Intervention

Behavior Based on Awareness

After this first success of turning down the potatoes and gravy, Frances was spurred on to engage her Adult even more about eating. She taped a 3" × 5" card to the refrigerator door: "My Adult can and will postpone gratification." She also decided that it would be useful to picture her weight loss. So she taped a picture of a skinny, bikini-clad woman on the refrigerator door next to her card. A week later a friend of Frances' husband was getting a cold drink out of the refrigerator. He started chuckling when he saw the picture of the bikini-clad woman next to the sign, "My Adult can and will postpone gratification." "Hey, Clark," he laughed, "what's the matter, have you been overdoing it lately?"

THE ADULT RAISES KEY QUESTIONS

A person moves toward autonomy through Adult evaluation of any new insights. Questions like the following are a good way to start sorting out some of the positive and negative elements of your ego states.

- Which of my ideas and feelings are constructive in my life today? Destructive?

- How closely do my ideas and feelings about myself match up to reality? In looking at what I'm doing with my life presently, what are the facts I'm basing my actions on?

- What is the healthiest thing for me to do now?

One of the goals of TA is not only to sort out the positive and negative—which gives us awareness—but also to *use the positive aspects of all three ego states.* This process means toning down, shutting off, or eliminating the destructive; and beefing up, turning on, and expanding the constructive.

Jackie's resentment toward her mother showed in a mobile she built of her Parent input from her mother. All the pieces were ugly and twisted. After studying it, Jackie laughed, "It looks as if I've thrown the baby out with the bath water. Because of my anger toward my mom, I've cut out all her good things. I remember she used to end her phone conversations with, 'May God bring you something good today.' That made people feel good. But I've never done it, because I didn't want to be anything like her. It's really all right to say something like that to people."

Many Parent ego states have lots of goodies. Some have only a few. But every little bit helps.

The appropriate use of all three ego states is necessary for the whole, healthy person. Such an individual cares about people like a good parent; has enough information to be effective like a productive, informed adult; and can laugh, cry, and be sensuous, charming, curious, and joyous like a healthy child.

Even though awareness is important in achieving a balanced and constructive use of all three ego states, awareness in itself is not enough. For example, one woman who had been in treatment for 14 years had a storehouse of information about her toilet training. After 14 years she was well informed but still unhappy. It had not occurred to her that she could redecide—that she could:

> write herself a new story,
>
> build her own scenery,
>
> find a new cast of characters,
>
> get off the pot and get on with her life.

**STEPS TO
AWARENESS**

Your Adult Interventions

Pick a sphere in your life that seems bothersome. It might be one of the following problem areas, or it might be something else:

Your relationship with a person of the opposite sex.

Your relationship with a person of the same sex.

A negative Parent tape.

A negative Child feeling.

A decision about whether or not to live together, to marry, or to divorce.

Whether or not to get a job or to change a job.

Listen to your inner messages and be aware of your feelings.

Write your inner dialogue here, showing your awareness of your Parent and Child messages:

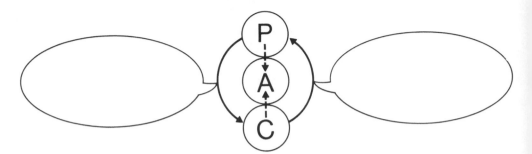

Use the Gestalt empty-chair technique, or double up your fists and have your right fist represent one part of your personality and your left fist the other. Develop a dialogue between these two parts of yourself. Continue this dialogue until you feel you can come to a new decision or can resolve a problem.

What did you learn from the experience? Summarize it in the diagram.

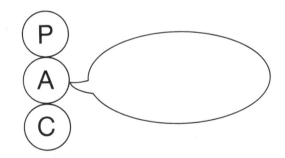

You may want to go through this procedure with other problems as they occur to you.

Learning to Give Strokes for the Adult

Women who have had their intelligence discounted since infancy are likely to perceive themselves as more childlike than womanly. As adults, they ignore their intelligence and some think of themselves as "girls" rather than as "women." They may even call themselves "girls."

With awareness, both women and men can recognize the importance of Adult strokes for many women. The attitudes on both sides of a transaction can change.

A male supervisor in a large manufacturing organization reported, "I really treat my girls well. I give 'em a smile and a 'hello,' and that keeps them happy. I even let them take long lunches. When they do something wrong, I get someone else to redo the work, so no one will get upset. They don't cause any problems here. But you know, I just haven't found a girl yet who could supervise. I give 'em a crack at a supervisory job and first thing I know, they're crying. They can't give their people tough news, and they're always coming to me to solve their problems."

This man gave Child strokes by calling women "girls," even though he expected most of them to function frequently in Adult ways as supervisors. Eventually he figured out that what he was doing was unproductive for his goals. He decided to start giving Adult as well as Child strokes. He began saying more things like:

"You did a good job preparing those reports."

"I appreciate the way you solved that problem independently."

"Thanks for making that decision. It showed good thinking."

"The information you've prepared isn't clear. Will you look at it again and then give me your thinking?"

"Based on what I've seen you do in the past, I know you can handle this assignment."

To his surprise, he found that by taking the talents of his women employees more seriously, he got a woman's day's work rather than a girl's. This change convinced him that strokes for Adult behavior pay off.

Balance in Your Personality

Now that you have studied the Parent, Adult, and Child ego states, you can work toward creating a more productive balance of your thinking, feeling, and doing. One way is to get in touch with both the negative and positive aspects of all parts of your personality. For example, the Nurturing Parent can be overprotective, too solicitous, condescending, and rescuing, thus inhibiting the growth of other people. Or the Nurturing Parent can take care of people who have genuine needs, provide protection, and give appropriate permissions for behaviors that are OK.

The Controlling Parent can be authoritarian, arbitrary, bitchy, and overcritical. Or it can establish fair rules that enable people to meet their needs in groups. This part of the Parent is also a source of ethical values, such as honesty and integrity.

The Adult can play calculated games, rationalize inappropriate behaviors, and figure out how to be destructive in relationships. Or it can search for truth. It can gather information, process it, and make decisions that take into account the caring aspects of the Parent and the needs and wants of the Child.

The Adapted Child can be overadapted in negative ways so that a person feels unduly inhibited and inadequate. Or it can learn to share, use good manners, and become aware of the needs of others.

The Natural Child can be self-centered, narcissistic, and insensitive. Or it can laugh, play, have fun, and express joy, sensuousness, curiosity, and affection.

STEPS TO AWARENESS

What is Your Egogram?

The Egogram, developed by John Dusay, can help you picture the balance in your personality.[2] Think of your psychic energy as flowing within and/or between ego states. If you invested equal energy in each aspect of your personality, your Egogram would look like the following adaptation of John Dusay's original idea.

NP   CP   A   AC   NC

NP = Nurturing Parent, CP = Controlling Parent, A = Adult, AC = Adapted Child, NC = Natural Child

(You might also want to include your Little Professor.)

What would a person be like if his or her Egogram looked like this?

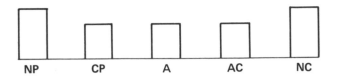

NP   CP   A   AC   NC

Or like this?

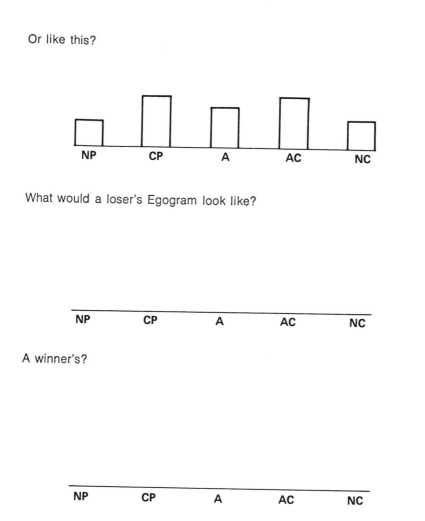

What would a loser's Egogram look like?

NP   CP   A   AC   NC

A winner's?

NP   CP   A   AC   NC

Think of how *you* use your psychic energy. How would *your* Egogram look?

NP   CP   A   AC   NC

Take another look at your own Egogram. Shade in the positive use as compared to the negative use, as in the following example.

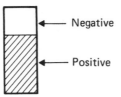

■ Are you satisfied with what you see?

■ Do you need to use any of your ego states more frequently? Less frequently?

If so, how can you do this?

■ What is your plan for today? Next week? Next year?

Redecisions need to be integrated with the Adult. In private, talk over your new decision with your other ego states. Using the empty-chair technique, be all of your ego states. Speak out loud to each about what you have decided to do. Is your Child in on the new decision? If so, you are likely to experience a deep feeling level. Your Child and Adult together make a good team—especially if your Parent offers protection.

THE AUTONOMOUS WOMAN LIVES FULLY

The autonomous woman experiences a growing awareness in all spheres of her life. She lives a continual process of discovering, perhaps for the first time, those internal and external pressures that shape her life. Through this process she learns to peel off archaic wrappings that bind her. She sheds any unrealistic feelings, such as guilt, ugliness, passivity, and perfectionism.

The aware woman filters old patterns through her Adult. She listens to her inner Parent tapes and evaluates the degree to which they are defeating, supporting, destructive, inspiring, or irrelevant. She makes decisions for herself. She stops blaming parent figures, realizing that her unhappy plight is now *her* own responsibility and that she can either manage it or let it manage her. She asserts herself to meet her needs and to get what she wants.

The autonomous woman listens to and feels her inner Child. She responds to her *genuine* needs and separates out irrational adaptations that defeat the enrichment of her life now. She also takes responsibility for her feelings. She recognizes that she (not others) depresses herself, kicks herself, angers herself, shuts off her feelings—all in her own head. She gives up the belief in a magical event or person that somehow, some day will make her life better, with no effort on her part.

She learns that she does not have to automatically respond to her past programming. She can become aware of it and strengthen her Adult by making new choices and doing what is best for her.

The autonomous woman also uses her Adult (with the help of her creative Little Professor) to discover new options. She grows, expanding those positive resources she already has. And she develops, adding new skills, insights, and knowledge to her personality repertoire.

She is not afraid to be the part of herself that is the woman. She strengthens her Adult by using it. She takes steps to bring more positive forces into her life.

The autonomous woman is in the process of becoming more fully herself. This process of awareness adds excitement and zest to her life. She accepts that she can be all that she was born to be—a total person, a winning person. She is not afraid to be her own woman. Her energy is not stuck in the past. It swells to meet the moment.

11

Thinking Straight About Women

- Why do men and women believe what they do about women?
- Why do some women discriminate against themselves?
- How can you confront and clear up confused thinking?

Look at me.
Tell me. What do you see?

You, there, say I can't drive.
And you, believe I'm fragile.

How do you know me?
How do you judge me?

Why do you judge
When you haven't seen
Past a million other faces
To really see what's behind mine?

Dorothy Jongeward

Some subjects are harder to think straight about than others are. But the subject of *women* is probably the most difficult of all. It hits us where we have invested our most primitive and basic sense of identity. The following incident illustrates how difficult it can be to see ourselves clearly.

After all the job applicants (five women and one man) had left the office Jack commented to a woman whose job was similar to the one being offered: "There must be something wrong with a man who'd want a job like yours."

The blind spot in Jack's thinking is obvious to those around him, but not to him. His blind spot distorts his objectivity and puts filters between him and reality. This same distortion in thinking shows up in this quip from an angry woman: "If they thought this equal-opportunity-for-women program was so important, they'd put a man in charge!"

Here is another illustration of this kind of unclear thinking:

Dru was meeting with a group of 15 divisional managers for a company with offices all over the West Coast. The purpose of the meeting was to examine ways of moving women into technical and managerial positions. As Dru presented some of the facts about working women and some avenues for ensuring equal opportunity, the discussion grew heated. One of the men listening to her briefing finally blurted out, "But would a man listen to a woman?"

THINKING CAN BE CONTAMINATED

Many distortions of reality result from the phenomenon of *contamination*. Contamination is an intrusion of the Parent and/or the Child into the Adult ego state. It inhibits and spoils the Adult's clear, objective thinking.[1]

Parent contaminations of the Adult contribute to *distorted cultural scripts*. Similarly, Child contaminations of the Adult are likely to result in *distorted personal scripts*. Thus contamination operates at both individual and group levels. Unrealistic cultural and personal scripts feed and foster each other.

Child Illusions

Contamination from the Child occurs if the person's self-imagery, decisions, positions, and feelings are unrealistic. For example, a woman who learns a contempt for her body sees herself as ugly. As a consequence, she has a difficult time thinking straight about what she really looks like. By the same token, a man who learns to always be strong and appear all-knowing may suffer from an illusion of superiority, in order to bolster a shaky sense of OK-ness.

Having Child illusions is like seeing oneself and the world through foggy glass. This kind of contamination can be diagrammed as follows:

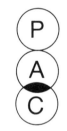

Child Contamination of the Adult

The unrealistic, unduly negating, destructive, or pompous elements of a person's script become illusions when they go unexamined by the Adult ego state. For example, the illusion of rescue is common to women.

- Cinderella seeks her Prince Charming.
- Rapunzel waits for her hair to be her rescue.
- And Sleeping Beauty lies on her back, asleep for a hundred years, waiting for her Prince to make his way through the thicket to turn her on again.

Parent Prejudice

If the Parent contaminates the Adult, the Adult accepts as valid many un-examined and unevaluated Parental attitudes. These attitudes are trans-mitted as facts. In turn, the Adult accepts these so-called facts without thinking. *Without thinking* is the key. The Adult, when misinformed by the Parent, lies dormant, does not seek more information, and fails to evaluate opinions and beliefs.

Parent contamination of the Adult can be pictured like this:

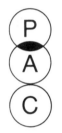

Parent Contamination of the Adult

Parent contaminations of the Adult result in a variety of prejudices. They range from politics to politeness, religion to race, food to fads, sanctimoni-ousness to sex. The severity of these prejudices spans the breadth from being suspicious of women doctors to hanging witches. The deepest forms are the prejudices that make up contaminated beliefs held by both sexes about femaleness and maleness.

Both chauvinism and sexism are rooted in contaminated thinking which deters healthy, viable relationships. Chauvinism is "prejudiced belief in the superiority of one's own group."[2] Sexism is "discrimination by members of one sex against the other, especially by males against females, based on the assumption that one sex is superior."[3]

If the members of one group believe themselves superior to members of other groups, they practice ways to keep the others "in their place." They band together to gain power and to produce a social setting which appears to prove and reinforce the contaminated belief. They flex their muscles and fall in love with sameness, feeling good only about what is like them in others. They fail to make contact, for contact implies an ap-preciation of differences. Also, there frequently exists a hidden collusion between the oppressor and the oppressed. One group acts powerless and gives a false sense of power to the other. Everybody pretends. Everybody loses.

If people in a group cling to traditional beliefs without question or evaluation, they produce a distorted *collective conscience*. Thus a culture evolves in which large numbers of people fail to check out their beliefs and actions, no matter how irrational, against available facts. Irrational cultural scripts lead to individual contamination.

Most of us have our Adult contaminated to some degree from both the Parent and Child. For example, a woman may have Parent contamination that says, "Men are able to fix broken machines." This same woman may have a Child contamination that says, "I am helpless when things break." These two contaminations can be diagrammed like this:

Parent and Child Contamination of the Adult

YOU CAN SPOT CONTAMINATION

As you eavesdrop on these comments, listen for the ways in which thinking is distorted.

One woman to another:

"If there's anything I hate, it's to be stuck with a batch of women for a whole afternoon."

Two people on a bus:

"Women should make up their minds. They should have either jobs or families."

Two people in a park:

"Look at that kid playing in the mud! Any woman who would let her child get that dirty is an unfit mother."

Neighbor to neighbor:

"Did you see Hank Jones actually hanging out the laundry? His wife must be sick."

Husband to wife:

"If you really want to have an evening out with the girls once in a while, why don't you just get a babysitter? After all, I play poker with the boys every Thursday night, and I wouldn't be home anyway."

Salesperson to salesperson:

"Women make me sick. They can't make up their minds about anything!"

One man to another:

"This men's club is one of the few places where we can talk about important deals. Chattering women would just be distracting."

Two people waiting in line for a restaurant cashier:

"Any guy who lets a woman pay his dinner check certainly isn't much of a man."

Two friends talking on the morning after:

"Did you see Charlie and Margie at the party last weekend? He's a real swinger all right, but *she* certainly has no business acting that way."

An executive mulling over two possible candidates for a new job as district manager:

"Walt is an up-and-coming man. He showed aggressive leadership on the Dallas project. Sue, on the other hand, gets the job done and has handled some big assignments. But she does seem a bit pushy. That's so unbecoming in a woman."

One friend to another:

"Isn't it a shame about Frances. She is college-educated, but she stays at home devoting all her time to two small children."

A male executive in a conservative company:

"Why, my secretary just called me by my first name. Sally can't do that to me!"

Irate woman to friend:

"The Department of Commerce defines the poverty level differently for men and women. For women, it's $2217; for men, $2396!"[4]

Husband to wife:

"You know, Carol, you never complained about being bored when the kids were small. Maybe we should have another baby."

One man to his woman's studies instructor:

"When women start doing all the inhumane things men have done for years, there will be no hope for the world!"

Fiancé to future bride:

"I've thought it over, honey, and decided it's OK for you to keep your maiden name."

**STEPS TO
AWARENESS**

Recognizing Contamination About Women

You can use this exercise to get a clearer image of what contaminated thinking is like and how it affects women and men. Although you can do this exercise alone, you may find it more fun to do with other people. To get the most out of it, do each part in the order presented.

Quickly list at least ten words or phrases *commonly heard* about women.[5] Start with "Women are. . . ." If you can't agree on an item, ask: "Would it commonly be heard around a dinner table, in a grocery store, on the job, in a church'"

Women are:

1.	6.
2.	7.
3.	8.
4.	9.
5.	10.

Now follow the same procedure, but finish the sentence, "Men are. . . ."

Men are:

1.	6.
2.	7.
3.	8.
4.	9.
5.	10.

As you look over your two lists, consider these questions:

■ Do you find any general sense of "OK" or "not-OK" for either men or women? If so, in what way?

Women are

Men are

■ Now look over the traits you listed and decide which ego state each is most likely associated with. For example, if one of the traits you listed was "weak," it would be most closely associated with the Child. In the same manner, "unemotional" is associated with the Adult; "authoritarian," with the Parent.

■ Tally up the numbers of traits you assigned for women to the Parent ego state, to the Adult, and to the Child.

■ Next, do the same with the list for men. If you find it difficult to decide, assign the traits to as many ego states as you can justify.

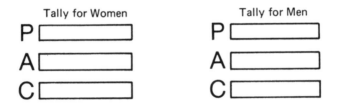

Tally for Women

P

A

C

Tally for Men

P

A

C

■ Use your tallies to draw comparative ego state portraits[6] for women and men. Increase or decrease the size of each ego state circle, depending on the number in your tally. (The ego state portrait shows the amount of use only, not whether or not a person *has* a particular ego state.) If five of the ten traits you listed are Parent, you would draw a very large Parent circle and small Adult and Child circles. For example:

231

Your Ego State Portrait of Women   **Your Ego State Portrait of Men**

Now look over the ego state portraits you drew and ask yourself:
- What are the differences between women and men in my typical portraits?

If these stereotypes were followed, how would they affect ego state development?

How might these differences affect such areas of life as:

Education?   Self-reliance?

Vocation?   Emotional expression?

Aspiration?   Sense of superiority or inferiority?

- How might these beliefs affect a woman's attitude toward herself?

Toward other women?

Toward men?

- How might these beliefs affect a man's attitude toward himself?

  Toward other men?

  Toward women?

- Is the relationship you see a dynamic one, based on two well-developed people capable of functioning both independently and interdependently?

- Is it a fixed relationship based on a dependency between ego states, in which one person is not "complete" without the other?

  If so, what ego state relationship seems to appear between women and men?

  What might this cause male/female relationships to be like:
  In marriage?

  On the job?

  Socially?

  What would be the impact on upward mobility for working women?

MANY WOMEN PUT DOWN OTHER WOMEN

One of the most destructive aspects of contamination is that it can be *internalized*. Thus a woman holding contaminated beliefs accepts all these things about herself. In addition, she may show contempt toward other women—their frivolities, erratic behavior, silliness, and undue emotionalisms. Or she may be caught in the double bind of being disgusted with "feminine ways" yet acting that way herself in order to appear feminine. She does not realize that she is taking her whole person and existence and stuffing it into a narrow, unexamined box.

Consider the implications in the following situations. A woman politician was asked by a newsperson when a woman might run for Vice-President. Ironically, she was reported as answering, "I don't know, but if they ever name one to be President, I'm going to leave the country." Similarly, in 1975 two out of three women legislators in one state voted against the Equal Rights Amendment.

Indeed, women have traditionally learned to be "their own worst enemies."

At a conference of 500 women employees, Dorothy raised the question, "How many of you would like to work for a woman?" When only a few hands went up, a brief argument ensued between two camps of differing opinions. However, most of the women in the crowd called out such things as: "Women are too emotional"; "They're too bossy"; "Women can never make up their minds"; "Who'd want to work for a woman? That's no fun!"

The next question was: "How many of you aspire to being a supervisor or a manager?" The many women who raised their hands in response to this question realized for the first time that most of the women present wouldn't want to work for them, including themselves. They were astonished at their own self-prejudice.

The small voice of dissent that was heard in this group represents a now growing number of women who are questioning traditional beliefs.

The Queen Bee Syndrome

The "Queen Bee" syndrome characterizes many women who have made it to the top in a man's world. This syndrome allows them to tenaciously cling to women's traditional legal and political positions and roles. Somehow they believe themselves to be exceptions. More ordinary women could not do their jobs. The attitudes of such "successful organizational women" toward those women joining together to better their lot came to light in the following survey:

> Many successful women . . . relish the fact that they are "special," that they have unique qualifications that allow them to get high-ranking positions normally denied to women. Nondiscriminatory policies become threatening: Queen Bees do not want competition for their jobs any more than the men do. . . .

> There is yet another powerful reason why Queen Bees denigrate the efforts of other women to make it into the system. Queen Bees are highly rewarded for doing so, for being special, for "looking so feminine" yet "thinking like a man." . . .

> Similarly, the Queen Bee who is successful in a male-dominated field feels little animosity toward the system that has permitted her to reach the top, and little animosity toward the men who praise her for being so unique. She identifies with the specific male colleagues who are her reference group, rather than with the diffuse concept of women as a class. . . .[7]

For a myriad of psychological and social reasons, the surge of feelings of sisterhood among women have been hard to come by. Contamination patterns pit women against women. The ability to organize characterizes people who feel power. The *inability* to organize—bickering, splitting into factions, failure to see common goals—characterizes those who feel powerless. In spite of this, many women are reality-testing and evaluating not only cultural scripts for women, but also their own personal scripts.

This renewal of the attitude of women helping women is a repetition of historical scripts. It is a rebirth of the spirit of the few, yet powerful and autonomous women who for nearly a century led the struggle for the franchise.

**STEPS TO
AWARENESS**

Discovering Women's Contempt for Women

This exercise can help you spot ways women put down other women. For example:

> "What can you expect from a woman!"
> "How can she stand working with women all day!"
> "If it's going to be a hen party, count me out!"

List some comments you have heard:

What effect would such comments have on the scripts of women?

For Women Only. Look over the list and ask, "Which of these comments do *I* use? If I talk about women in this way, what does that say about me as a woman?"

For Men Only. Ask yourself, "What are the implications for me as a man, if the women in my life say and hear these messages?"

CONTAMINATIONS IN SUBCULTURES DIFFER

It is likely that many of the stereotypes you discovered in the "Recognizing Contamination About Women" exercise are typical of the white middle class. Yet most subcultures traditionally delegate women to even lesser positions. Just think for a moment of the women who still live under the machismo ethic or women who still mentally, at least, walk ten paces behind their men. But in America, it is the black woman who holds a unique historical position.

Because many black women have learned to feel not-OK because of their color, not their sex, most cultural contaminations that are put on the shoulders of women in general—weak, emotional, fragile, dependent—do not typically describe black women. In fact, black women are often *expected* to work, to be strong, to be a central figure in their families. And indeed women head three out of ten black families and six out of ten *poor* black families.[8]

This "strength" that many black women exhibit may contribute at least in part to the findings of Cynthia Fuchs Epstein. According to her research, college-educated black women have more confidence in their abilities than a comparable group of white women graduates. She reports: "Black women seem to have acquired a sense of confidence in their competence and ability. Interviews with these black professional women revealed a strong feeling of self-assurance."[9] When women were asked if they thought their personalities were suitable for careers as business executives, only 49% of white women interviewed responded positively, whereas 74% of the black women did.

These differences in contaminations also place the black woman in a unique position as she progresses toward her own personal freedom. If she is to be liberated as a person, her race must also be liberated. Such a movement holds the potential of bringing black men and women closer together as they reach out for common goals.

If, however, black men, as they are more and more able to accept the family roles of mates and fathers, script themselves after white men, they fall into the trap of holding sexist attitudes toward the women in their lives. Black women lose. In contrast, as white women and those of some other subcultures move toward personal autonomy, wedges work their way into traditional relationships between women and men.

As a consequence, in order for the contamination to be cleaned away, men of all ethnic groups need permission to examine the basis for their own self-images as men. What does it really mean to be masculine? What does it mean for men to be freed from measuring their male OK-ness against female not-OK-ness? Does a man become something less if a woman becomes something more?

> Is it healthy for
> any relationship between
> any two people
> to be based on the fragile grounds
> of a false feeling
> of either power or powerlessness?

Feeling OK only as superior to women requires men to adorn themselves with many masks. This keeps men and women apart. Such hiding encourages men to play games, avoid intimacy, and stifle personal growth.

MALE SCRIPTING CAN HAVE LETHAL ASPECTS

Men who are falsely expected to always be strong, courageous, brave, intelligent, logical, stoic, and mechanically inclined are likely to be put under unrealistic pressure. Their bodies literally strain under stress. Stress for a prolonged period of time causes deterioration of the body. Sidney Jourard highlights some of the lethal aspects of the male role:

> Men die sooner than women. . . . Biology provides no convincing evidence to prove that female organisms are intrinsically more durable than male ones or that tissues or cells taken from males are less viable

than those taken from females. A promising place to look for an explanation of the perplexing sex differential in mortality is in the transactions between men and their environments, especially their interpersonal environments.... What aspects of being a man in American society are related to man's faster rate of dying?

The male role requires man to appear tough, objective, striving, achieving, unsentimental, and emotionally unexpressive. But seeming is not being. If a man *is* tender (behind his persona), if he weeps, if he shows weakness, he will probably regard himself as inferior to other men....

Man's potential thoughts, feelings, wishes and fantasies know no bounds, save those set by his biological structure and his personal history. But the male role, and the male's self-structure will not allow man to acknowledge or to disclose the entire breadth and depth of his inner experience to himself or to others.... It is as if being manly implies the necessity to wear ... neuromuscular "armor" of which Reich wrote with such lucidity....

Naturally, when a person is in hostile territory, he must be continually alert, tense, opaque, and restless. All this implies that trying to seem manly is a kind of work, and work imposes stress and consumes energy. Manliness, then, seems to carry with it a chronic burden of stress and energy expenditure which could be a factor related to man's relatively shorter life span.

If self-disclosure is an empirical index of openness and if openness is a factor in health and wellness, then research in self-disclosure seems to point to one of the potentially lethal aspects of the male role. Men keep their selves to themselves and impose thereby an added burden of stress beyond that imposed by the exigencies of everyday life.[10]

The process of male scripting starts early. The pressures to be strong, athletic, virile can show up in a boy's schooling. Leo Buscaglia describes this pain:

Drawing from personal experiences, I remember my physical education classes in junior and senior high school. If there are any physical education teachers reading this, I hope they hear me loud and clear. I remember the striving for perfection. Physical education should be a place where we all should have an equal opportunity, where our only competition should be with ourselves. If we can't throw a ball, then we learn to throw a ball the best we can. But that wasn't it—they were always rewarding perfection. There were always the big muscular guys standing up there. They were the stars. And there I was—skin and bones, with my little bag of garlic around my neck, and shorts that didn't fit and always hung way down my little skinny legs. I'd stand there in line while we were being chosen in games, and I used to die every single day of my life. You remember! We all lined up, and there were the athletes standing there with their big chests out, and they'd say, "I choose you." "I choose you." And you saw the line dwindling away, and there you were, still standing there. Finally they got down to two people, one other little skinny guy and you. And then they'd say, "OK, I'll take Buscaglia," or "I'll take the wop," and you'd step out of line dying because you were not the image of the athlete, you were not the image of perfection they were striving for.[11]

Contamination about the sexes hurts not only women, but also men. It hurts the old. It hurts the young.

CLEAR AWAY THE COBWEBS

Contaminations can be cured by examining old information and gathering new information. This process of clearing away the cobwebs may take the form of raising questions, getting facts, or being open to new observations. Acquiring new information is not enough, however. The information must be thought through, evaluated, accepted, and then integrated into the personality. The end products of decontaminated thinking are changed attitudes which lead to changed behavior.

The process of decontamination looks like this:

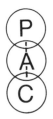
Adult gathers information about the Inner Parent and Child.

Then the Adult raises questions and seeks current information.

Decontamination takes place as Adult thinking clears.

As decontamination occurs, it often sounds like this:

"I didn't know that!"

"I used to think that . . ."

"I remember when I felt like . . ."

"Well, that certainly changed my mind."

"I can't believe it, but it's true."

Clearing up thinking means different things for different people. For some women it can mean:

Feeling good working for a woman

Feeling good about not being a parent

Feeling good about having a large family

Enjoying an elderly person's living in the home

Feeling good about nursing a baby

Confidently and assertively seeking a promotion

Enjoying being paid well for good work

Enjoying helping women grow personally and professionally

Feeling that men are OK

Enjoying sexual intercourse

Feeling good about being single

Appreciating the talents of women.

Confronting Contamination

Since contamination is a blind spot in the Adult, encouraging people to think rationally takes skill. Peeling back the layers of contamination sometimes needs to be done gently.

Sharing Adult information and making observations and raising questions help break the barriers of contamination. In the following illustration, a senior executive in a government agency skillfully impelled his staff to become aware of prejudice against women, by asking just the right question at just the right time.

Awareness training for women was the first item on the agenda for the regional director's staff meeting. The subtitle of the training session was "Helping Women Contribute From Their Full Potential." John, the Regional Director, was immediately confronted with mixed, but loud, opinions about the necessity of this special training.

The loudest disclaimer came from Marilyn, the only woman on his ten-person senior staff. As she disputed the need for any such training for women, Marilyn referred to her own staff: "Just look at the number of women in high-level jobs. We have plenty. Women who are management material don't need hand-holding!" *Several of the nine men voiced their support of Marilyn's position; several others heatedly asserted their contrary opinions.*

As the all encompassing "shoulds," "oughts," "musts," and "everybody knows" were hurled back and forth across the conference table, John sat back, listening and observing. The discussion about whether women were already accurately represented in management grew louder but less productive. Finally John leaned forward, and the attention of the nine men and one woman turned toward him. He said, "I've been hearing a lot of opinions pro and con about how fairly women are represented at top management levels. Will you look around this table right now and then give me your thinking?"

John was skillful at recognizing contamination and confronting it. You may want to use the following exercise to check out how you would confront contamination.

**STEPS TO
AWARENESS**

Dealing with Contamination

You are at lunch with George Smith, a colleague from another department. He is just relating:

"I'll sure hate to lose my secretary. She's such a bright, capable girl. She hasn't said anything yet, but I know her husband just got out of the Army, so she'll probably quit. I'll have her a few months or maybe a year and then she'll quit to stay home and have a baby. That's the way it always is. And you know, she's happy in her job, and she makes good money for a woman."

How would you respond to George?

Women's history gives us a dramatic example of confronting contamination. Sojourner Truth, a rangy black woman who was born a slave, became active as a revivalist, abolitionist, and suffragist.

In 1851 at a woman's rights convention in Akron, Ohio, none of the women seemed able to answer an outbreak of heckling, and it looked as if their cause would be worsted at their own gathering. Sojourner Truth came forward and sat on the steps of the pulpit from which Frances Dana Gage was presiding. Many women, apprehensive that the abolitionist leader would harm their cause, begged Mrs. Gage not to give her the floor. Mrs. Gage, fortunately, thought otherwise: "[Sojourner] moved slowly and solemnly to the front, laid her old bonnet at her feet, and turned her great speaking eyes to me. There was a hissing sound of disapprobation above and below. I rose and announced 'Sojourner Truth' and begged the audience to keep silent for a few moments."

Sojourner turned the full force of her eloquence against the previous speaker, a clergyman who had ridiculed the weakness and helplessness of women, who should, therefore, not be entrusted with the vote:

"The man over there says women need to be helped into carriages and lifted over ditches, and to have the best place everywhere. Nobody ever helps me into carriages or over puddles, or gives me the best place—ain't I a woman?"

With a gesture that electrified the audience, she raised her bare black arm:

"Look at my arm! I have ploughed and planted and gathered into barns, and no man could head me—and ain't I a woman? I could work as much and eat as much as a man—when I could get it—and bear the lash as well! And ain't I a woman? I have born thirteen children, and seen most of 'em sold into slavery, and when I cried out with my mother's grief, none but Jesus heard me—and ain't I a woman?" Then she shifted to another, shrewder vein: "If my cup won't hold but a pint, and yours holds a quart, wouldn't ye be mean not to let me have my little half measure full?"

Mrs. Gage wrote of her achievement:

"Amid roars of applause she returned to her corner, leaving more than one of us with streaming eyes, and hearts beating with gratitude. She had taken us up in her strong arms and carried us safely over the slough of difficulty, turning the whole tide in our favor. I have never in my life seen anything like the magical influence that subdued the snobbish spirit of the day and turned the sneers and jeers of an excited crowd into notes of respect and admiration."[12]

THINKING STRAIGHT ABOUT WOMEN
HELPS EVERYONE

Thinking straight about what it means to be a woman is tough for most of us. Child contaminations distort self-imagery, which in turn stifles personal growth. This type of distorted thinking encourages compulsive living that defies reason and denies the realities of femininity.

Without knowing why, a woman may, in the name of her concept of femininity, play the Victim role and wait for a rescue. She fulfills her script by play-acting roles rather than by being the woman she was meant to be.

Parent contaminations often fester into sexism and chauvinistic attitudes. They shadow our thinking about sex roles, ethnic differences, and foster power plays to maintain the status quo.

Stereotyped sex roles hurt people. They encourage women to vegetate and men to die before their time—the ultimate way for the underdog to get even.

Contamination separates people inwardly from themselves and outwardly from each other. The aware person—woman or man—progressively peels back its layers. Though this journey may be painful and at times seems to lead nowhere, the journey itself often holds rich rewards. A moment of awareness renews us, endorses us, and refreshes us like a cool breeze blowing through a stuffy room.

Decontamination happens when we make evaluations, gain new information, and raise questions. This process is not always easy. Consider how the facts about women in history have been discounted. The immense contributions of outstanding women frequently go unheralded, unknown, or unnoticed. In the next chapter you will discover some new insights into women in American history—insights that confront contaminations you may unknowingly hold.

12

A
Hundred
Years
Hence

- How has contaminated
  thinking contributed to
  women's status in
  history?

- How have women in the
  past dealt with distorted
  thinking?

- What can you learn from
  the lives of some significant women in American
  history?

- What do you see when
  you look at women in
  history from a TA view-
  point?

Then woman, man's partner, man's equal shall stand,
While beauty and harmony govern the land;
To think for oneself will be no offense,
The world will be thinking a hundred years hence.[1]

With these words, composed by Frances Dana Gage, suffragists' spirits swelled in the hope that their personal sacrifices, their dedication to freedom for all—regardless of sex—would reap great benefits for the grateful generations to come. Since these women courageously raised their voices to sing in the mid-1870s, it was fitting to speak of 100 years hence. We are those for whom they sang.

STEPS TO
AWARENESS

History and Women and You

Who are six *men* you admire from history?

Who are six *women* you admire from history?

Which list did you have an easier time with?

Begin to think about why one list may be easier than the other.

Now think about yourself in the center of a historical circle, with the significant women in your life surrounding you. Go back into history as far as you can. Write in the names of women significant to you now and those from history with whom you identify. Perhaps you will pick Queen Esther, Joan of Arc, Florence Nightingale, or Harriet Tubman. Or perhaps you might not think of any.

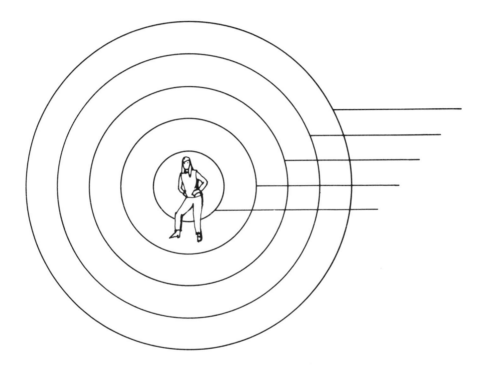

If you could not think of many women from the past, what may that mean for you now?

American Women in History

1.

2.

3.

4.   5.

6.   7.

You might have fun checking out your knowledge about some significant women in history and what they did. How many of these questions can you readily answer?

1. Who was Anne Hutchinson? Why is she important in American history?

2. Who was Emma Willard? To what field did she contribute?

3. What happened in Seneca Falls, New York, in 1848? Why is that event still important for us today?

4. Why was Harriet Tubman known as "Moses"?

5. Who was Elizabeth Cady Stanton? What did she do?

6. With what cause do you associate Susan B. Anthony?

7. You may be a member of an organization founded by Carrie Chapman Catt. What is the name of that organization?

8. What did Alice Paul write that is still of concern to many people today?

9. How many of the women pictured on pp. 246–247 do you recognize? (The women in the photographs are identified on p. 268.)

You are not alone if you could not answer all of these questions or identify all of the pictures. Recently we asked a bright 16-year-old woman what she had learned in history class about Susan B. Anthony. "Susan who?" was her wide-eyed response.

The way history books have been written, until quite recently, has denied many of us an opportunity to get to know exceptional women in the past. Not only are some of us unaware of the *exceptional* women, but also *lesser heroines* may go completely unsung. Did you know:

- that of the 18 married women who landed with the *Mayflower* in 1620, only four survived the first bitter winter?[2]

- that the trials in New England in 1692 led to the execution of 20 "witches"—most of them women—all of whom had deviated in some way from the Puritan mode of behavior?[3]

- that of the women who usually made up one-third of a slave ship's human cargo of some 500 to 700 blacks, one slaver wrote dispassionately, "I saw pregnant women give birth to babies while chained to corpses which our drunken overseers had not removed. . . ."?[4]

- that the appalling situation of women working in factories screamed for attention when, in the Triangle Shirtwaist Co. fire of 1911, 146 young women workers lost their lives in flames? Their paths for escape from the loft in which they worked had been barred.[5]

Yet as philosopher George Santayana observed, "Those who do not remember the past are condemned to relive it." To this we might add, "Those who do not know the historical script of their group cannot learn from it." Contamination blurs their vision. Their values remain distorted. And the same scenes and acts crop up in different generations to repeat themselves again and again.

Just as individuals can gather facts about their personal scripts to prevent repeating and passing on defeating patterns, so can groups. For example, men and women can confront old contaminations and collective scripts by gathering new information about women in history. We hope that this brief journey back into the past will pique your interest in discovering more about what women in American history have done and about what they have had done to them.

You will be reading factual but admittedly sympathetic portrayals of a few of the many women we admire.

You undoubtedly will find yourself closely identifying with particular women.

As you read these brief profiles, ask yourself questions similar to those in the beginning of the book:

Is this woman like someone in my life today

who needs my support?

who works with me?

who is my friend?

who is related to me?

Or is she like me?

ANNE HUTCHINSON (1591–1632)

Speaking Out for Religious Freedom for Women

Picture a pregnant woman on trial for heresy and brought to court to testify on her own behalf. Even though she is pregnant, she is forced to stand throughout the long proceedings until it becomes obvious she can no longer stand at all. To establish her heresy beyond question, she is forced to stay in the home of one of her opponents. Even though ill most of the time, she is still subjected to weeks of inquisition. As the trial continues, her strength fades, and so does her eloquent and lucid defense of her beliefs. As you picture this incident in Anne Hutchinson's life,[6] consider also the cultural scripts in which she grew up and lived.

Every society suffers those who deviate from the norms of the group scripts, yet there always seem to be a few people who in their spirit of autonomy and independence dance to their own tune. Some people are able to disagree with their majority culture and remain respectable and even acceptable. Benjamin Franklin is an example of this. Others, however, are considered radicals to be disposed of. Anne Hutchinson is an example of the latter.[7] Radicalism among women has always seemed more repulsive.

The role of the woman was clear to everyone in Puritan New England. She was to be an unquestioning follower. Men were to lead. Any woman who tried to lead, other than in the domestic domain, was a disgrace to herself and to her community and was also accused of going against the wishes of God.

Women received little or no education. Even the *thought* of women studying theology was abhorred. What a strain it would be for those tiny female minds to grapple with such heady thoughts!

However, Anne Hutchinson exhibited anything but a "tiny mind." She was intelligent, strong-willed, and devoted almost totally to her religion. In fact, she uprooted her entire family in 1634 to follow her favorite minister, John Cotton, to the New World.

Her insights and stands on religion were major deviations from her time and for her place. For example, it was her deep belief that God's grace dwells inside us. As a consequence, she professed the Covenant of Grace. She saw faith as a human being's most basic link to God. She held strong feelings that each person feels inwardly the power of God's grace. She saw this as the most important path to true salvation.

Even though it was unheard of in her day, she began to hold meetings that were separate from the church. Some 80 people, many of them women, attended these meetings. She would often point out that those ministers who preached the Covenant of Good Works (salvation through good behavior and self-control) were not proper ministers. The numbers of women listening to her increased. As a consequence the numbers of ministers aroused by fear and anger also increased.

Anne Hutchinson also began to question the status of women in the church. The assumption that no woman could have a voice in church affairs did not seem rational to a woman who felt so personally close to God.

She soon was in battle with the church authorities in her community. Although the battle appeared to be drawn along strictly theological lines, there was little question that the strongest undercurrent grew out of the fact that she was a woman. Anne Hutchinson made the unprecedented demand that women be permitted to think for themselves about God. She not only did this herself, but also encouraged other women to do the same.

The governor, John Winthrop, became provoked and eventually turned into one of her worst enemies. He and other community leaders feared that Anne Hutchinson with her radical ideas would tear apart the whole fabric of their society. Even though he represented the state, he also represented the church. At the time there was no distinction between the two. Anne Hutchinson had questioned the validity of *the place assigned to her sex* by both the church and the state for the first time in the New World. She was banished from the colony—an almost certain death sentence.

It is reported by some that her husband supported her as best he could. He did go with her and their family when they left the colony. Eventually, though, she and her family were killed in an Indian uprising. To the Puritan leaders this confirmed their view. She was, after all, a sinful woman, and it was God's will that she meet a gruesome death.

Following the break that Anne Hutchinson made from the religious fathers, women continued to remain silent in public. Though there were dissenters against the Church of England, all remained united in their belief about woman's place in the church. As punishment for the original sin of Eve, women suffered limitations of both mind and body. Yet to make them fit for motherhood, they had been bestowed such special virtues as meekness, compassion, affability, modesty, and piety.

In the Colonial period the Quakers were the only group that even permitted women to speak in meetings. They also ordained them as ministers. The attitude of St. Paul continued to be followed by other Protestant churches: "Let the women learn in silence with all subjection. . . . I suffer not a woman to teach, nor to usurp authority over the men, but to be in silence. Let your women keep silent in the churches, for it is not permitted unto them to speak."[8]

This attitude was not unique to churches. It reflected a society that did not allow women a say. Anne Hutchinson was one of those women.

Do you know a woman today who dedicates herself to religious freedom?

SOJOURNER TRUTH (1797–1883)

In Her 40s Building a New Career after Slavery

Sojourner Truth clearly stands out as a powerful voice against her culture's contaminated thinking toward both black slaves and women. Through her work as an abolitionist, revivalist, and suffragist speaker, she challenged many to change.

We admire her not only for that, but also for her courage and confidence to start an entirely new career when she was in her mid-40s. At this point in her life, her personal energy and commitment were unquenched, despite her birth into a slave household.

Sojourner Truth's exact birthdate is not known, since no record was kept of the birth of slaves. Slave parents did not usually know the calendar year, and since most of them did not know how to write, 1797 is a guess.

Her parents were owned by one of the many New York state families of Dutch descent. One writer reports that when Sojourner Truth was born, her owner stopped by and commented, "She'll make a good worker."[9] Little did he know what he was predicting at the time!

The new baby was named Isabelle, which the slaves soon shortened to Belle. Her mother taught her a respect for God. When rumor had it that her master was about to die, Belle's mother kneeled with her children. Together they said the Lord's Prayer in low Dutch, which was the only language they knew. Belle did sometimes ponder that if God answered prayers, as her mother had said, why didn't she pray for her children not to be sold?

Their owner did die. Within a week, cattle, horses, and slaves were put up for sale. Before she know it, Belle was standing alone on the platform as the auctioneer's gavel hit with, "Gone, gone, gone."

Her new master, Neely, being an outsider and a newcomer in the community, thought that owning a slave child might give him and his wife some status. But he was determined to "beat the Dutch" out of Belle and insisted that she speak English. One day when Belle was ordered to go to the barn, her master was there, ready with a handful of smooth reeds. He ordered her to bare her back, and then he thrashed her brutally. With her hands tied, she had no way to ward off his blows.

After the beating, Belle lay in a stupor on the cold, rough, wooden floor. She was aroused from her semiconsciousness with an order to go back into the house and get to work.

With this forecast of their relationship, Belle soon learned to find peace away from the house. She searched out a place where she could cry out to God in her agony. In her lifetime other masters were to come, each a different experience.

Belle was eventually set free when New York freed its slaves in 1827, a fact that was barely mentioned in the newspapers. When Belle was 46 a spiritual "message" came to her. Now a tall, gaunt woman, she left the home where she was working and marked the start of her new life's work by adopting the name Sojourner Truth. From then on she traveled the country, speaking out as a revivalist, abolitionist, and suffragist.

Sojourner Truth's courage and directness revealed themselves in the following incident:*

---

* From *Journey Toward Freedom: The Story of Sojourner Truth* by Jacqueline Bernard. Copyright © 1967 by Jacqueline Bernard. Used by permission of Grosset & Dunlap, Inc.

Sojourner traveled from Battle Creek into Indiana on a speaking tour with her old friend from New England, Parker Pillsbury. Indiana was a rough place for abolitionists. The rolling hills and rich black earth had attracted many settlers from the South. More than once hecklers made it impossible for the tall Negro woman and the stocky black-bearded ex-minister to hold their meetings.

In Kosciusko County, a rumor was circulated that Sojourner was an impostor, a man disguised in women's clothing. A large number of proslavery people turned up at one of the meetings. Their leader, a local doctor, had bet forty dollars that Sojourner was a man. Just as she started to speak, he stepped forward, hands raised above his head.

"Hold on," he shouted. "There is strong doubt in the minds of many persons here regarding the sex of the next speaker. A majority of us in fact are convinced that the speaker is not a woman but a man disguised as a woman. For the speaker's own sake, we demand, if it be a she, that she expose her breast to the gaze of some of the ladies present so that they may report back and dispel the audience's doubts."

Sojourner noticed many of the women flushing with embarrassment and anger at the man's suggestion. Pillsbury, who was hearing the rumor for the first time, strode quickly toward the doctor. His hand was raised and his face above the square black beard was crimson. Sojourner feared he would hurl the doctor to the ground. She rose hastily.

"Why do you suppose me to be a man?"

"Your voice is not the voice of a woman," replied the doctor. "It is the voice of a man and we believe that you are a man." He turned to face the audience and called out, "Let's put the matter to a vote. Is this person a man?"

The crowd roared "Aye."

Quietly, her fingers steady, Sojourner began to untie the white kerchief across her breast. Slowly her hands moved to undo the buttons at the top of her dress.

"I will show my breast," she announced as the last button came undone, "but to the entire congregation." And as she opened her blouse, she added with slow emphasis, "It is not my shame but yours that I do this."[10]

This kind of presence of mind under pressure typifies Sojourner Truth's unstinting work for what she believed in. Even today her life and words serve as a model for many people.

Do you know a woman who despite an adverse background, shows a strong personal autonomy?

HARRIET TUBMAN (1820–1913)

Risking Her Life to Free the Oppressed

Another black woman remembered by history is the famous and infamous Harriet Tubman. Harriet Tubman's physical smallness—she was only five feet tall—belied her possibilities. She possessed uncanny gifts of sagacity and courage.

She was known for her piercing eyes and the turban which always swathed her head. This turban concealed the dent in her skull caused by an overseer who threw a metal weight at her when she was 15 years old. For the rest of her life she suffered from spells of unconsciousness, even while she was helping others to escape to freedom.

Though born a slave, Harriet Tubman's spirit thought freedom. She begged her husband to flee North with her, but he refused. She chose to risk her chance for freedom without him. Alone, she faced the hazards along the way to Pennsylvania.

At 30 years old, Harriet Tubman became a "conductor" on the Underground Railroad. In childhood she had learned of Moses, who had set his people free. And for ten years she was a "Moses" to her people, leading them to freedom. Snatches of the song, "Go down, Moses," were signals on the Underground Railroad.

During her rescues Harriet Tubman was often sought by men using guns and dogs; yet she stayed in the home of Ralph Waldo Emerson and was befriended by Louisa May Alcott. Her 10 journeys netted freedom for 300 men, women, and children. The price on her head grew to an unbelievable figure for that day—$40,000. But she was never caught or harmed, nor were any of her "passengers."

One of her most heroic rescues was of a fugitive slave, Charles Nalle, who was in custody and being returned to his owner. Harriet Tubman gathered a crowd to make his return difficult. As the excitement rose, the abolitionists dragged the prisoner away from his captors. However, Nalle was recaptured and locked in the office of the Justice of the Peace.

One of the huge men moved forward from the crowd and splintered the door. A few moments later he dropped to the floor, felled by a deputy's hatchet. Harriet Tubman stepped over his body and bore Nalle out into a buggy which carried him to freedom.[11]

During the Civil War Harriet Tubman rendered further service. She was both a military scout and a nurse to Union armies. However, her devotion to the cause of freedom and to her country went unrewarded. She spent her later years in dire need, struggling to get a pension from the government. Congress grudgingly granted her $20 per month when she was 80 years old.[12]

Do you know a woman whose contributions are going unrewarded?

EMMA WILLARD (1787–1870)

Helping to Turn the Tide in Women's Education

Young Emma's relationship with her father was most fortunate. He supported her and endorsed her intelligence. He found Emma to have a lively mind, especially because she enjoyed tackling mathematical problems just for the delight of solving them.

She finally, however, came to the realization that most women were not allowed even to study higher mathematics. It was believed to be a strain on their brains. In fact, Jean-Jacques Rousseau's (1712–1778) ideas on education were still the rule of the day.

> The whole education of women ought to be relative to men. To please them, to be useful to them, to make themselves loved and honored by them, to educate them when young, to care for them when grown, to counsel them, to console them, and to make life sweet and agreeable to them—these are the duties of women at all times, and what should be taught them from their infancy.[13]

Emma Willard knew that women must study in a systemized, orderly way if they were to ever overcome such prejudice. Since universities were for men only, she requested the privilege of attending a men's examination at the University of Middlebury. Her request was denied. As a consequence, she began to study long hours each day to develop her own teaching and training methods. She involved other women and began training them to become teachers. Lacking textbooks to teach solid geometry, she taught with the aid of pyramids and cones carved out of turnips and potatoes.

It was an almost universal belief by both women and men that since women's brains were smaller in capacity to men's, therefore they were also inferior in quality. Even women who demanded more educational advantages for women held this belief. The subsequent lack of education curtailed many of their dreams. People did not desire greater opportunities for women. They merely felt that if women had more knowledge, they could be better mothers and more efficient housewives.

Therefore, even as late as 1812, the education of women had made little progress. Women from wealthy families who were considered educated had most likely studied painting, French, embroidery, singing, and playing the harpsichord.

Although there was still an emphasis on domestic education, Emma Willard continued to explore new horizons at the Troy Female Seminary. This school, which she founded, was the first endowed institution for the education of girls. Physiology stood out as one of her most daring subjects.

She taught such classes at a time when any mention of the human body by ladies was considered highly indelicate.

> Mothers visiting a class at the Seminary in the early 30's were so shocked at the sight of a pupil drawing a heart, arteries and veins on a blackboard to explain the circulation of the blood, that they left the room in shame and dismay. To preserve the modesty of the girls, and spare them too frequent agitation, heavy paper was pasted over the pages in their textbooks which depicted the human body.[14]

The experiences and contributions of women who fought for women's education go largely unheralded. Emma Willard's valiant efforts to provide educational opportunities for young women are unknown to many people even today.

Do you know a woman who unselfishly works for quality education for women?

ELIZABETH CADY STANTON (1815–1902)

Integrating the Demands of Home and Career and Personal Growth

"Trapped in the suburbs with small children and a husband gone much of the time" is how Elizabeth Cady Stanton might have described her life if we could talk with her today. Much of her contribution to the feminist movement came when she and her family moved to Seneca Falls. It was here that she came face to face with the realities of the drudgery that many. housewives faced who were isolated in small towns.

Her husband was gone much of the time, and she was left with a growing family of robust and lively children. With servants in short supply, she found herself immersed in an immense amount of work—caring for her babies, cooking, washing, and sewing. In spite of the reading she managed to do, her bright mind began to find the situation intolerable.

> I now fully understood the practical difficulties most women had to contend with in the isolated household, and the impossibility of woman's best development if in contact, the chief part of her life, with servants and children. . . . Emerson says: "A healthy discontent is the first step to progress." The general discontent I felt with a woman's portion as wife, mother, housekeeper, physician, and spiritual guide, the chaotic condition into which everything fell without her constant supervision, and the wearied, anxious look of the majority of women,

impressed me with the strong feeling that some active measures should be taken to remedy the wrongs of society in general and of women in particular. My experiences at the World Anti-Slavery Convention, all I had read of the legal status of women, and the oppression I saw everywhere, together swept across my soul, intensified now by many personal experiences. It seemed as if all the elements had conspired to impel me to some onward step. I could not see what to do or where to begin—my only thought was a public meeting for protest and discussions.[15]

Elizabeth Cady developed her sensitivity to human problems and inequities early in life. Her experiences as a child crouched in a corner of her father's law office schooled her for sizing up difficult situations. Since her father was a judge, there was a steady stream of people with problems through his office. Many of his clients were wives or daughters of men who had dissipated their money on drink. Even if a woman earned a little money from sewing or raising chickens, her husband could take it and spend it any way he wanted. Elizabeth heard her father explain to women again and again that *because of the law*, the man had complete control of all property. The husband also held sole right to the children in case of separation.

Sometimes Judge Cady would even take his books from the shelves and point to the law which said that a woman wronged by drink or abuse had no legal redress. Elizabeth confided to a friend that she planned to get rid of the offensive laws by cutting them out of her father's books with scissors.

Her father's law office was also the site of a visit with an escaping slave in the 1830s. Hearing this black woman tell her story spurred Elizabeth's strong commitment to become an abolitionist.

Elizabeth's education went beyond that which took place in her father's law office. She attended Emma Willard's school in Troy and received what was then some of the finest education available.

When Elizabeth was in school, a terrible accident happened to her brother, the only boy in a family of five girls. Her brother was her father's pride and joy, and Judge Cady was severely saddened by the loss of his only son. Eleven-year-old Elizabeth grieved for her father and her lost brother. She attempted to console her father by telling him, "We all miss him so deeply but you know we love you too, and we will strive all the more to be the kind of children you would like us to be." Her father sighed and answered, "Oh, my daughter, I wish you were a boy!"[16]

It did not take long for young Elizabeth to decide that a crucial difference between boys and girls was that boys could ride horseback and study Greek. The story goes that she went next door that day and asked the family's neighbor, a minister, to start teaching her Greek. Determined, she became skilled at both Greek and horseback riding. In addition to becoming an accomplished horseback rider, she also won a coveted prize for Greek scholarship at Johnstown Academy. Bringing the prized Greek Testament home for her father's approval, she hoped he would accept her at last as much as a son. His devastating response was, "My daughter, it's a pity you were not a boy."[17]

In 1840 Elizabeth Cady married Henry B. Stanton, an abolitionist leader who had faced many an angry mob. Shortly after their marriage, she and her husband traveled to London to attend a World Anti-Slavery Convention. Lucretia Mott, another woman keenly interested and active in the abolitionist movement, also traveled to London. To their dismay and to the heated objection of some of the American leaders, the convention ruled that *only men delegates could be seated.*[18]

Although both women were active in the abolitionist movement and were delegates to the convention, they were not allowed to sit in the meeting room with the other delegates. Instead, they had to remain seated behind a screen for the next ten days.

As a result, the two women found themselves walking the streets of London, dealing in misbelief with a shocking reality. Women who were devoted workers to the antislavery cause could have no voice in a world meeting about slavery, *because they were women!* What a rude awakening for two intelligent women to discover that their femaleness pushed them into a powerless position in the fight against the subjugation of others.

The meetings in London served as a spark to what many historians call the beginnings of the women's rights movement. Some years later, Elizabeth Cady Stanton spent a day with the Motts, whom she visited in a town near Seneca Falls. During that day she also met Jane Hunt, Martha Wright, and Mary Ann McClintock, all of them Quakers. Elizabeth expressed her discontent and indignation about the plight of women. The group was moved to take a step. On this important occasion, these five women, sitting around a small, mahogany table, made a momentous decision to call a convention, a Women's Rights Convention.

They then pondered what to do at their conference. But after reading the Declaration of Independence, they began to see an already established framework within which they might declare themselves. Excerpts from the resulting Declaration of Principles look like this:

> We hold these truths to be self-evident: that all men and women are created equal; that they are endowed by their Creator with certain inalienable rights; that among these are life, liberty and the pursuit of happiness. . . .

The history of mankind is a history of repeated injuries and usurpations on the part of man toward woman, having in direct object the establishment of an absolute tyranny over her. To prove this, let facts be submitted to a candid world.[19]

Out of these beginnings, Elizabeth Cady Stanton dedicated more than 50 years of her life as a leader in the suffragists' struggle. She became a brilliant philosopher of the movement. Her work with her lifelong friend, Susan B. Anthony, focused the nation's attention on the political status of women.

In her later years, Elizabeth Cady Stanton returned to a view of women's rights that went beyond the vote and authored a book called *The Woman's Bible*.[20] This work, motivated by her desire to show the intended equality of the sexes, attacked biblical passages which she considered negative or degrading to women.

However, given the puritanical and religious nature of America in the 1800s, *The Woman's Bible* made many enemies among both men and women. As a result of the overwhelming storm that grew up around her *Woman's Bible*, Elizabeth Cady Stanton became disassociated from the women's movement—a movement close to her heart for most of her life.

Do you know a woman who is combining demanding family responsibilities with active political reform?

SUSAN B. ANTHONY (1820–1906)

Living a Single Life Rich with Purpose

A most significant historical example of cooperation between women grew out of the long working relationship between Elizabeth Cady Stanton and Susan B. Anthony. Their equal but different talents and the different circumstances of their personal lives made them ideal complements to each other. Elizabeth Cady Stanton was the philosopher, the thinker, the writer; Susan B. Anthony, the speaker and hard-working organizer. In fact, the precinct political system grew out of a scheme she designed.

Whereas Elizabeth Cady Stanton seemed to always be pregnant and tied down with her family, Susan B. Anthony, remaining single, was much more mobile. As a consequence, she could either travel or be available to serve as a babysitter for the many Stanton children when their mother needed to get away to prepare a speech. Though the two women had differences, their union of spirit remained constant. Elizabeth Cady Stanton speaks of this when she writes as follows.

She supplied the facts and statistics, I the philosophy and the rhetoric, and, together, we made arguments that stood unshaken through the storm of long years; arguments that no one has answered. Our speeches may be considered the united product of our two brains.[21]

Susan B. Anthony chided her friend for her large family. But the two women were destined to make their mark, even though Elizabeth Cady Stanton was a prolific mother. Once she wrote to Susan B. Anthony:

> You must come here a week or two, and we will do wonders. Courage, Susan—this is my last baby, and she will be two years old in January. Two more years and—time will tell what! You and I have the prospect of a good long life. We shall not be in our prime before fifty, and after that we shall be good for twenty years at least.[22]

Susan B. Anthony was the daughter of a strong-willed Quaker abolitionist who believed in equal upbringing for his sons and daughters. He supported her in her quest for gaining skills and education, attributes that were normally reserved for men.

Young Susan helped on the farm and then became a teacher. At the time, teaching was the only vocation open to a woman who had schooling. Becoming "Headmistress" of the Female Department at Canajoharie Academy, she found this a dead end. The inequities heaped on a woman teacher compelled her to go back to the family farm.

Through her father, she met many prominent antislavery leaders. She supported this cause and also tried working as a paid agent for the temperance movement. However, like many women who work to undo injustices today, she encountered prejudice against any kind of equal participation by the women employees.

Susan B. Anthony grew aware of and concerned about the circumstances of women. As a consequence, she sought signatures for a petition to the New York legislature seeking reforms. She believed that women should be able to control their own earnings, that women should have rights to guardianship of their children in case of divorce, and that women should have the vote—all of which were then denied them by law and practice.

Her mother's and sister's acclaims about having gone to a women's rights convention in Rochester in 1849 aroused in her the desire to meet and to know Elizabeth Cady Stanton and Lucretia Mott. Compared with these others, Susan B. Anthony was a late-comer to the movement for suffrage. But she was destined to become a potent force. When she met Elizabeth Cady Stanton in 1851, she joined the ranks for women's rights.

If Lucretia Mott typified the moral force of the movement, if Lucy Stone was its most gifted orator and Mrs. Stanton its outstanding philosopher, Susan Anthony was its incomparable organizer, who gave it force and direction for half a century.[23]

In the style of the organizer that she was, she selected 60 women to serve as "captains." These women, who represented every county in New York, went out in midwinter of 1854 to start collecting names.

Winter travel was difficult, and the physical hardships borne by women like Susan B. Anthony were many. She started out on Christmas Day, 1854, with her literature, petitions, and a small pittance of money lent to her by a friend. In most of the towns where she stopped, she had to make all of her own arrangements, even to seeing that there were lights and ushers in the meeting place. She never knew what the next stop would bring. One stop was particularly painful.

The snowdrifts are over the fences in many places and the roads are so badly blocked with snow that vehicles have to take to the ice-covered meadows. Susan's feet, frost-bitten no doubt, begin to give her serious trouble. She soaks them in cold water, then wraps them in woolens, but the pain merely transfers itself to her back. All the way to Malone she has to sit doubled over, clinging to the seat in front in order not to groan aloud. She holds her meeting in spite of suffering, gets to Ogdensburg, then to Canton. But when the time arrives to leave this point, she has to be carried to the stage. Ten miles from Watertown she changes to the train, barely able to walk, and arriving at the hotel in the late afternoon, she determines to give the "water cure," sovereign remedy of the age, a final test. She sends for the chambermaid, orders two buckets of ice water, and sitting in a coffin-like tin tub, has both buckets poured over her aching body. Wrapped in hot blankets she sleeps through the night and, believe it or not, wakes in the morning as good as new.[24]

Susan B. Anthony and the other women had to travel in an era when a woman traveling unescorted was a rarity. Women who did so were not only subjected to public ridicule, but also, of course, lacked the things so much a part of travel today—automobile air conditioning, in-flight movies, and polyester double knits. Nineteenth-century women traveled in open conveyances and were frequently exposed to bitter weather. Their long skirts, sometimes weighing 10 to 15 pounds and weighted with rocks, in addition to their corsets, which constricted their every movement, added even more difficulty to their daily lives. Women who were alone found it hard to secure decent food and respectable accommodations. They faced prejudice, hostility, and apathy, often from the very women they sought to help.

Like itinerant tin pedlars or book agents they tramped the streets and country roads, knocking at every door, presenting their petitions, arguing with women who half the time slammed the door in their faces with the smug remark that they had husbands, thank God, to look after their interests, and they needed no new laws to protect their rights. After each rebuff the women simply trudged on to the next street, the next row of houses, the next grudgingly opened front door.[25]

Most women, particularly those married to working men, were still not ready to support a change. Susan B. Anthony frequently suffered the brunt of contempt from other women. If she had a proper husband, she was told, she would not have embraced such a cause.

Even with such an affront, Susan B. Anthony remained keenly aware of the affects of "civil death" on the power and status of women. Under British common law, which was the law that governed the majority of states, a woman ceased to exist when she married. Legally, this meant that her signature was no longer valid. She had no right to her own earnings. She had no right to her children in divorce. And, indeed, she was the property of her husband.

Susan B. Anthony's contribution to the women's emancipation movement came partly because she was single. As a single woman, her signature was valid. She had not suffered the civil death of her married sisters. She could still sign legal documents, including rental agreements for halls in which to hold meetings.

Facing daily hardships, Susan B. Anthony lived into her 80s and devoted most of her life to gaining the vote for women. But as fate would have it, she died 14 years before the fruits of her labor became reality. Both she and her long-time friend, Elizabeth Cady Stanton, went to their graves not having seen their dream and vision of a better future for women come true.

Do you know a woman who singlemindedly devotes herself to a cause?

ALICE PAUL (b. 1885)

Sparking New Life Through Militant Tactics

Alice Paul was a Quaker and a veteran of the English suffrage campaign. Her militant spirit and tactics were offensive to many of the "old-line" women. However, her antics injected new energy and excitement into an ailing struggle for a federal amendment giving voting rights to women.

Arriving in Washington in 1913, she and Lucy Burns gathered important women around them. There was still energy in the movement, but it needed a new impetus. Within two months, this tiny group organized a parade of some 5000 women.

Even though Alice Paul had a police permit, she and her marching women received little protection when things degenerated into a near riot. It was reported in the news that these 5000 women fought their way foot by foot up Pennsylvania Avenue.[26] The crowd had completely defied the police. They swamped the marchers and broke the procession into little companies. It was noted that no other presidential inauguration had been accompanied by such scenes. One newspaper recorded the event as follows:

> The women had to fight their way from the start and took more than one hour in making the first ten blocks. Many of the women were in tears under the jibes and insults of those who lined the route. At Fourth Street progress was impossible. Commissioner Johnson called upon some members of a Massachusetts National Guard regiment to help clear the way. Some laughed, and one assured the Commissioner they had no orders to act as an escort. At Fifth Street the crowd again pressed in and progress was impossible. The Thirteenth Regiment, Pennsylvania National Guard, was appealed to and agreed to do police duty.... Very effective assistance was rendered by the students of the Maryland Agricultural College, in guarding the women marchers. It was where Sixth Street crosses the avenue that police protection gave way entirely and the two solid masses of spectators on either side came so close together that three women could not march abreast. It was here that the Maryland boys formed in single file on each side of the "Pilgrims" and became a protecting wall. In front a squad of the boys locked arms and formed a crowd-breaking vanguard. Several of the "war correspondents" were forced to use their fists in fighting back the crowd.... The parade itself, in spite of the delays, was a great success. Passing through two walls of antagonistic humanity, the

marchers, for the most part, kept their tempers. They suffered insult, and closed their ears to jibes and jeers. Few faltered, though some of the older women were forced to drop out from time to time.[27]

When such accounts hit the news, public opinion became outraged, provoking an investigation. Contrary to the belief of many of the more traditional feminists, this tremendous publicity aroused sympathy and pushed toward progress.

On July 31 a procession to the Capitol presented a group of senators with 200,000 signatures. In the face of such reaction, President Wilson could hardly respond as he had before. Previously, he had remarked that the matter of women's suffrage had never been brought to his attention.

When the country entered World War I, Carrie Chapman Catt, respected leader and pragmatist that she was, was aware that the ability of the suffragists to plead their cause would depend on whether or not they had joined in the national war effort.

This was not true of the more militant group led by Alice Paul. She and her followers had picketed the White House, and mob violence broke out. Once the suffrage arrests began, it was not hard to see where government sympathies lay. Invariably, the picketers were arrested, rather than those men who attacked them and ripped the banners from their hands, often physically maltreating the women.

As picketing and violence continued, women were sentenced to jail. Terms gradually increased from a few days to six weeks and eventually to six months. Some 218 women from 26 states were arrested during the first session of the 65th Congress. Ninety-seven of them went to prison.[28]

Women who were illegally imprisoned suffered brutal conditions. They responded by going on hunger strikes. And the authorities retorted by forced feeding—an ugly procedure requiring tubes to be forced down the throat, and for those women who refused, hard rubber tubes were forced through their noses.

Of course, the Carrie Chapman Catt camp disavowed this "violent action." But the pickets showed no sign of giving up. As a result of the arousal of public outrage, all pickets were unconditionally released.

Alice Paul organized, marched, threatened, carried posters, and even proposed to form an independent political force composed of women only. Chafe reports:

The Women's Party (formerly The Congressional Union) constituted the militant wing of the suffrage movement. Its adherents adopted radical tactics, chaining themselves to fences, picketing the White House, and engaging in hunger strikes in prison. The National American

Women's Suffrage Association, on the other hand, sought to cooperate with the government and to work from within to achieve its goals. Alice Paul and the Women's Party burned President Wilson in effigy, while Carrie Chapman Catt invited him to address the NAWSA convention. Although both organizations were seeking the same end, they frequently worked at cross purposes, and many women traced the subsequent conflict within the women's rights movement to the residual distrust of the earlier struggle.[29]

Do you know a woman who asserts herself in radical ways for the benefit of women?

Beyond Suffrage

Even after the Nineteenth Amendment was finally ratified in 1920, giving women the vote, the two suffragist factions had different goals. Mrs. Catt immediately formed the League of Women Voters. The League felt that since women had won their full rights with the Nineteenth Amendment, they could turn their attention to other areas of reform—such as child welfare, disarmament, and working hours—and align themselves with like-minded groups. According to one leader of the League: "we are not feminists primarily; we are citizens."[30]

Alice Paul's Woman's Party, still militant, held a very different view: "Women today [in 1921] are still in every way subordinate to men before the law, in the professions, in the church, in industry, and in the home."[31] Alice Paul and other members of the Woman's Party had tried filing bills in state legislatures to end the various discriminatory practices women still faced. But very few of these bills were ever passed. What was needed, they insisted, was an amendment to the Constitution ensuring equal rights for women.

In 1923 Alice Paul authored the Equal Rights Amendment: "Equality of rights under the law shall not be denied or abridged by the United States, or by any state, on account of sex."[32] The proposed amendment did not pass Congress until 1972. Within nine months, 26 states had ratified the E.R.A. But then opponents of the amendment gained strength. By April 1, 1976, only 34 states had ratified the E.R.A. Ratification by 38 states amends the Constitution.

More than 50 years after she proposed this amendment, Alice Paul at 90 years old was still waiting, waiting for approval of what she spent her life fighting for—equal rights for women.

Contemporary American Women

1.

2.

3.

4.

5.

6.

7.

8.

9.

WHAT DID IT ALL MEAN?

Alice Paul's waiting strikes a chord of symbolism. The question that emerges is: "Was it all worth it?" Do most women today appreciate the struggle their nineteenth-century sisters endured?

The women into whose lives and work you have just taken a glimpse appeared to be thinking women pushed by a passion to make the world a more rational and better place. Thinking and feeling spurred them on to *doing*. These women had the confidence and courage to take stands, to move against the daily waves of prejudice, and to not allow their drive to be dampened by efforts to humiliate or degrade them. They kept their eyes and energy focused on their dreams.[33] What dreams do you have for 100 years hence?

There are contemporary women who have achieved significantly in their chosen fields, although their numbers still remain unreasonably small. A few of these women are pictured on pp. 266–267. You may recognize some or all of them. See if you know what each woman is noted for—speculate about what each holds as her own private dream. (Check below to see how accurate you are.)

DID YOU RECOGNIZE THE WOMEN IN THE PHOTOGRAPHS?

American Women in History (from pp. 246–247)

1. Carrie Chapman Catt
2. Elizabeth Cady Stanton
3. Emma Willard
4. Lucy Stone
5. Susan B. Anthony
6. Alice Paul
7. Sojourner Truth

Contemporary American Women (from pp. 266–267)

1. *Sarah Caldwell,* opera producer and conductor. As founder and artistic director of the Opera Company of Boston, Ms. Caldwell has received international acclaim for her innovative musical interpretations.

2. *Yeffe Kimball,* artist. Of American Indian and pioneer ancestry, she is widely known for her work in American Indian art and education. Her paintings have been displayed in more than 75 solo exhibitions, and she has lent her professional assistance to innumerable public and educational projects.

3. *Chien-Shiung Wu,* nuclear physicist. Not only is Dr. Wu professor of physics at Columbia University, but she has also served as president of the American Physical Society. She is especially well known for her discovery of nonconservation of parity in beta decay.

4. *Barbara Boyle Sullivan,* businessperson. One of the founders and president of Boyle/Kirkman Associates, Inc., New York City, she is well known for her leadership in affirmative action.

5. *Barbara Jordan,* U.S. Representative. Of modest background, Ms. Jordan entered law and politics almost simultaneously. Now representing the 18th District, Texas, she began her political life as the first black woman in the Texas Senate. As a member of the House Judiciary committee, she rocketed to national prominence during the Watergate hearings.

6. *Billie Jean King,* tennis player and businesswoman. Three-time Wimbledon champion and leader in American tennis circles, Billie Jean King was instrumental in the founding of World Team Tennis.

7. *Shirley Chisholm,* U.S. Representative. As a Democrat representing the 12th District, New York, Ms. Chisholm is especially well known for her work in the fields of child welfare, higher-education legislation, and the relations of our government with the nations of the Third World.

8. *Barbara Walters,* TV personality. Well known for her appearances on NBC as co-host of the Today Show, she is also moderator of Not For Women Only.

9. *Cynthia Wedel,* community and religious leader. Currently Ms. Wedel is one of six international presidents of the World Council of Churches. She is also National Chairman of Volunteers of The American National Red Cross. Among many past appointments, she has served as president of the National Council of Churches, on President Kennedy's Commission on the Status of Women, and on the Citizen's Advisory Council on the Status of Women.

Whom would you add to your own list of significant women?

13

Daring
to
Dream

- Do you know where you have blind spots in your awareness?
- What are the thoughts and feelings you keep hidden from others?
- How can you turn the power of your fantasies and dreams into a positive life force?

THINK like a mountain
Think like the sky
Ever expansive with
Thoughts soaring high.

Think like a river
Think like a stream
Letting thoughts flow to
A possible dream.

Maria Monahan[1]

Think of all the great things and all the small things made real by people who dared to dream. Think of the people who disclosed themselves, who took a stand, who saw through the distortions of their backgrounds and their times. Think of the people who were not afraid to *think big*.

You have probably heard someone comment something like, "Why I can't even *imagine* going to the moon!" Fuel for propulsion seldom explodes from such thinking.

On the whole, women are seen by the people around them as having feelings, innermost thoughts, fantasies, and dreams more frequently than men. In fact, sometimes women's ability to dream things up gets put down. Women may even be thought of as unrealistic "daydreamers," unable to separate their own subjectivity from reality.

Women can turn what is attributed to them already into a great source of growth—for learning, solving problems, understanding more clearly their true natures, and getting more of what they want. So can men who admit to feelings and fantasies.

Many of us are not aware of the blind spots we have about our own behavior or of the way we hide from others those things we feel deep inside ourselves. Also, we are often not aware of the power we hold within ourselves to create a positive force in our own lives.

WE EACH HAVE SEVERAL LEVELS OF AWARENESS

Each of us seems to have at least four levels of awareness about our behavior, feelings, and motivations. These levels change, depending on who knows what is happening.

- *The Blind Self:* Sometimes we are not aware of what we are doing. But others know.

- *The Hidden Self:* Sometimes we hide what is going on inside us. We know, but others do not.

- *The Closed Self:* Sometimes what motivates us is not known to anyone —including ourselves. No one knows.

- *The Open Self:* Sometimes we are open and sharing with others. We all know.

Our Blind Selves

Other people were aware of what Phyllis was doing, but she was not.

As Phyllis worked on the design of a new model home, she often thought about how nice it would be to show the finished house to her mother. "I've worked so long to get architectural accreditation, I can hardly wait to show Mom what I can do."

As soon as the new home Phyllis had designed was completed, she brought her mother over to see it. When her mother saw the building, she laughed, "Who'd live in a place like that! It's such a strange shape and looks so boxey! Nobody'd ever want to stay there. It looks like a child built it. Really, Phyllis, it looks downright weird!" At this, Phyllis's feelings of elation gave way to pain. For days she stewed about her mother's lack of approval. And her bad feelings dulled her creative energies.

Phyllis was not aware of what motivated her to take her mother to see the house she had designed. She hurried to get her there, even though she knew from past experience that her mother would be disapproving.

Although other people might look at Phyllis's situation and predict her mother's reaction, Phyllis continued to have a blind spot that kept her from seeing how she set herself up to be let down. Early in her childhood, Phyllis had learned to get strokes from her mother that were painful "kicks." She was still doing it.

In doing the "Ego State Exercise," you may have discovered some Parent behaviors and Child feelings that used to be in your blind spots. For instance, other people may have been aware when you were "coming on Parent." But *you* may not have been. Now that you have this new level of awareness, you also have a new level of consciousness.[2]

Our Hidden Selves

Sometimes what we are feeling, thinking, and daydreaming about is hidden from other people. We know what is happening inside us—that pictures flash through our minds, that butterflies flutter in our stomachs, that we calculate what to say next while someone else talks, or that we want to cry. But we manage to hide these feelings from others. Even though *we* may be aware of what is happening inside of ourselves, we mask it. This is our hidden level of conscious awareness.

For example, Phyllis felt hurt by her mother's reaction. However, she never shared this feeling. She kept it inside. She had never attempted to work it out, and as a consequence, it remained a continuing problem. It also allowed Phyllis to be depressed and eventually mad (her blind spot). Because of her mother's behavior, Phyllis felt justified in having bad feelings.

Another example of this level of awareness is reported by many public speakers. They say that just before they speak, their palms sweat, their hearts beat fast, and their nerves are on edge. Yet to their audience they appear calm, confident, and in good control. Perhaps most of us have experienced something similar to this at some time or other.

You may have discovered in doing some of the "Steps to Awareness" that you feel a particular way inside over and over again. And perhaps at least sometimes you manage to hide or mask this feeling from the people around you. Once a hidden area is brought into your awareness, it is then much more a matter of your personal choice. For very wise reasons you may choose not to share your inner self with other people. On the other hand, you may decide that you can share much more of your feelings, thoughts, and fantasies than you ever allowed yourself to dream of.

Our Closed Selves

Sometimes our behavior, feelings, and motivations are so primitive that nobody knows what is going on. Our lost and forgotten dreams, like primitive impulses, seem bewildering. They may be unconscious or preconscious. We do not know or understand them, and neither do the people around us. Suppressed events from childhood often lie here—just below the surface of our conscious awareness. Phyllis's script motivation to "be a successful career woman but don't enjoy it" is likely closed off from both Phyllis and her mother.

You may do things you do not understand. You may have dreams that return night after night, but which hold little meaning for you now. Your closed self contains those things about yourself that remain shut off from everyone's awareness—impulses and experiences you do not want to remember and those that other people want you to suppress.

Our Open Selves

We also experience an area of consciousness that is open to ourselves and to others. We are aware of what is motivating us and how we are feeling and what we are doing. And other people are aware too.

The more we are able to be open, the better we communicate with others. As we are able to accept more and more of ourselves and to share ourselves with others, most people in turn accept more of us.

For example, Phyllis told her mother about how hurt she felt when her mother disapproved of what she did. Her mother retorted, "For heaven's sake, Phyllis, why should it make any difference how I feel? It's your work. You should do what you want to, no matter what anyone thinks."

Sharing this bit of herself, even though painful, gave Phyllis a new insight. She finally decided that her mother's often repeated negative comments were not likely to change. She was indeed taking on her mother's problems as her own. In addition, she realized that her mother sent her a combination of messages—some very positive—which she had never sorted out before. When she went through this process, she moved something from her hidden area of consciousness (her inner feelings) into the open area. Now both she and her mother know how she felt. She also moved information about herself from the blind area of her awareness to her open area. She has freed herself to invest more energy in a new level of consciousness. Growth for Phyllis, like growth for all of us, comes through exploring, understanding, and expanding our levels of awareness about our thinking, feeling, and doing.

FANTASIES CAN HELP YOU CHANGE AND GROW

To help her overcome her bad feelings, Phyllis put her ability to fantasize to work. Now, instead of repeating in her mind over and over again what her mother had said in the old scene, she pictures what she would *like* to see. She exaggerates what she wants from her mother by imagining her exclaiming, "What a beautiful building! I'm so proud of you—doing something like this. It's spacious and modern-looking. I'd love to live here."

This exaggeration helped Phyllis put her problem in perspective. She used her Adult to direct the creative power of her Child. Her new fantasy helped to appease her Child needs for approval from her mother. She had fun taking care of herself the way she expected her mother to. This enables her to respond more frequently to her mother from her Adult. As Phyllis put it:

"I'm better with my mother when I have a supply of positive feelings before I talk with her. It's like not going to the grocery store when I'm dieting and hungry. And, too, after visualizing this new scene many times,

I was pleased with how I actually began to treat my mother. Later, when I took her to one of my other architectural projects, I felt more kindly toward her and was more rational. Instead of feeling depressed and mad, as before, I felt calm.

I knew what her reaction would probably be. I could predict it. So when she started saying how strange the building was and how any six-year-old could do something like that, I didn't feel hurt and angry. I just repeated back to her what I thought she felt. I calmly said something like: 'It seems like the design isn't one you particularly care for.' To my surprise, she quipped, 'Well, I wouldn't want to live in it. But I have to say it's interesting.'"

"It really hit me how much of my energy I had spent trying to get my mother's approval. I decided not to put unrealistic demands on her any more. I could be me and she could be herself. I really started practicing what I already knew—that I'm the one responsible for taking care of me. And taking care of me is the best way to be kind to someone else."

Directing Fantasies

People use the power of their fantasies differently. Here is how some women have used theirs.

Rosella had not worked outside her home for 17 years. It scared her to even think about going for an interview. She always found one more "reason" not to go to the employment agency. She did not have the right thing to wear. She needed to get her house thoroughly clean before she could go to work. She had not made out a resumé. One day when she realized she had been talking about getting a job for almost a year, she decided she needed to get over being scared.

She began to imagine herself getting dressed for the interview, taking her completed resumé, and confidently answering each of the interviewer's questions. After doing this for several days, she felt ready to actually do what she imagined. It took her five interviews to get a job, but the first "wasn't nearly as bad as I thought it would be."

Eleanor's 20-year old daughter wanted to move away from home. She worried, "I know she'll have to move eventually, but just the thought depresses me."

Eleanor imagined on two levels. On one level, she thought about how happy her daughter would be in her new apartment. She pictured her going about the apartment saying, "What a great housekeeper Mom is, I sure learned a lot from her."

On the second level, Eleanor started imagining what she would do with her own time now that she did not have to wash, iron, and pick up after her daughter. "I just picture myself in my garden, or tucked away in a comfortable spot reading a lot of those books I've bought over the years."

Claire, a university instructor and family counselor, used her imagination to bring about things she wanted to do. In one instance she had visited a high school senior girls' homemaking class when the students were working on their term projects. They were picking out wedding gowns and selecting wedding invitations, china, and silver patterns. Out of her experience Claire knew that the needs of young women were quite differ- ent from this. Many of the students were from low-income families and needed information on nutrition and budgeting. Several of them had little information about their sexuality, yet had problems related to sex. In fact, some of them had suffered from venereal disease. These current, severe problems seemed a far cry from expensive gowns and china. So Claire decided she could make a significant contribution by sharing some of her information and insights with homemaking teachers, a group she had never reached before.

She began to imagine how and where she might do this. She mentally pictured the hall in which she might give a lecture—a place where she had not spoken before. She saw herself standing in front of the group and even imagined what she was wearing. Three weeks later she received a telephone call from the state homemaking teachers association requesting her to give a weekend workshop for the university. Two hundred sixty- five educators came to the class, which was held in the very hall which she had envisioned. She even decided to wear the dress that she had selected for her fantasy! The program was a great success.

Ruth decided that she wanted a different kind of surroundings to live in. The home she was in was comfortable, but she enjoyed the outdoors and longed to be closer to trees and birds and the things of nature that she loved. Since she lived near a congested urban area, such places were in short supply. Real estate brokers held out little hope.

To compound the problem, she had a family and a demanding job which required travel. As a consequence, she had little time for house-hunting. She began to look on her own in spare moments. She also began imagining exactly what she wanted—large windows, trees, wildlife, and an open view of the green hills.

Ruth kept being drawn to one particular area. Although she did not see a home she liked there, she saw an interesting one under construction. Several times, while driving back and forth to the city, she drove up the hill to see how the house was coming along. One time she discovered a little street that was not easy to see. Tucked on a hillside at the end of the court was a brand-new home that had just been completed by a private builder. It was amazingly close to what she had imagined—large windows with an exceptional view of a small valley surrounded by green hills. The trees on the property were filled with birds. She called the builder and was told that the home was to be listed on the open market the very next day. Needless to say, she made an offer.

Being Realistic

In all these cases, the women were capable of doing what they imagined themselves doing. Their fantasies were realistic in terms of what actually could happen. For example, Rosella was *capable* of looking for a job, even though she was afraid to do so. Ruth desired a home that though difficult to find, *was possible* to find. Claire's request to speak to homemaking teachers was unusual, but she was accredited to teach at a university.

The ability of these women to picture clearly in their minds what it was they wanted or wanted to do undoubtedly facilitated their directing their activities in ways to get what they wanted. They mobilized their psychic energies.

Your fantasies have tremendous pulling power. You can discover and direct that power.

STEPS TO
AWARENESS

Letting Your Fantasies Help You

Think of a situation or relationship you want to improve.

- Think what the situation or relationship will be like when it is better.
- Begin to visualize in your mind how this could look when it happens.

- Now build a sequence of events in your mind portraying the fulfillment of your wish. Get your Adult and your Child together.

- Once you have your fantasy designed, decide on a time every day when you will repeat it in your mind. This time might be when you get up or go to sleep or look at your watch or fix breakfast. Find a convenient hook to hang your fantasy on.

- Continue to exercise your fantasy until you feel comfortable trying out part of it.

- You will find that as you clarify for yourself what you want and live with it mentally for awhile, it does not seem so hard to do.

DREAMS CAN ALSO WORK FOR YOU

An exciting way to learn more about yourself is to be aware of and learn more about your dreams. Current research shows that dreams can mean many things. Ann Faraday, in her book *Dream Power*, points out that the important messages in your dreams come from the person who knows you best—you!

She sees at least three levels, or three kinds, of dreams. The first kind looks to the world outside you. Your dreams often call to your conscious attention things that you were not aware of noticing during your waking hours. The second type reflects your attitudes and prejudices. The third type looks inward. These dreams hold existential messages that help you to discover hidden sources of your problems and regain long-buried parts of your personality.

You can learn to be more aware of and to direct more fully the power of *your* dreams.

Looking Outward

The content of many dreams comes from recent waking experiences. In such dreams there will always be elements of objective reality. These elements of reality can serve as warnings, reminders, or even predictions.

It is useful, then, to take a good look at any dream to see if it reveals information about things happening outside yourself—things perhaps that your conscious mind has not figured out or absorbed.

One of the first things to do with a dream is to look at it from this point of view. Ask yourself: "Is there something in my dream that relates to the everyday events of my life? Is there something that I need to be reminded of or perhaps be cautious about? Or am I subtly aware that something is about to happen?"

- Marion's dream was a helpful reminder. The night before she was due to present a major budget proposal, she dreamed that the president came in at the last minute and wandered around the room, unable to find any place to sit. As a result of this dream, Marion decided to check out the room ahead of time. Sure enough, there were not enough chairs. But because of her advance reminder, Marion had things well in order before the meeting started.

- Ellen's dream was more of a warning. Soon after moving into a new house, she dreamed that she saw her toddler fall screaming from a porch. She woke up startled and fearful, her heart pounding. The next day, she checked around the house and yard and found that indeed the fence near a long drop to the ground had blown down. She repaired it immediately. During the hubbub of the move, she had not consciously noticed the break in the fencing on the side of the house. Evidently her brain was telling her through the dream that something needed to be done for the safety of her child.

- Alice dreamed that she was standing in front of a large audience and that people were applauding and cheering her. Soon, one by one, people in the audience rose to their feet, and someone handed her a bouquet of roses. Shortly after that, she was actually given an award for having made a significant improvement in the local school. The award was presented in a school auditorium, and she did receive a standing ovation. Although she did not receive flowers, she was given a trophy in the shape of a school bell. Even though Alice swore she had no idea that she was going to receive the award, she may have responded to looks and glances of other people in a subliminal way. Also, perhaps her brain knew that she had indeed worked on very difficult and special projects for the school.

- Doreen's dream foretold something she could not believe. She dreamt she walked across the bedroom and opened her husband's closet. She was stunned to see that all of his things were gone, except for an old tie hanging at the back. She fretted about the dream for several days, but passed it off with, "It must mean that I need to do the spring cleaning." Three months later, she was shocked when her husband, without any forewarning, asked her for a divorce. Soon after that, his empty closet became a reality. He had also emptied the shelf containing his photograph collection, leaving only the album of their wedding pictures propped against a box of old clothes to go to the Salvation Army.

  Looking back, Doreen recalled that she had felt a strange tension in their evenings home together and that her husband seemed strained and more aloof. But she really could not put her finger on anything concrete.

During our dreams, our brains do great detective work below the surface of consciousness. Our dreams are not always a hundred percent accurate, but they certainly point out to us things well worth pursuing. Check the next dream you have. Is there any truth to it?

SOME DREAMS SPRING FROM DEEP RECESSES

Dreams can be like windows into the innermost corridors of our minds. Dreams thus offer a fertile source for answering the question, "Who am I?"

Many of our primitive, recurring, and problem-solving dreams are products of childhood experiences. Some deep expressions of the Child ego state take the form of dreams.

The Dream As Part of the Dreamer

Ultimately, we all must take responsibility for our dreams, for the dream is often the dreamer. Dreams that go deeper into ourselves, that are puzzling, and that seem more than reminders frequently hold a disguised and vital message. Frederick Perls says, "Any dream appears to be real and this is justified because the dream is a reality. It is an existential message, though coded in cryptic language."[3] A dream is "the most spontaneous expression of the existence of the human being."[4]

To discover the parts of ourselves that our dreams are, we need to *become* the parts of these dreams. The Gestalt approach is not to analyze dreams, but to integrate them by reliving them, by accepting responsibility for them, and by opening ourselves to their messages. The focus is on *how* rather than *why* we do what we do.

Tell the Dream. If you want to learn from your dreams, use some way to recall them immediately upon waking. Immediately relate your dream into a tape recorder or write it down. Let nothing interfere with this. Dreams fade quickly from our memories. They are wiped away with the slightest interruption. Even getting up and walking across the room for paper and pencil can cause us to lose our dreams. Any interruption, such as talking with someone or answering a phone, seems to sweep the fragile fragments of dreams from our memories.

Contrary to common belief, dreams seem to be remembered more readily if we wake up while dreaming. Since we seem to dream in 90-minute cycles, those of us who are seriously motivated to come in touch with our dreams can arrange to be awakened by alarm at 90-minute intervals. Then immediately record the dreams. Whatever method you choose, record not only the people but also the objects, places, and physical surroundings in the dream.

The next step is to pick the part of your dream that has the least emotional content, progressing to what seems the most emotional to you. Either part might be an object rather than a person. Then begin your dialogue. Speak out loud and act out each part of your dream.

- Florence's recurring dream was of a long road that seemed to stretch out interminably. When she became the road, she spoke out loud as if she were the road. She started her dialogue with "I." "I'm a road, I lie here, still. I go some place but I can't move, and everybody walks on me. People walk on me. Animals walk on me. Everybody just walks on me." With surprise, Florence said, "Yeah, that's the way I feel. Everybody walks on me. But it never occurred to me before how I pave the way for them to do it."

- For years, Beth had a recurring dream of a car accident. The dream disturbed her, but she could not seem to find the key to its meaning. When she learned the Gestalt method, she became the accident and started her dialogue: "I'm a wreck." She explained, "My whole life's been turned upside down for years. It's about time I straightened this wreck out."

- Renee had a recurring dream of driving around in a car aimlessly and endlessly. "A man sits beside me giving me directions which keep me going in circles. In the back seat there is a dead body and I'm supposed to dump it someplace. But I keep listening to the man and just keep driving around. I never find the right place."

  When Renee progressed to acting out the dead body, her dialogue sounded like this: "I am dead weight. I'm what you think you're supposed to be. I'm a drag on you and you need to unload me. You keep following other people's directions and not making your own decisions. As long as you do that, you're never going to get rid of me." Renee said whimsically, "That's true. That's what I've been doing. I've been carrying around a load of dead weight. I've been doing what everybody else tells me to do. I haven't listened to myself."

Anna recorded in *vivid* detail the dream she had two months after she was widowed. The parts of the dream she recalled were a filmy nightgown, a frightening face in the window, and a pair of black shoes. The pale face peering through the window was the most emotional part. So in working through her dream, she saved that for last.

In the dream I'm standing in the bedroom I had as a child, but I'm grown up. I am straightening clothes—hanging some and putting some away. One garment is a long, filmy nightgown. It's wrinkled, and the bottom of the hem hangs down. I take the nightgown down from where it is hanging in the middle of the room and straighten it by running my fingers through the folds of the skirt. Then I put it away in the closet, and I say, "Here is where you belong—you have space to hang free and I know just where I can get you when I want to."

I pick up a pair of shoes out of the shoe drawer. They are sturdy, black shoes with open toes and laces up the front. I look at the shoes and say, "Oh, my mother gave me these shoes a long time ago. She must have bought them on sale. I've never worn them. They don't go with anything." As I pick them up again, I look at them and see that they are very well made of nice leather with fine details. Then I realize they would go beautifully with a knit outfit I have. I look at them with the outfit and say, "You know, these really are lovely shoes. I know I'll enjoy them and they'll wear well for a long time. I just need to put them with the right things."

Toward the end of the dream I look up and through a small window at the end of my bedroom, I see a round pale face with wild, nonfocusing eyes looking into the room. I feel terrified, I feel that the face is going to kill me. Eventually the figure sticks a hand holding a pistol through the open window. I look at the hand and the gun, figuring out how I can hide. As I look at the face and decide how to hide, the hand drops the gun on the floor.

When I acted out the dream, I took the item with the least emotional attachment first—the shoes. I began my dialogue: "I am very well made out of good leather. I am an odd but classic cut. I came from your mother. I haven't been worn, but I can go well with certain things. I'll provide pleasure when I'm used in the right places."

The second thing in the dream was the nightgown, and when I became the nightgown, I said: "I am filmy and flowing, but I'm beginning to feel frayed at the edges. I'm getting in the way, and part of the hem is sticking out and getting stepped on and torn. I am going to be put away in the closet, where I can hang free but be ready to use."

And in the third part, where I became the face, I said: "I'm a scary face, and I'm looking into the room that you grew up in. I'm not really seeing anything, because my eyes don't focus. I'm just here because I've always been here. I have a gun in my hand. I thought I was going to kill you, but now I don't know what to do. I point the gun around the room, but I decide to drop it. As I drop the gun I realize I don't fit any more. I don't really want to pull the trigger and kill you. I'm just hanging around this old place because that's where I always hang around. I'm really a stupid old scary.

The meaning of a dream can bring a past unresolved problem to closure. For example, Anna started seeing her mother in a new perspective. "Just like the shoes, she's great when I put her in the right spot in my life. She doesn't go with everything, but she's quality, well put together, and I know I'll enjoy her for a long time."

Since Anna had been widowed, she realized that the nightgown represented her putting her sexual expression away so that she could give herself time to decide what was best for her. Two of her husband's closest friends had already approached her. She knew she was not thinking clearly about men right now and that she needed time to gain perspective about that part of her life.

Anna realized that the scary face represented her own feelings about suicide. She had thought of it as an out when she felt she could not go on alone. She knew now that suicide really was not what she wanted to do.

Act Out the Dream. Sometimes our dreams represent conflicting forces or polarities in our personalities. Becoming these conflicting forces and acting them out can help to integrate the problem. One useful way to act out these polarities is to use the empty-chair technique.

Mary Louise had a recurring dream about water spurting out from under the sink. She reported the dream: "I'm standing in the kitchen and washing the dishes. Water spurts out from under the sink. I call for a plumber and the plumber tries to fix the leak, but the water keeps spurting and spurting."

In acting out the dream, Mary Louise set two chairs facing each other. In one chair she was the plumber; in the other, the spurting water. Her dialogue went like this:

PLUMBER: I'm going to fix you; I'm going to stop you from spurting.

WATER: I am going to spurt.

PLUMBER: You need to be held back; you need to be stopped. I am going to stop you.

WATER: No you're not. Leave me alone. I want to spurt. I will keep going no matter what you do.

PLUMBER: I've got tools. I'm going to put a cap on you so you won't spurt any more. You've got to stop moving!

WATER: I won't be fixed. *I won't let you fix me.* I am going to keep moving. I am going to spurt. I am not going to let anybody put a cap on me.

In the last dialogue Mary Louise's voice rose to a loud crescendo, and she was asked to repeat the last few sentences. As she shouted out these words, she broke into tears. "The plumber is my father. I always felt that he didn't like me the way I was and that whenever I tried to express my-self or talk to him, I was just shooting off at the mouth and he told me to be quiet. I may have had to be quiet then, but I certainly don't need to be quiet any more. I can keep spurting. I can keep moving. There is not something wrong with me that has to be fixed just because I want to burst out of myself."

With that dialogue, an old unresolved conflict between her Inner Parent and her Inner Child was brought to closure for Mary Louise.

"Like floating" is how Emily described her feelings after getting clo-sure on an early childhood decision. She discovered she had decided to not be better than others—to never make it. She wrote down her dream as if it were happening right now.

I'm walking down the side of a little stream that is trickling along a rocky, grassy bank. As I'm walking along the sides of the stream, I realize that it's a little stream that I played near when I was a child. I see a huge pile of rocks that form a dam against the ocean. I wonder what's in back of all those rocks and boulders. Rather than the stream trickling into the ocean as I remember it, the ocean is flowing into the stream. As I see the ocean building up in back of the dam, I start to climb the pile of rocks to get to the top. But when I do get to the top, I feel frightened at the size and power of the ocean.

In acting out my dream, the first part I portrayed was the stream: "I'm a little stream next to a big ocean. I'm quiet and flowing. I'm familiar. People come and play along my banks and in my water. They move the rocks and sand and rechannel me. They come around me because I'm small and they can do what they want with me."

Then I portrayed the part of the dam of rocks: "I am a collection of rocks and boulders piled at the edge of the ocean. I'm damming and holding back my power and my greatness. I'm hiding the power of the ocean. I don't let the people who are playing down in the stream know how big the ocean really is."

Finally, I took the part of the ocean: "I am immense and powerful. I am what I am, regardless of other people. I have waves that roll and crash on the shore. I am big and great."

After I portrayed the parts of the dream, I realized: "I don't have to hold back my greatness from the people I've been around a long time. Stifling my talents doesn't help me, and it isn't good for them either. I can be as great as I am. I can be all that I can be!"

Emily made a dramatic redecision of her childhood decision to not be better than anyone else. With this closure of an old problem, she began to sense and appreciate her own power as a person.

The Feeling of Closure or Gestalt

As you look at this line, you may find that you want to complete it and make it into a full circle. It appears to be human nature to bring things to closure or to complete them—to form a gestalt. The word "gestalt" is derived from German. There is no exact English translation. The word does, however, carry the meaning of completeness or an organized whole.

If you have ever had it cross your mind that you may have left the stove on, you are probably keenly aware of the discomfort you felt until you actually checked out the stove. The same feeling occurs when we have unresolved conflicts or problems. We continue to feel unsettled and undirected until the issue is finished—brought to closure.

Our dreams serve as one way to bring past issues that are still "on our minds" to closure. Dreams can reveal to us some of our innermost feelings, prejudices, beliefs, and fears.

Once a conflict or problem has closed, there usually is a great feeling of relief. It is like, "Whew. That's finished!"[5]

CLARIFY YOUR GOALS AND MOBILIZE YOUR PSYCHIC ENERGY

We block potential personal power by keeping our fantasies fragmented and undirected and by suppressing our dreams. The Child in us brims with limitless imagination and a clarity of vision that experience blurs. As a result, what we want out of life is often vague and unclear to us. In fact, some of us have never even thought about it.

What is it that *you* want? What are your desires? What is it that you want to be able to do? What is it you want to happen?

One way to more fully direct your own life is to *deliberately* mobilize your psychic energy. You can do this by consciously planning what it is that you hope to feel or to attain or to do or to be. Let your creative Child work for you with the positive trust of your Parent and the intelligence of your Adult.

When mobilizing your energies for positive change, it is most important that the things you desire for yourself in life do indeed and can indeed exist. They must be realistic. Check this out by looking around at the realities of other people. See their relationships, what they have, what they do, who they are. Then ask yourself: "Are the things I want really possible?" You may find that much more is possible than you ever dreamed of before.

**STEPS TO
AWARENESS**

Mobilizing Your Energy for Change

Think about what you really want. Now take a step beyond just thinking about it and write it down. Be specific rather than general. For example, "Be a better person" is too general to deal with. "Make two new friends" is specific and measurable.

- Study carefully those things that you wrote down that you really want.
- Now ask yourself: "Do these things exist in other places for other people?" (For example, if what you want is a close friend, look around your circle of relationships to see whether other people are close friends with one another.)
- Eliminate from your list those things that, when you look at them from a realistic point of view, are not possible.
- Restate those things that are possible and write out vividly and in detail exactly what you want.

- Keep your list in a private place. It is yours alone. Sharing this kind of list may open you to the direction and the forces of other people that may not be the best for you right now.

Look at the things on your list two or three times a day.

- Begin imagining yourself in these situations.
- Picture yourself doing what you want to do, having what you want to have, being with the people you want to be with, creating what you want to create, looking the way you want to look.
- Before retiring for the night, think of one of these things and direct some of your dreams around this issue in your life.
- If a dream comes to you, act it out. Be the parts of the dream. Look for the objective realities in the dream. Look for the guidance, the warnings, the cautions, and the deeper messages.

Now start looking for facts:

- What information do you need?

    Where can you get it?

    With whom could you talk?

- Do you need special training?

- Who are the best people you can learn from?

    How can you get to them?

Now begin to get in touch with your energy flow. Keep in mind that excitement generates energy.

- What are you excited about?

- What or who helps get your energy flowing?

- Who do you think experiences you as a source of energy?

- How much of your time is spent in dull or low-energy activity?

- How could you invest more time in energetic people and activities?

How much of your energy do you invest in thinking? Feeling? Doing?

- Does any area not function as well as the others?

- How can you pay more attention to this area?

- Set out your major goals and your minigoals.

- Reward yourself for doing what is best for you.

Believe in yourself and your own power to bring about change. Use your fantasy and dream life and your good sense to check out reality and bring what you want into your life. But first know what it is you *do* want.

You can enrich your life by directing your fantasies and working through your dreams. The detective of your mind works diligently through the night, putting together the pieces of the puzzles of your being.

Doing this brings you in touch with the realities that lie below the surface of your conscious awareness. You can move many of the hidden things of your personality, the blind things, and the closed things into the open area where you have choice and responsibility. Discovering how these pieces fit together can be great moments of "Ah-hah" as you click things into place. You may suddenly feel like a new person.

The New Woman

The new woman arises
full of confidence
she speaks eloquently
and thinks independently

Full of strength
she organizes efficiently
and directs proudly

She is the new woman
capable of changing
the course
of society

   Susan Polis Schutz[6]

14

Living Your Dream

- What can you do to focus on your dreams?
- What are some steps you can take to bring your dreams into reality?

I am woman, hear me roar
in numbers too big to ignore,
and I know too much to go back to pretend
'cause I've heard it all before
and I've been down there on the floor,
no one's ever gonna keep me down again.

Oh, yes, I am wise
but it's wisdom born of pain.
Yes, I paid the price
but look how much I gained.
If I have to I can do anything.
I am strong, I am invincible, I am woman.

You can bend but never break me
'cause it only serves to make me
more determined to achieve my final goal.
And I come back even stronger
not a novice any longer,
'cause you've deepened the conviction in my soul.

I am woman, watch me grow
see me standing toe to toe
as I spread my lovin' arms across the land.
But I'm still an embryo
with a long, long way to go
until I make my brother understand.
Oh, woman! I am woman! I am woman!

Helen Reddy[1]

So sings Helen Reddy of a dream becoming reality for many women. Her song describes the inner confidence and deep sense of purpose and vision that are part of being a winner. Allowing yourself to be more of the winner you were born to be means:

dropping old, negative self-images,

dropping unrealistic pressures of "What will people think?"

stepping off of paths that lead nowhere,

becoming more and sharing more,

caring about yourself and others with real affection.

Laying aside these weights leads to living with more spontaneity and awareness: more here, more now.

Living more with your full awareness focused on what is happening around you right now may not always be easy. Past memories, decisions, and ways you have learned to treat yourself and others can all get in the way of clear vision.

Deciding on growth means getting in touch with what is really important to you. What do you really value? Once you have a fix on this, you can make contracts for change. Maybe you want to stop putting down your intelligence, lose weight, stop yelling at someone, get a better job, appreciate your body for what it is, take better care of your health, or start learning something new. Maybe you want to change something else.

The important thing is to clarify for yourself what you really want to have happen in your own life. Know what it is that you value enough to put your energies into making it happen. For whatever it is, your commitment demonstrates what you value. When you decide to commit yourself to something new, learning to contract for change helps.

YOU CAN CONTRACT FOR PERSONAL GROWTH

Pick a friend who you know will support your change. Working with a friend has a number of advantages. You can verify with each other that your contract is specific and concrete enough for someone else to know when you have achieved it. If you both have contracts, it is a great opportunity for mutual support in personal growth.

When you draw up a contract, you will each need a copy. It might look like this one, or you may want to make up your own.

I,_____, am going to

_____

I shall start this right now, and by the date of _____

_____ I will have _____ .

This contract will be fully completed by the date of

_____.

Witnessed on _____

Witnessed by _____

_____
                                        signature

Success is OK

Your Inner Saboteur

Another part of the contract process is looking at how you might scuttle your good intentions to set yourself on a better path. Most of us have learned ways to subvert many of our good qualities. To avoid this self-sabotaging and to increase your chances for growth, think about these questions.

- How have I sabotaged my "good intentions" in the past?
- What are ways I might sabotage my present contract?
- What can I do to be more aware of and to deal with my methods of defeating myself?
- How can I treat myself better along the way so that I do not invite negative strokes by not living up to my contract?

Getting Support

We all need other people. We need good strokes. We need validation. Going it alone is not always necessary. You and your friend may want to check with each other to reward yourselves for your accomplishments.

When you fulfill a contract, have a ceremony. Do something good and fun for yourself and the person who helped you.

Celebrate!

FIND YOUR FLOW OF LIFE

Whether you decide to do what others recommend or whether you decide on a path for yourself, your life will end where you take it. If you allow yourself to experience life, your essence is forever in flux. You are never the same from one moment to the next. You never look the same. You never feel the same. You never think the same. Finding yourself and being yourself are hard things to do. But it helps to have the confidence to make up your own mind about what is right for you, what fits the goals and dreams you have chosen, and what helps you to be more fully the person you are.

Enjoy your body. Let it feel good. Know it. Take care of it. It is you.
Know how you feel. Express your feelings. Be your feelings.

Allow your intelligence and your feelings to work together. Take what tools you can from others, but *be your own guru.* Be your own person. Experience your own successes.

The History of Your Successes

Imagine that people are reading about you and your successes in a history book a hundred years from now. What kinds of things do you want to be remembered for? Now give yourself some time to write out what you would like people to read.

Success takes many forms and arouses many feelings. It means something special to each of us. Ralph Waldo Emerson writes of success:

To laugh often and much
To win the respect of intelligent people and the affection of children;
To earn the appreciation of honest critics and endure the betrayal of
   false friends;
To appreciate beauty;
To find the best in others:
To leave the world a bit better, whether by a healthy child, a garden
   patch, or a redeemed social condition;
To know even one life has breathed easier because you lived.
THIS is to have succeeded.

We leave you to your own life with this thought:

The more you are,
the more you become,
the more you have to share.
Your life filled to the brim
spills over, enriching the lives of others--
all the more
because
you chose to be more--you chose to be a winner.

References

PREFACE

1. *See* Eleanor Emmons Maccoby and Carol Jacklin, *The Psychology of Sex Differences*, Stanford, Calif.: Stanford University Press, 1974.

2. For further information about Dr. Frederick Perls and Gestalt therapy, refer to: *Gestalt Therapy Verbatim*, Lafayette, Calif.: Real People Press, 1969; *In and Out the Garbage Pail*, Lafayette, Calif.: Real People Press, 1969; *The Gestalt Approach and Eye Witness to Therapy*, Ben Lomond, Calif.: Science and Behavior Books, 1973.

CHAPTER 1

1. Judith Viorst, "A Woman's Liberation Movement Woman" (excerpt), *People and Other Aggravations*, New York: World, 1969, p. 16. Reprinted by permission.

2. Abigail Heyman, *Growing Up Female: A Personal Photojournal*, New York: Holt, Rinehart and Winston, 1974, n.p. Reprinted by permission.

3. U.S., Department of Health, Education, and Welfare, Public Health Service, National Center for Health Statistics, Health Resources Administration, *Monthly Vital Statistics Report*, (HRA) 76–1120, Dec. 29, 1975, pp. 2–3.

4. Of every 1000 married women 15 years old and over in 1960, 92 were divorced. By 1972 this number had increased to 169. U.S., Bureau of the Census, "Marriages and Divorces: 1940–1973," *Statistical Abstract of the United States: 1974*, No. 93, 1974, p. 66.

5. Elwood Carlson, "Working Wives and Unstable Marriages," Ph.D. diss., University of California at Berkeley, cited in the *Oakland Tribune*, February 15, 1976.

6. Alfred Allan Lewis with Bonnie Berns, *Three Out of Four Wives: Widowhood in America*, New York: Macmillan, 1975, p. 3.

7. *Ibid.*, p. 9.

8. *Ibid.*, p. 11.

9. U.S., Bureau of the Census, "Money Income in 1973 of Families and Persons in the U.S.," *Current Population Reports,* Series P-60, No. 97, pp. 112–113. We appreciate the special help of Donald G. Fowles, National Clearinghouse on Aging, Division of Data Analysis and Dissemination, U.S. Department of Health, Education, and Welfare, Washington, D.C., in his letter of March 13, 1975.

10. *Monthly Vital Statistics Report,* p. 1.

11. U.S., Department of Labor, Employment Standards Administration and Women's Bureau, *The Earnings Gap,* 1975, p. 4.

12. U.S., Department of Labor, Employment Standards Administration and Women's Bureau, *Fact Sheet on the Earnings Gap,* rev., 1971, p. 3.

13. U.S., Department of Labor, Employment Standards Administration and Women's Bureau, *Twenty Facts on Women Workers,* 1973, p. 2.

14. *The Earnings Gap,* p. 2.

15. *Ibid.,* p. 3.

16. *Ibid.*

17. *Fact Sheet on the Earnings Gap,* p. 1; *The Earnings Gap,* p. 2.

18. U.S., Department of Labor, Employment Standards Administration and Women's Bureau, *The Myth and the Reality,* rev., 1974, p. 1.

19. U.S., Department of Labor, Employment Standards Administration and Women's Bureau, *Why Women Work,* rev., 1975, p. 2.

20. U.S., Department of Labor, Wage and Labor Standards Administration, *1969 Handbook on Women Workers,* Women's Bureau Bulletin 294, 1969, pp. 7–8.

21. U.S., Department of Health, Education, and Welfare, *Report of the Women's Action Program,* January 1972. *See also* Carl D. Chambers, Ph.D., and Dodi Schultz, "Housewives and the Drug Habit," *Ladies Home Journal,* July 1972.

22. Contra Costa County Mental Health Services Research and Evaluation, "Preliminary Report on Drug-Related Emergency Room Contacts at County Hospital," Martinez, Calif., October 22, 1975.

23. U.S., Department of Health, Education, and Welfare, *Alcohol and Accidental Injury Conference Proceedings,* Superintendent of Documents Classification No. FS 1.2: AL 1–2, 1965, p. 17.

24. Dorothy Jongeward, "The Disease of the Delicate Ego," rev., *Marriage Counseling Quarterly* 1, 4 (May 1967): 33–35.

25. Robin Morgan, ed., "Know Your Enemy: A Sampling of Sexist Quotes," *Sisterhood Is Powerful: An Anthology of Writings from the Women's Lib Movement,* New York: Random House, Vintage Books, 1970, pp. 31–32.

26. *Ibid.,* p. 34.

27. Cf. Ecclesiastes 3:1–8.

28. Adapted from Muriel James and Dorothy Jongeward, *Born to Win: Transactional Analysis with Gestalt Experiments,* Reading, Mass.: Addison-Wesley, 1971, pp. 1–3.

CHAPTER 2

1. Sara Rath, *What Ever Happened to Fats Domino,* Madison, Wisc.: Wisconsin House, 1971, p. 15. Reprinted by permission.

2. U.S., Bureau of the Census, *Statistical Abstract of the United States: 1974,* No. 93, 1974, p. 38.

3. Dr. James Morgan, Director of the Maryland Association for Transactional Analysis, contributed many useful ideas on the waiting theme.

4. Eric Berne, M.D., *What Do You Say After You Say Hello?* New York: Grove Press, 1972, p. 418. *See also* Muriel James and Dorothy Jongeward, *Born to Win: Transactional Analysis with Gestalt Experiments,* Reading, Mass.: Addison-Wesley, 1971, p. 79; Eric Berne, M.D., *Principles of Group Treatment,* New York: Oxford University Press, 1964, p. 310.

5. Dorothy Jongeward, "What Do You Do When Your Script Runs Out?" *Transactional Analysis Journal* 2, 2 (April 1972): 78–80.

6. Dorothy Jongeward and Dru Scott, *Affirmative Action for Women: A Practical Guide,* Reading, Mass.: Addison-Wesley, 1973, p. 6.

7. Mary Bralove, "Runaway Wives: More Women Fleeing from Home, but Most Return to Husbands," *Wall Street Journal,* October 1, 1975.

8. Abraham Maslow, *Motivation and Personality,* 2d ed., New York: Harper & Row, 1970.

CHAPTER 3

1. Stephen B. Karpman, "Fairy Tales and Script Drama Analysis," *Transactional Analysis Bulletin* 7, 2 (April 1968): 39–43.

2. For additional study of women's scripts, see the writings of Hogie Wycoff: "The Stroke Economy in Women's Scripts," *Transactional Analysis Journal* 1, 3 (July 1971): pp. 16–20; "Radical Psychiatry and Transactional Analysis in Women's Groups," *Transactional Analysis Bulletin* 9, 36 (October 1970): 128–133; "Banal Scripts of Women," *Scripts People Live,* ed. Claude M. Steiner, New York: Grove Press, 1974, pp. 176–196.

3. Eric Berne, M.D., *What Do You Say After You Say Hello?* New York: Grove Press, 1972, pp. 231–243.

4. Cf. Muriel James and Dorothy Jongeward, *Born to Win: Transactional Analysis with Gestalt Experiments,* Reading, Mass.: Addison-Wesley, 1971, p. 93.

5. Judith Viorst, *People and Other Aggravations,* New York: World, 1971, pp. 36–37. Reprinted by permission.

6. Berne, *What Do You Say After You Say Hello?* pp. 42–47.

7. *Ibid.*, pp. 420–421. Reprinted by permission of Grove Press, Inc. Copyright © 1972 City National Bank, Beverly Hills; Robin Way; Janice Way Farlinger. All rights reserved.

8. *Ibid.*, pp. 214–215. Reprinted by permission of Grove Press, Inc. Copyright © 1972 City National Bank, Beverly Hills; Robin Way; Janice Way Farlinger. All rights reserved.

CHAPTER 4

1. Muriel James and Dorothy Jongeward, *Born to Win: Transactional Analysis with Gestalt Experiments*, Reading, Mass.: Addison-Wesley, 1971, p. 38; Dorothy Jongeward and Dru Scott, *Affirmative Action for Women: A Practical Guide*, Reading, Mass.: Addison-Wesley, 1973, pp. 30, 35.

2. Robert Goulding, M.D., "New Directions in Transactional Analysis: Creating an Environment for Redecision and Change," *Progress in Group and Family Therapy*, New York: Brunner/Mazel, 1972, p. 107.

3. Robert Goulding and Mary Edwards Goulding, "Injunctions, Decisions, and Redecisions," *Transactional Analysis Journal* 6, 1 (January 1976): 41–48.

4. Goulding, *Progress in Group and Family Therapy*, pp. 105–134. Much of Mary Edwards Goulding and Robert Goulding's work is done at the Western Institute for Group and Family Therapy, 262 Gaffey Road, Mount Madonna, Watsonville, California. See also a new book by Robert Goulding for professional therapists, to be published in 1976 by Brunner/Mazel.

5. Muriel James and Dorothy Jongeward, *Born to Win*, p. 79.

6. Muriel Schiffman, *Gestalt Self Therapy and Further Techniques for Personal Growth*, Menlo Park, Calif.: Self Therapy Press, 1971. This book helps you learn to use gestalt methods in your personal life.

7. Edith Hamilton, *Mythology*, New York: Mentor/New American Library, 1971, pp. 255–256.

8. Matina S. Horner, "Femininity and Successful Achievement: A Basic Inconsistency," in Judith M. Bardwick, Elizabeth Douvan, Matina S. Horner, and David Gutmann, *Feminine Personality & Conflict*, Belmont, Calif.: Brooks/Cole, 1970, pp. 46–47, 55, 60–61.

9. Shirley Chisholm, "A Visiting Feminine Eye," *McCalls*, August 1970, p. 6.

10. William H. Grier, M.D., and Price M. Cobbs, M.D., *Black Rage*, New York: Basic Books, 1968, pp. 42–44. © 1968 by William H. Grier and Price M. Cobbs, Basic Books, Inc., Publishers, New York.

CHAPTER 5

1. Robert A. Raines, "Waiting for a Hug," *Lord, Could You Make It a Little Better?* Waco, Texas: Word Books, 1972, p. 18. Reprinted by permission.

2. R. Spitz, "Hospitalism: Genesis of Psychiatric Conditions in Early Childhood," *Psychoanalytic Study of the Child* **1** (1945): 53–74; *Second Chance* (a film), Nutley, N.J.: Hoffman-LaRoche Laboratory.

3. Eric Berne, *Games People Play,* New York: Grove Press, 1964, p. 15.

4. Eric Berne, *What Do You Say After You Say Hello?* New York: Grove Press, 1972, pp. 137–139.

5. Claude M. Steiner, *Scripts People Live: Transactional Analysis of Life Scripts,* New York: Grove Press, 1974, pp. 114–117.

6. *Ibid.*

CHAPTER 6

1. Eric Berne, *Transactional Analysis in Psychotherapy,* New York: Grove Press, 1961, p. 32.

2. Eric Berne, *Principles of Group Treatment,* New York: Oxford University Press, 1964, p. 364.

3. Quoted in Richard Gilman, "Where Did It All Go Wrong?" *Life Magazine* **7,** 71 (August 1971): 51.

4. *Ibid.,* p. 52.

5. Quoted in Richard Gilman, "The Women Problem," *Life Magazine* **7, 71** (August 1971): 45.

6. Richard Gilman, "Where Did It All Go Wrong?" p. 51. *Also see* Dorothy Jongeward and Dru Scott, *Affirmative Action for Women: A Practical Guide,* Reading, Mass.: Addison-Wesley, 1973, pp. 24–26.

7. Cf. Janice Kay, "What Do I Do Next?" in Dorothy Jongeward and Dru Scott, *Affirmative Action for Women,* pp. 260–261.

CHAPTER 7

1. Reprinted with permission of Blue Mountain Arts, Inc., from *I Want to Laugh, I Want to Cry,* p. 61, by Susan Polis Schutz, © 1973 by Continental Publications.

2. Ashley Montagu, *The Natural Superiority of Women,* New York: Lancer Books, 1943, pp. 42, 1952. Reprinted by permission.

3. Vivian Gornick and Barbara K. Moran, eds., *Woman in Sexist Society,* New York: Basic Books, 1971, p. 341.

4. *Ibid.*

5. *See* Madeline Stern, ed., *Behind a Mask: The Unknown Thrillers of Louisa May Alcott,* New York: Morrow, 1975.

6. For more on the topic of sexual preference, see: Muriel James and Dorothy Jongeward, *Born to Win: Transactional Analysis with Gestalt Experiments,* Reading, Mass.: Addison-Wesley, 1971, pp. 152–178; Merle Miller, "What It

Means to Be a Homosexual," *San Francisco Chronicle*, Jan. 25, 1971; Peter and Barbara Wyden, *Growing Up Straight*, New York: Stein and Day, 1968; Del Martin and Phyllis Lyon, *Lesbian/Woman*, San Francisco: Glide Publications, 1972; Sidney Abbott and Barbara Love, *Sappho Was a Right-On Woman*, New York: Stein and Day, 1972.

7. Muriel James and Dorothy Jongeward, *The People Book*, Reading, Mass.: Addison-Wesley, 1975, p. 135; John James, "The Game Plan," *Transactional Analysis Journal* **3**, 4 (Oct. 1973): 14–17.

8. Cf. John Dusay, "Egograms and the Constancy Hypothesis," *Transactional Analysis Journal* **2**, 3 (July 1972): 37. *See also* Chapter 10 of this book.

CHAPTER 8

1. Judith Viorst, "The First Full-Fledged Family Reunion," *People and Other Aggravations*, New York: World, 1971, pp. 60–61. Reprinted by permission.

2. Aaron Wolf Schiff and Jacqui Lee Schiff, "Passivity," *Transactional Analysis Journal* **1**, 1 (January 1971): 71–78.

CHAPTER 9

1. Bergen Evans, ed., *Dictionary of Quotations*, New York: Delacorte, 1968, p. 101.

2. Harry Harlow, "The Nature of Love," *American Psychologist* **13**, 12 (1958): 673–685. *Also see* H. F. Harlow and M. K. Harlow, "Social Deprivation in Monkeys," *Scientific American* **46**, 207 (November 1962): 136–146.

3. Margaret Mead, "Some Theoretical Considerations on the Problem of Mother-Child Separation," *American Journal of Orthopsychiatry* **24** (1954): 471–483; *see also* U.S., Department of Health, Education, and Welfare, Welfare Administration, *Children of Working Mothers*, Children's Bureau Publication No. 382, 1960, pp. 18–25.

4. U.S., Department of Commerce, Bureau of the Census, "Population Characteristics," *Current Population Reports*, Series P-20, No. 282, July 1975.

5. Parents Without Partners is an organization to help solve this problem. There are affiliates in most major cities.

6. Claude M. Steiner, "The Treatment of Alcoholism," *Transactional Analysis Bulletin* **6**, 23 (July 1967): 69–77; cf. Leonard P. Campos, "Transactional Analysis of Witch Messages," *Transactional Analysis Bulletin* **9**, 34 (April 1970): 51; also see Eric Berne, M.D., *What Do You Say After You Say Hello?* New York: Grove Press, 1972, pp. 279–283.

7. Planned Parenthood, "World Population Letter from Cass Canfield in New York," October 1974.

8. See Lisa Aversa Richette, *Throwaway Children*, Philadelphia: Lippincott, 1969.

9. Planned Parenthood, "World Population Letter." For more information about battered children, *see also* Hans Forssman and Inga Thuwe, "One Hundred and Twenty Children Born After Application for Therapeutic Abortion Refused," Psychiatric Departments of the Goteborg University at the Sahlgren Hospital and at St. Jorgen's Hospital; "When to Suspect Parental Assault," *Resident and Staff Physician*, August 1973; "Dysfunctioning Families and Child Abuse," *Public Welfare*, Fall 1972; Parents of Battered Babies," *British Medical Journal*, November 1973; "Battered Children," *Transaction*, July-August 1971; "Battered Child Syndrome," *Bulletin of the New York Academy of Medicine*, September 1970; "Violence Against Children," *Journal of Marriage and the Family*, November 1971.

10. Planned Parenthood, "World Population Letter."

11. One organization that provides this type of help is Parents Anonymous, 2810 Artesia Boulevard, Suite F, Redondo Beach, CA 90278.

12. *See* Muriel James, *TA for Moms and Dads*, Reading, Mass.: Addison-Wesley, 1974.

13. For information, contact Parent Effectiveness Training Courses, 110 South Euclid Avenue, Pasadena, CA 91101.

14. Reprinted with permission of Blue Mountain Arts, Inc., from *I Want to Laugh, I Want to Cry*, p. 31, by Susan Polis Schutz, © 1973 by Continental Publications.

CHAPTER 10

1. Jacqui Lee Schiff with Beth Day, *All My Children*, New York: M. Evans, 1970, pp. 210–211.

2. John Dusay, "Egograms and the Constancy Hypothesis," *Transactional Analysis Journal* **2**, 3 (July 1972): 37–41. *See also* Dorothy Jongeward and Muriel James, *Winning with People: Group Exercises in Transactional Analysis*, Reading, Mass.: Addison-Wesley, 1973, p. 89.

CHAPTER 11

1. Eric Berne, *Transactional Analysis in Psychotherapy*, New York: Grove Press, 1961, p. 62. *See also* Muriel James and Dorothy Jongeward, *Born to Win: Transactional Analysis with Gestalt Experiments*, Reading, Mass.: Addison-Wesley, 1971, pp. 231–234.

2. William Morris, ed., *The American Heritage Dictionary of the English Language*, New York: American Heritage Publishing Co. and Houghton Mifflin, 1973.

3. *Ibid.*

4. U.S., Department of Commerce, "Consumer Income: Characteristics of the Low-Income Population," *Current Population Reports, 1973*, Series P-60, No. 98, issued January 1975, p. 161.

5. Cf. Dorothy Jongeward and Muriel James, *Winning with People: Group Exercises in Transactional Analysis*, Reading, Mass.: Addison-Wesley, 1972. *See also* Dorothy Jongeward and Dru Scott, *Affirmative Action for Women: A Practical Guide*, Reading, Mass.: Addison-Wesley, 1973, p. 28.

6. Muriel James and Dorothy Jongeward, *Born to Win: Transactional Analysis with Gestalt Experiments*, Reading, Mass.: Addison-Wesley, 1971, p. 256.

7. Graham Staines, Carol Tarvis, and Toby Epstein Jayaratne, "The Queen Bee Syndrome." Reprinted from *Psychology Today* Magazine, January 1974, pp. 55–56. Copyright © 1973 by Ziff-Davis Publishing Company. All rights reserved.

8. U.S., Department of Labor, Employment Standards Administration and Women's Bureau, *Twenty Facts on Women Workers*, 1973, p. 2.

9. Cynthia Fuchs Epstein, "Positive Effects of the Multiple Negative: Explaining the Success of Black Professional Women," *American Journal of Sociology* **78,** 4 (January 1973): 912–935.

10. Sidney M. Jourard, *The Transparent Self*, 2d ed., New York: D. Van Nostrand, 1971, pp. 34–36. Reprinted by permission.

11. Leo Buscaglia, *Love*, Thorofare, N.J.: Charles B. Slack, 1972, pp. 22–23. Reprinted by permission.

12. Eleanor Flexner, *Century of Struggle: The Woman's Rights Movement in the United States*, Cambridge, Mass.: Harvard University Press, Belknap Press, 1959, pp. 90–91. Reprinted by permission.

CHAPTER 12

1. Elizabeth Cady Stanton, Susan B. Anthony, and Mathilda Joslyn Gage, eds., *The History of Woman Suffrage*, Vol. III, Rochester, N.Y., n.p., 1886, p. 39. Quoted in Eleanor Flexner, *Century of Struggle: The Woman's Rights Movement in the United States*, Cambridge, Mass.: Harvard University Press, Belknap Press, 1959, p. 172.

2. Flexner, *Century of Struggle*, pp. 4, 5.

3. *See* June Sochen, *Herstory*, New York: Alfred, 1974, pp. 46–49.

4. George F. Dow, *Slave Ships and Slaving*, Salem, Mass., n.p., 1927, p. 242. *Also see* Flexner, *Century of Struggle*, p. 19.

5. Flexner, *Century of Struggle*, p. 363.

6. *See Antinomianism in the Colony of Massachusetts Bay, 1636–1638*, Prince Society Publications **XXI** (1894): 284. Cited in Flexner, *Century of Struggle*, p. 11.

7. *See* Sochen, *Herstory*, p. 49.

8. New Testament, 1 Corinthians 14:34, 35.

9. Jacqueline Bernard, *Journey Toward Freedom*, New York: Norton, 1967, p. 2.

10. *Ibid.,* pp. 181–183. Reprinted by permission.

11. *See* Dorothy Sterling, *Freedom Train,* New York: Doubleday, 1954, pp. 126–129.

12. Flexner, *Century of Struggle,* pp. 95–96.

13. Jean-Jacques Rousseau, *L'Emile, or A Treatise on Education,* ed. W. H. Payne, New York and London, 1906, n.p., p. 263. *Also see* Flexner, *Century of Struggle,* pp. 23–24.

14. Alma Lutz, *Emma Willard,* Boston, n.p., 1929, p. 56. *Also see* Flexner, *Century of Struggle,* p. 26.

15. Elizabeth Cady Stanton, *Eighty Years and More,* New York, n.p., 1898, pp. 147–148. Quoted in Flexner, *Century of Struggle,* pp. 73–74.

16. Quoted in Mary Ann B. Oakley, *Elizabeth Cady Stanton,* Long Island, N.Y.: Feminist Press, 1972.

17. *Ibid.* Quoted in Dorothy Jongeward and Dru Scott, *Affirmative Action for Women: A Practical Guide for Women and Management,* Reading, Mass.: Addison-Wesley, 1972, p. 26.

18. Charles Remond to Charles B. Ray, June 30, 1840, in *Documentary History of the Negro People in the United States,* ed. Herbert Aptheker, New York, n.p., 1951, p. 196. *Also see* Flexner, *Century of Struggle,* p. 71.

19. Susan B. Anthony, Mathilda Joslyn Gage, and Elizabeth Cady Stanton, eds., *The History of Woman Suffrage,* Rochester, N.Y., n.p., 1881. Quoted in Flexner, *Century of Struggle,* p. 75.

20. Andrew Sinclair, *The Better Half: The Emancipation of American Women,* New York: Harper & Row, 1965, p. 201. *See also* William H. Chafe, *The American Woman,* New York: Oxford University Press, 1972, p. 7.

21. Stanton, *Eighty Years and More,* pp. 165–166. *Also see* Flexner, *Century of Struggle,* p. 89.

22. Quoted in Alma Lutz, *Created Equal,* n.p., n.d., p. 104. Mrs. Stanton was sanguine, but not quite sanguine enough. She lived to be 88, and Miss Anthony to be 87, and both can be said to have died with their boots on. Quoted in Flexner, *Century of Struggle,* p. 89.

23. Flexner, *Century of Struggle,* p. 84.

24. Rheta Child Dorr, *Susan B. Anthony,* New York, n.p., 1928, p. 98. Quoted in Flexner, *Century of Struggle,* p. 87.

25. Report of General Instructor and Director of Women's Work and Wages, *Proceedings of the Knights of Labor, 1888,* p. 5. Quoted in Flexner, *Century of Struggle,* p. 86.

26. *See* Chafe, *The American Woman,* pp. 19–20.

27. *Baltimore Sun,* March 4, 1913. Quoted in Flexner, *Century of Struggle,* p. 264.

28. Flexner, *Century of Struggle,* p. 285.

29. *See* Mrs. Frank Vanderlip to Maud Wood Park, October 11, 1922, LWV Papers, Library of Congress, Series II, Box 43. Quoted in Chafe, *The American Woman*, p. 113. Reprinted by permission.

30. Quoted in Chafe, *The American Woman*, p. 115.

31. *Ibid.*, p. 114.

32. Maria Karagianis, "Alice Paul Still Waits for Equal Rights," *Boston Globe*, February 1, 1976.

33. For further information on women in history, see: Maren L. Carden, *The New Feminist Movement*, New York: Russel Sage, 1974; Robert E. Riegel, *American Feminists*, Lawrence: University Press of Kansas, 1968; Haig Bosmajian and Hamida Bosmajian, *This Great Argument: The Rights of Women*, Reading, Mass.: Addison-Wesley, 1972; Miriam Schneier, ed., *Feminism: The Essential Historical Writings*, New York: Random House, 1972.

CHAPTER 13

1. "Think Big," from *Everyone Needs a Tree House*, a collection of poems by Maria Monahan. Reprinted by permission.

2. For more information about the Johari Awareness Model, see Joseph Luft, *Of Human Interaction*, Palo Alto, Calif.: National Press Books, 1969.

3. Frederick S. Perls, *In and Out the Garbage Pail*, Lafayette, Calif.: Real People Press, 1969, n.p.

4. Frederick S. Perls, *Gestalt Therapy Verbatim*, Lafayette, Calif.: Real People Press, 1969, p. 66. Also see pp. 67–70.

5. For further information about dreams, see: Ann Faraday, *Dream Power*, New York: Berkeley, 1972. We highly recommend this book. Ann Faraday is not only knowledgeable, but also uniquely sensitive to women. *See also* Ernest Hartmann, *Sleep and Dreaming*, Boston: Little, Brown, 1970; Frederick Perls, *Gestalt Therapy Verbatim*, Lafayette, Calif.: Real People Press, 1969; Ralph L. Woods and Herbert B. Greenhouse, *The New World of Dreams: An Anthology*, New York: Macmillan, 1974.

6. Reprinted with permission of Blue Mountain Arts, Inc., from *I Want to Laugh, I Want to Cry*, p. 39, by Susan Polis Schutz, © 1973 by Continental Publications.

CHAPTER 14

1. Copyright 1971, 1972, Irving Music, Inc., and Buggerlugs Music (BMI). All rights reserved. Used by permission.

Picture Credits

p. 267: (6) Russ Adams; (7) Courtesy of Shirley Chisholm; (8) National Broadcasting Company; (9) The American National Red Cross

p. 294: (top left) Jack Prelutsky/Stock, Boston; (top right) Frank Castello; (bottom right) John Pearson

p. 295: (top) Dorothy Jongeward; (bottom left) Donald C. Dietz/Stock, Boston; (bottom right) John Pearson/BBM

Index

For Pam,
who brought out the dog in me

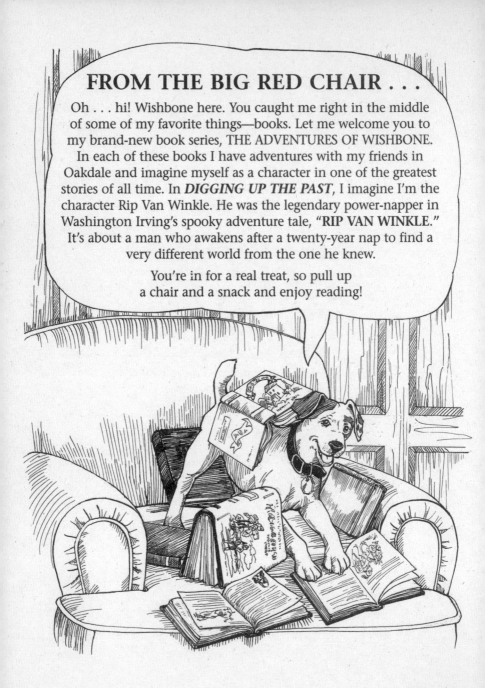

FROM THE BIG RED CHAIR . . .

Oh . . . hi! Wishbone here. You caught me right in the middle of some of my favorite things—books. Let me welcome you to my brand-new book series, THE ADVENTURES OF WISHBONE. In each of these books I have adventures with my friends in Oakdale and imagine myself as a character in one of the greatest stories of all time. In *DIGGING UP THE PAST*, I imagine I'm the character Rip Van Winkle. He was the legendary power-napper in Washington Irving's spooky adventure tale, "**RIP VAN WINKLE.**" It's about a man who awakens after a twenty-year nap to find a very different world from the one he knew.

You're in for a real treat, so pull up
a chair and a snack and enjoy reading!

Chapter One

Wishbone smiled in his sleep. He lay stretched out on the kitchen floor, his stomach still full from breakfast. The sunlight streaming through the window warmed his fur, and the dream in his head was terrific. *Hmm . . . chase cats. Go. Go! Adventure! I love it!* He felt good all the way from the tip of his nose to the tip of his tail.

It was a perfect morning. Almost.

Brown-haired, twelve-year-old Joe Talbot, Wishbone's close friend and housemate, stepped over the Jack Russell terrier. Wishbone had been right in the middle of a good dog snore.

The dog's head popped up. "Hey! Joe . . . buddy . . . pal—it's me down here. Man's best friend. More important, *your* best friend. I'm right where you almost stepped."

Stopping at the counter, Joe poured himself a bowl of cold cereal. Wishbone dropped his head back to the linoleum and closed his eyes. But Joe banged the cupboard door shut. And the silverware drawer rattled when he opened and closed it. Then Joe stepped over Wishbone again.

Wishbone sighed as he heard Joe finally sit down at the table. "Ah, silence at last."

But within seconds, Joe rustled the newspaper, which caused Wishbone to raise his head up off the floor. He glanced toward the table.

"I know you like to read the sports section, Joe. But let's have some peace and quiet, *pleeease*, and thank you." He dropped his head down again.

Just as Wishbone was starting to nod off, Joe's mom, Ellen, came into the kitchen. She, too, stepped over him.

"Breakfast for you, Ellen?" Wishbone mumbled sleepily. Each time her shoes clicked against the linoleum, Wishbone's ears twitched.

A short screech caused when Ellen pushed down the toaster lever startled Wishbone. His head popped up.

"Nobody ever listens to the dog." He pawed his ear. "Boy, do I dislike that toaster sound." Relaxing again, he sighed. "Ahhh. Sleep is coming . . . full speed ahead." He was almost ready to nap once more.

But Wishbone heard Ellen step over him again. She picked up his water bowl and walked to the sink.

Soon she was back. "Here you go, Wishbone." She set the bowl down next to his head with a loud clunk.

"Helllooo! I'm *trying* to sleep. *Humph!* Water. No,

thanks." He yawned. "Sleepy, not thirsty." His head dropped back to the floor, his eyes already half closed.

He heard Ellen searching through the cupboard. She was probably looking for her favorite mug. Wishbone tried to ignore the sound of the clinking cups as she moved the china around.

Finally Ellen picked out a mug and poured herself coffee. She grabbed her toast and went to the table. "I have to go in to work for a while, Joe. Did you make any plans for today?"

Joe glanced up from the football article he was reading. "Not yet. Sam was talking about having a street-hockey game down by the park." Joe turned the page. As he snapped the newspaper straight, it rustled loudly.

"Noise again." Wishbone sat up abruptly.

I'm not getting much sleep here, so I may as well fill you in. Samantha—Sam, for short—is one of Joe's best friends. She loves adventure as much as I do. We get along great! Joe and Sam have another good friend named David. He is one smart dog cookie, always building things to help out others. The four of us spend a lot—*repeat*—a lot of time together. It's usually when we're on some kind of adventure. I love it!

Ellen picked up her mug and sipped from it. "Just make sure you straighten your room before you leave the house."

"Mom, it's Saturday," Joe reminded her. "Can't I do that tomorrow?" He took a bite of cereal.

Wishbone cocked his head. "I think tomorrow is good, Joe. Ellen, you don't really want Joe to spend our day together cleaning, do you? I've already looked in his room, and there isn't even a ball or Frisbee lying around. And food crumbs are cleaned up daily." He wagged his tail proudly. "The Wishbone Crumbmaster, at your service."

Wishbone stood and slowly stretched. "Ohh, that feels good on my back. Would either of you care to give it a scratch? . . . No? Well, then, if you two will kindly excuse me, I'll be off. I believe I hear the big red chair in the study calling my name." He headed to the doorway. "I have a cat nap to finish." He hesitated. "Or would that be a *dog* nap?"

10

Joe rolled his eyes, but he nodded as Ellen tugged his sleeve for an answer.

"Great, Joe!" Wishbone said. "I love the library—except for the 'no-animals-allowed' rule."

"See you later," Ellen said. She walked from the study to the front door.

Joe waved. "'Bye."

After Ellen had shut the door and left the house, Joe sat down on the arm of the red chair. He scratched Wishbone behind the ears. "Hey, do you want to help me clean up?"

Wishbone cocked his head. "Hmm. Watch you work . . . or get some sleep? Let me do some deep thinking about this." Wishbone stood up. He quickly paced a circle on the chair cushion, then flopped back down. "No, I thought about it. I choose the nap. Wake me up when you're finished."

Dropping his chin to his paws, Wishbone closed his eyes halfway. He watched Joe shake his head as he walked out of the room.

"Gimme a dog's life any day," Joe mumbled.

Wishbone yawned.

A dog's life, indeed. How lovely! There's nothing like a good nap—the kind of nap old Rip Van Winkle used to take. Rip originated the *power nap*, and he remains the patron saint of lazybones everywhere. There's even a book about him. The title is—

Wishbone jumped into the red chair, lay down, and dropped his chin to his paws. "Ahhh. Comfort *and* quiet. The two go together like bacon and eggs. Like cake and ice cream. Like ginger snaps and me!" His tail thumped against the chair.

Joe and Ellen's voices drifted from the kitchen to the study. With his superb hearing, Wishbone picked up every word they said, clear as a doorbell.

"What about your social-studies paper?" Ellen asked. "Isn't it due on Monday?"

"Yeah, I guess so," Joe said.

Ooh. Wishbone perked up his ears. He bet some sort of a face came with that answer. "Your tone of voice gives you away, Joe."

"Well, when are you going to work on the paper?" Ellen asked.

Wishbone heard a crunch, then the clink of a spoon against a mug. *A bite of toast, and a drink of coffee—it must be Ellen*, he thought, pleased with his guess.

"Tomorrow," Joe answered.

Wishbone detected a spoon-against-bowl scrape. *Joe, spooning cereal into his mouth*, Wishbone guessed. *A good excuse for a brief answer.*

Ellen sighed.

"Oh, oh, Joe," Wishbone said. He'd heard that exact sigh before, and he knew what it meant. It meant, *Perhaps you should rethink this.*

Ellen went on. "You know, Joe, you can't put everything off until tomorrow. Have you even started the paper?"

Joe sighed, too. "No."

Wishbone raised his head and pawed the air. "I feel for you, buddy." His ears picked up the sound of Ellen's hands rubbing together. Wishbone heard toast crumbs hitting the floor. "Thank you, Ellen. I'll get to them a little later."

"What's the subject of your paper?" Ellen asked Joe.

Joe rustled the newspaper.

That's Joe, folding up the paper, Wishbone guessed. *I'm getting pretty good at this game,* he thought. He wagged his tail at another sound and spoke in a low voice. "Welcome to 'Dog Jeopardy,' the game where you're given the answer and you ask the question. In the 'SOUNDS category, for 100,' what is, 'Sliding the paper to the center of the table'?" Wishbone wagged his tail. "Correct for 100 chew bones!"

Joe's voice interrupted Wishbone's thoughts. "We're supposed to write about something our grandparents had—something we wish was still around today."

"Oh. Well, did you pick a topic yet?" Ellen asked.

"No," Joe said. "I'm still thinking."

Cocking his head to listen to a soft thump, Wishbone made another guess. "What is, 'Ellen tapping the newspaper'?"

"Look at this front-page headline, Joe," Ellen said. "'EMISSIONS VIOLATIONS CLOSE HOBROCK PLANT.' What about this?"

Wishbone raised his paw. "The dog scores again! Two hundred squeaky toys!"

"Naaah," Joe said. Wishbone heard him drink the last of his milk from his bowl, then get up from the table. "It's supposed to be something that we wish was still around."

More clinking and a chair scraping against the floor made Wishbone guess again. "What is, 'Ellen carrying her dishes to the sink'?" He rolled onto his side and stretched out his hind legs. "The cute little dog is *sooo* good! He's just earned 300 rubber balls!"

Wishbone heard footsteps approaching, and he looked up.

"Hello, Ellen."

Entering the study, Ellen glanced this way and that, in search of something. "So, Joe, do you have any ideas on *getting* a topic idea?"

Joe followed Ellen into the room and shrugged. "No, not really. I'm sort of stumped."

"Aha!" She sounded relieved. "There's my backpack—under Wishbone." Ellen made a bee-line to the red chair. With a tug, she pulled her pack out. "Excuse me, Wishbone."

Wishbone raised his head slightly off the chair cushion. "Pardon me, but did I leave a wake-up call?"

Ellen dug her keys out of her backpack; they jingled. "Why don't you come to the library, Joe, after you've straightened up your room? Doing a little research might give you some ideas."

you guessed it—"Rip Van Winkle." It was written in the early 1800s by Washington Irving, one of America's first great authors.

The story takes place in colonial America—just before the Revolutionary War, which started in 1776. At that time, the country was still a province of Great Britain and was under the rule of the King of England.

Now, lads and lassies, turn the page and head off on an adventure!

Chapter Two

With his imagination running at full speed ahead, Wishbone imagined himself as Rip Van Winkle. He was a good-natured farmer living in a little village at the foot of the Catskill Mountains. The mountains rose high into the sky, standing like guardians over the countryside. Sometimes a gray mist gathered thickly around their peaks. When the strong rays of afternoon sun speared through the mist, they cast an eerie glow on the mountains.

Like the Indians before them, the Dutch colonists from Holland who founded the village thought the mountains were haunted by spirits. Some people even believed the spirits controlled the weather, and that they caused good or bad hunting seasons in the mountains. Spooky, huh? Rip lived right next door to all this! I think I'm starting to smell adventure already.

This was an old village, located near the mighty Hudson River. Up the road in one direction stood

16

houses of the original settlers. They were built from small yellow bricks brought all the way from Holland. Beautiful latticework—long strips of wood—crisscrossed the windows. Old metal weather vanes, often made in the shape of a rooster, were mounted on rooftops. They turned squeakily in the wind.

Down the road in the other direction stood the village inn. That was Rip's favorite hangout. The King George Inn was a small place, but easy to spot. Above the door hung a portrait of His Majesty George the Third. He was the King of Great Britain.

I met a King once, at the vet clinic. Pretty nice fella. He was a Great Dane, and he looked nothing at all like this English King.

17

Inside his house, Rip Van Winkle jumped up into the chair nearest the window and sat on his haunches. Tucking his tail close to his side, he did nothing but listen to the birds chirp and watch the grass grow. It was a beautiful morning . . . until he heard the thundering footsteps of his wife, Dame Van Winkle.

"Dame" was a term that people at that time used to describe the lady of the household. It was like the way Ellen Talbot is the lady of the Talbot house.

"Rip Van Winkle, ye are a lazy man!" Grabbing a broom, she headed toward him threateningly.

Rip leaped out of the chair. He landed on all fours, just in time to duck her swinging broom.

"The only work ye do is for the people of the village. Always lending *them* a hand, ye are." Dame Van Winkle followed Rip around the room, nearly stepping on his hind feet. Her skirts swished around him, catching on the tip of his tail. "Why do ye sit idle when there is so much to be done right here? Open those big eyes of yours, Rip Van Winkle, and look at this place. 'Tis falling apart. Do ye not see that the fence needs mending? I'm tired of chasing after the cow. And the cart? It needs a wheel before it will be of any use. How else am I to carry things?"

As always, Rip Van Winkle maintained his good mood. He reached out a paw and he patted his wife gently. "But isn't it a good day to relax and enjoy the gifts of nature? Perhaps I should go to the river and fish." He'd spent many a happy hour fishing—or what he called "fishing." Most times he didn't even use bait. Actually, catching a fish would have interrupted his peace and quiet.

Dame Van Winkle swung her broom again, this time before Rip could scamper away. Bristles clawed across his brown ear like a cat's paw. "Perhaps ye should go outside and work! There's nothing like an honest day's work to make an honest day's pay."

Rip shook his head until his ears flopped down. "Perhaps you are right, wife." He strapped his musket across his shoulder and placed his hat upon his head.

Dame Van Winkle pulled open the door and waited for Rip to walk over the threshold.

Rip moved quickly to step outside, reminding himself that his wife's bark was worse than her bite.

As soon as he padded through the doorway, the door slammed shut behind him.

Rip adjusted his gear, began to walk, and cast his eyes around the farm.

Work? Here? Excuse me, but I don't think so. This place is a mess.

Why, his farm was the worst piece of ground in the country. For every rock he cleared away, six more appeared. Weeds grew all around, but crops wouldn't. And there weren't enough trees for his liking. His land was so bare that his soil blew away with every breeze. And what hadn't already gone wrong with the house soon would.

Rip turned and glanced back at his shabby farm-house. Giving the house a fresh coat of paint would be as useless as it would be to wash the dirt on the ground. The roof sagged like the back of an old plow horse. He shook his head with disappointment. No, his place wasn't worth any more than a water bowl with a hole in it.

Rip pawed his chin in thought. He decided to make his way to the village inn to gossip with his friends. Instantly a smile spread across his furry face. He loved chewing the fat with his buddies. *Perhaps a traveler from far away has left a newspaper for us to read from,* he thought. *That always makes for good talk. It also gives me fresh ideas for my storytelling.*

Rip sighed. Yes, the inn was where he enjoyed spending most of his days. There he was able to avoid hard work and the shouts of his wife.

"Father!" His daughter, Judith, raced around a corner of the house. She pulled on his coattail.

"Father, look!" said Judith. She held up the most-recent wooden doll that Rip had carved for her. "I've used some of Mother's cloth to make a fine gown for my doll."

Rip took the doll in his paws. He oohed and ahhed as he examined his daughter's handiwork. A worn-out piece of cloth was tied around the doll's neck. The cloth hung down, covering her arms and legs.

"A fine job you have done, Judith. Yes, a fine, fine job."

Judith's face lit up like the brilliant morning sun.

Rip winked. "And does she like her new set of clothes, lass?"

"Oh, yes, Father, she certainly does."

The door to the house burst open. Dame Van Winkle, broom in hand, rushed outside toward Rip. "I told ye to stop wasting time!" She swung her arms, and the broom sliced through the air like a sword.

Rip jumped out of the way just in the nick of time. "All right, my good woman." He handed the doll back to Judith. Then he pointed a paw at a leaning fence post, as if he planned to fix it.

Dame Van Winkle nodded her approval at Rip. Then she focused her attention on her daughter. "Come, Judith. Ye will only be a distraction," she said, bustling inside.

Judith hugged Rip. "Good-bye, Father."

"Good-bye, lass." Without a second glance at the fence post, Rip headed down the lane that led away from his property. Soon he spotted his son, young Rip. Clothed in tattered trousers, he lay on his back, staring up at the sky.

"Cloud-watching, are you, son?" Rip called.

"Yes, Father, I am."

Young Rip didn't come running the way his sister had. He just leaned on one elbow, gave a lazy wave, then lay back down again.

But Rip understood. Young Rip was like his father, appreciating nature every time he could.

Rip Van Winkle pointed upward with his paw to a

small cloud overhead. "What does that cloud look like?" he called to young Rip.

Young Rip studied the cloud for a while. "A chicken. And the tiny piece of cloud below it is an egg."

Rip Van Winkle nodded and wagged his tail. "I do believe you're right. That's quite a talent you have, lad, for picturing things."

"Thank ye, Father," young Rip replied, without even raising his head.

Rip trotted off toward the center of the village. He sniffed the air, enjoying the clean, crisp aroma of early autumn. Ahh. It was a mixture of earthy smells floating down from the Catskill Mountains, and of a fresh sea scent coming up from the Hudson River.

Catskills—poorly named, indeed! Cats do not have skills!

How he loved those special scents! It was times like this that Rip was thankful for his keen sense of smell.

At the edge of the village, Rip came upon the Van Felders' house. Dame Van Felder stood out front, pounding wildly at her door frame with a heavy hammer. She stopped for a moment, grumbled, then pounded some more.

"Good morning to you, Dame Van Felder." Rip sniffed at a bush on his way over to her. "Could I be of help?"

Dame Van Felder sighed. "It's this old hinge."

Rip took her hammer in his mouth. He whacked away at the hinge until the door swung freely.

"Thank you, Rip," said Dame Van Felder. She took the hammer from him, then gently scratched the fur between his ears. "This old door has needed attention for a long time. I have asked my husband a hundred times to fix it. Poor man, he's always busy with other work. And I was having a terrible time doing it myself." She smiled. "You are such a kind soul, Rip Van Winkle, to help me out."

Rip wagged his tail, pleased with her compliment. "I am glad to be of help, my good woman."

Dame Van Felder briefly dashed to the side of the house. She pumped some cool, refreshing water from the well to reward Rip for his hard work.

Moving back a bit from the house, Rip sat tall on his haunches, looking all around the place. His glance rose to the smoke curling from the chimney. Then his gaze dropped down to focus on the rest on the roof. "Alas." He pointed upward with his paw. "I shall return yet another day to make you some shingles. I see several are missing."

"You are truly a good man—a blessing to our village! Good day, Rip Van Winkle."

"A good day to you, Dame Van Felder." Before leaving, Rip lapped up the cup of water she had put down for him. Then, turning, he made his way merrily down the road.

Suddenly Rip stopped and pricked up his ears. He heard voices—children's voices! He trotted around a corner of an abandoned house. There he spotted three of his friends. His tail went into a high-speed wag.

"Hello there, lads! You're playing marbles again, I see. Are you all having fun?" He jumped into a pile of fallen leaves and barked with joy.

"Rip Van Winkle!" The children stopped their game to call out to him.

"Won't you play with us? Please?" begged the oldest.

"Oh, perhaps tomorrow," said Rip, who had joined their games many a time. "And I might even come with a story or two."

"Ooh, yes!" the children answered as one voice. They briefly put aside their game and went over to Rip.

Rip loved to tell stories to the children. He wasn't sure who enjoyed the telling more, the lads or himself. "I'll tell you about Indians and witches." Then he lowered his voice until the children leaned in close to him. "Or maybe I'll tell you about the *ghosts* that live up there." He gestured with a paw toward the mountains.

The children gasped with delight.

Reaching out with his paw, Rip tousled the youngest lad's hair. Then he dug into his pocket. He pulled out a small dog, a terrier, carved from wood. "Here you go, Delmond."

The child looked at the dog. Then he held it to his heart. "Thank you, Rip Van Winkle."

"You are most welcome."

When Rip pulled out nothing else, looks of disappointment crossed the other lads' faces.

Rip winked and pointed to the oldest boy. "Remember, it was I who gave you the kite last spring.

I taught you how to fly it, too. You learned well, I might say."

The boy smiled. "Will you fly it with me again soon?"

Rip stood on his hind legs and put his paw on the boy's waist. "Yes, as soon as the wind is right."

Then Rip looked to the middle child.

"And your toy, Martin—I am working on it. It's a puppet. It will be done soon enough. Then I look forward to a wonderful puppet show."

Brightening, Martin nodded.

To amuse his young friends, Rip jumped high into the air and flipped. Their laughter filled Rip's ears; the sound was like music. Happily, he wagged his tail.

Rip said good-bye to the boys and then continued toward the inn. He started to chase a falling leaf. All of a sudden, he caught sight of the Van Hatters' house. Rip stopped in his tracks—all four of them.

Dame Van Hatter stood outside her house, mumbling, pushing and pulling on a strip of her window latticework. In her frustration, she threw something across the yard. Rip briefly thought about chasing it, but instead, he trotted over to Dame Van Hatter.

Standing on his hind legs, he pressed a paw on the strip of wood. "Let me mend this lattice for you, Dame Van Hatter. I shall have it fixed in no time."

She nodded thankfully at Rip. "You have a big heart, Rip Van Winkle. A big, big heart."

Whoa! Have you noticed? Everybody seems to love Rip, *except* for his wife!

26

Rip picked up some tools. First he worked with one in his paws; then he worked with one in his mouth. Pounding and pulling, then tugging some more, Rip labored until the lattice was completely mended.

Dame Van Hatter stood back and admired his work. "This is so neighborly of you, Rip Van Winkle. Now stay put, and I'll get you a reward." She hurried into her house.

Well, he certainly knew what "stay" meant. And he liked people who brought him gifts—especially the kind that might come from the kitchen. A bowl of stew? A meaty bone? Biscuits? Those would all be very appreciated. Rip licked his lips in anticipation.

When Dame Van Hatter came back outside, she gave Rip a piece of johnnycake, a kind of bread made with cornmeal. "It's still warm from the pan," she said.

Rip took it in his teeth and chewed. "Mmm. Wonderful." Gulping, he gave his whiskers a quick lick for crumbs. *What? No seconds?* he thought, still hoping.

Rip wagged his tail. Helping the villagers gave him a good feeling. A bright day seemed even brighter when you were appreciated. Rip wished a good day to Dame Van Hatter, then padded off.

Down the lane he trotted, giving each dog he passed a neighborly wave of his paw. Not a one was displeased. All, in fact, gave him a friendly tail wag in return. Not once, in all Rip's days, had a village dog ever barked out against him.

Finally, Rip reached the King George Inn. His friends, Derrick Van Bummel and Nicholas Van Vedder, were already engaged in gossip. They sat outdoors on one of the inn's long wooden benches. Derrick Van Bummel was the local schoolmaster. Nicholas Van Vedder was the village patriarch—the oldest male in the village; sort of like the father or head honcho of the place. Van Vedder was also the landlord of the inn. The two men raised their tankards to Rip.

Tankard. There's a word we don't use every day. A tankard is a tall silver or pewter mug with a lid. It was a very common item back then. These men had their tankards filled with ale.

Rip jumped up on the bench to join his good friends. Another jump landed him on top of a large barrel of ale.

Derrick Van Bummel slapped Rip on the shoulder, knocking off his hat. "What say ye, Rip Van Winkle? Have ye been run out of the house again by your wife?"

"*Run* out of the house? Helllooo! *Swept* out of the house is more like it. Have you seen that broom of hers?" Rip asked.

Derrick chuckled.

Nicholas Van Vedder nodded and puffed on his pipe. Wide, lazy smoke rings rose into the air. Rarely had Rip heard Nicholas speak. But still, he usually knew the man's thoughts. The wide, lazy smoke rings meant that Nicholas agreed with a remark. Short, quick puffs meant he was displeased.

The men chatted, not about anything special; it was just small talk. Another fellow, Brom Dutcher, stopped by and joined them. Leaning against the big tree that sheltered the inn, he waved a newspaper in the air. "This was left behind by one of the inn's guests." He passed the paper on to Derrick Van Bummel, their usual reader. Being the schoolmaster, Derrick could pronounce even the most difficult words.

Derrick released a long, loud belch. He pointed to the headline. "We've not seen the likes of this since Peter Stuyvesant!"

Peter Stuyvesant was the last Dutch governor of colonial New York. His nickname was Old Silver-nails, because a stick of wood took the place of his right leg. The wooden leg was decorated with silver nails. What a grouch Peter Stuyvesant was! When people disagreed with him, he swore and stomped his wooden leg.

He was about as well liked as a cat in a dog-house. He was so unpopular, in fact, that when an English fleet landed in New York Bay in 1664, the Dutch settlers refused to defend their own land! The Dutch would rather live under English rule than have Peter Stuyvesant be their leader! All this happened more than a hundred years before this story takes place. Speaking of this story, let's return to it!

Rip brushed a paw across his nose as he breathed in Derrick's old-ale-breath burp. Disgusting! It was at a time like this that he wished his nose wasn't quite so superbly sensitive.

Rip didn't much care for talking about politics. He wagged his tail happily when the subject changed and the men chattered on freely again. Each one repeated all the gossip he'd recently heard around the village.

Rip's ears suddenly pricked up at the sound of footsteps approaching from behind him. They were the same thundering clomps he'd heard before he was shooed out of his house.

He thought about jumping down and hiding under the bench. Before he could make a move, a beefy, work-hardened hand grabbed him by the scruff of his neck. It was the hand of Dame Van Winkle!

She swung around in front of him, her face red and pinched with anger. She put her face close to Rip's wet nose. "I knew I'd find ye here, whiling away the hours storytelling. Spinning tales is about as useful as trying to chase yesterday. It won't get ye nothing or nowhere."

Dame Van Winkle gave the other men the evil eye. She pointed a sausage-like finger at Nicholas Van Vedder.

"It is ye who encourages my husband in these wicked ways. And it is ye who has helped bring ruin to our family! Shame. *Shame!*"

Nicholas uttered not a word, but short, angry puffs of smoke rose rapidly from his pipe.

Even before that moment, Rip knew what Nicholas's mood was. With his keen nose, Rip could smell Nicholas's anger. It was as strong as the scent of a startled skunk.

When no one spoke, Dame Van Winkle turned back to her husband. She pinched his spotted ear, making his head tilt. "Your children, too, are running around as ragged as urchins. What do ye have to say for yourself?"

In answer, Rip tucked his tail between his legs and cast his eyes upward. What could he say?

Dame Van Winkle stomped off, spitting out parting remarks. "Ye are no good a'tall. None of ye are. Idle hands are the devil's workshop!"

Rip's friends began to laugh. Even Nicholas Van Vedder broke down, bringing more creases to his old, well-wrinkled face.

But Rip did not laugh. He felt himself flush from the tip of his nose to the tip of his tail. He wanted to dig a hole and bury his head in it. Never before had Dame Van Winkle scolded him so mercilessly.

"It has been said," said Derrick Van Bummel, "that a man's good attitude and patience come from having a sharp-tongued wife." He winked and raised his tankard toward Rip. "If so, my friend, ye are three times blessed." He threw back his head and laughed heartily along with the others.

Rip buried his face in his paws. Alas, he felt like an absolute fool in front of his friends.

He jumped down from the keg. "After years of practice, that woman is a grand master at hounding me. I can take no more."

Positioning his hat comfortably over his ears, he turned to face his buddies.

"Today, my good men, I will go off and enjoy the solitude of the mountains."

With that, Rip set off down the lane, shooing off the chickens that stepped in his path. Soon he was alone, making his way along the banks of the Hudson River. Tree branches rustled in the breeze, occasionally sending a red or yellow leaf down for him to chase. High above him, to the west, a rope of gray mist appeared and snaked its way from tree to tree across the slope. Soon a thick, eerie fog began to descend over the mountains.

Chapter Three

Rip wound his way along the riverbank, through patches of cattails and low-lying wild plants and bushes. Now and then he stopped to lap up a mouthful of the cool, clear river water.

He stepped back from the rippling edge and searched his pockets. "I could sit and fish if only I'd brought something to make a hook." He pawed through his pockets a second time. "Oh, well, perhaps another day."

Rip pushed up his hat and readjusted his musket. He strolled on until he came to a clearing that led up the side of the mountain. An occasional bright wildflower, left over from summer, peeked out from the bushes along the trail.

Eagerly, Rip started up through the clearing. After he had gone a few steps, he suddenly hesitated in his tracks. He looked around, sniffing first the air, then the ground. "This is a nice path, but it's one I've not traveled before."

As he continued up the mountain, the air became cooler and the trees were more plentiful. Rip shook off a chill. Cocking his head, he released a contented sigh. "Ahh, I love listening to the mountains. All I hear is the wind whispering and the birds chirping. There's no nagging from Dame Van Winkle, and no laughter from the gentlemen at the inn."

Gentlemen, ha! Those guys were laughing like a bunch of hyenas.

Rip slowed down to sniff a bush. "It is a true pleasure to be amid the peace of the Catskills."

Suddenly Rip's ears perked up. From somewhere far below there came a growl. Rip's heart sped up as he sniffed the air. *A bear,* he thought.

"Bear? Excuse me. I don't want to become an afternoon snack. I'd better shake a leg." *Shake a leg?* he thought. *Try all four of them! Go, go, GO!*

Rip took off, racing up the path. Suddenly he stopped short; the path divided, forming a fork. Rip looked first one way, then the other. *Which way should I go?* he wondered. *Left? Right? Does one go up and the other down? Hmm . . .*

A squirrel darted out in front of him and headed straight up the mountainside between the two paths. Pushing off with his hind feet, Rip tore off after him.

Well, maybe there's safety in numbers! he thought. *Or maybe the squirrel knows something I don't—like where the bear-free zone is.*

Before long, the squirrel raced ahead and disappeared up a tree. Rip continued hotpawing it up the mountain until his four legs felt heavy as logs cut from a dogwood tree. His tongue was dry and hanging out of his thirsty mouth. He dropped to his belly on a grassy mound.

"I'm sure to be safe here!" Rip said, panting. He glanced around, then belly-crawled forward. The grass was so cool against his stomach fur that it almost felt damp. At the edge of the mound, Rip stopped and peered down through the trees. Below, through the thickening mist, the Hudson flowed silently. "Hmm, this mist is sort of yellowish, almost glowing." He sniffed the air but smelled nothing unusual.

Excuse me. Could this possibly be the same eerie glow that made the Indians and early settlers believe this place was haunted?

"I don't think I've trekked this high up the mountain before," said Rip between pants, looking longingly at the river. "A drink of that water would be most welcome after my climb." Alas, he sighed, and put his chin on his paws. Soon he dozed off.

Visions of Dame Van Winkle filled his dream. She was twice her regular size and had two heads, side by side. Her ears came to points, and catlike whiskers grew from each nose. She held Rip by a leash.

"Fix the roof, Rip," said one face.

"Plow the field," said the other with a scowl.

Rip tugged against the leash, so she shortened it.

"Build a fence!" hissed the first head.

"No, hunt for food!" said the second one.

Again Rip struggled against the leash that held

him, and again it was shortened. Before either head could give another command, Rip reared back, then lunged into the air, jerking free from the leash and his two-headed wife. He raced off into the distance.

"Riiip Vaaan Wiiinkle!" The scream of his wife pierced the air.

She could call if she wanted to, but he was not going to stop. He pumped his four legs harder, not even slowing to smell the best-looking trees.

"Rip Van Winkle! Rip Van Winkle!" The shouting continued.

"What?" Jolted from his sleep, Rip bolted up to all fours. He looked around for Dame Van Winkle. Finally realizing what had happened, he sighed with relief. "It was only a dream," he said, wagging his tail.

But his relief was short-lived. The lengthening shadows told him it would be dark soon. "I'll never make it home before nightfall now. Dame Van Winkle will have my spotted hide! And this time it won't be just a dream!"

The call that he thought was imaginary came to him a third time. "Rip Van Winkle."

The voice seemed to make the air around him vibrate. The fur on his back was bristling like that of a porcupine, and Rip looked down to a nearby glen, an isolated, narrow valley. All he saw was trees. "Helllooo! Who's there?"

It can't be the bear, he thought, *unless he's had a crash course in English.*

"Oh, come out, come out, wherever you are . . .

36

whoever you are," Rip added in a whisper. He didn't want to be considered a scaredy cat, but *brrrr!* This weird voice stuff, added to the glowing mist, gave him the shivers from his nose to his tail.

A tall man dressed in old-fashioned Dutch clothing stepped out from behind a pine tree. He started up the hill toward Rip. The fellow's breeches were decorated with a row of metal buttons down each leg. Oddly, they were oversized and dirty, even by Rip's standards. His doublet, too, was ill-fitting—much too large.

Here's a fashion flash from me, Wishbone. A doublet is a close-fitting jacket. Breeches are short trousers that stop just at, or below, the knees. Boy, am I glad I don't ever have to worry about wearing the right-size coat!

The man's face was as pale as milk, as if he hadn't seen the sun for quite some time. On one shoulder he carried a cider keg. It was so large and heavy that he bent from the weight. A smaller keg was tucked underneath his other arm.

The man motioned to Rip with his head.

Hmm . . . Rip pawed his chin and thought. *He's a strange-looking fellow. Let me see . . . his clothes are a bit out of style. He's got a big beard, bushy eyebrows, and wind-whipped hair. Nope, nobody I know. Should I be scared?*

As Rip continued staring, the man wound his way up a path through the pine trees. His right arm, which came in contact with the sunlight streaming through the branches, faded in and out of sight.

"Hmm . . ." Rip took a step back.

Finally the man's arm was exposed to an area of very bright sunlight, and the arm completely disappeared from Rip's vision. The small keg hung in the air at the fellow's side all by itself!

"Look, Ma, no hands!" Rip cried. "This is not good." He rubbed his face with his paws. "My eyes are playing tricks on me."

When Rip opened his eyes and looked again, the man's arm was back. But as Rip tried to release a sigh, his breath caught in his throat like a chicken bone. The man's entire head had dissolved away! Rip let out a howl.

Oh, boy! Things are getting exciting. Who is this guy with the vanishing body parts, and what does he want with Rip? I wonder how he knows Rip's name. Spooky! And did you get a load of his outfit? We're talking way out of style here, and not exactly sparkling-clean.

Speaking of clean, I wonder how Joe is coming with his room. I think I'll see if he's finished tidying it up yet. We have places to go, people to see, and lawns to explore!

Chapter Four

"Whazzat?" The sound of footsteps interrupted Wishbone's nap in the study.

"Let's go, Wishbone." Joe held up a leash.

"Go? You bet! Go where?" Wishbone jumped down from the chair and held perfectly still while Joe clicked the leash onto his collar.

It's not that I like the leash. In fact, I *don't* like it. But it's the only way I get to go for walks. And I love walks. Walks can lead to adventure!

"Come on, Joe!" Wishbone hurried to the front door.

After locking the door behind them, Joe headed straight for the sidewalk.

Wishbone tried to stop and sniff the lawn. "Hey, Joe, what do you say we dig in the dirt first? I've got a great bone buried next to the mums."

Joe kept going, giving the leash a gentle tug.

"Is that a 'no'?" Wishbone trotted up alongside Joe. "Nobody ever listens to the dog. Sometimes being cute just isn't enough."

As soon as Joe and Wishbone reached the library, Wishbone jumped up on the bench just outside the door.

"I know the routine."

He circled three times, then lay down on the old coat Joe had spread out for him. His head dropped down onto his paws. "Ooooh . . . sunshine and a bench. Lovely. It looks as if I might get a nap, after all."

As Joe bent over to tie the leash to the bench rails, his backpack swung forward and bumped Wishbone.

Wishbone sat up abruptly. "Hey! I'm assuming that was an accident."

Joe patted him. "Now, wait here. I won't be long." Then turning, Joe walked into the library.

Wishbone wagged his tail and used his best and deepest watchdog voice. "Never fear. While I'm on guard, the perimeter is secure."

Wishbone yawned. Before he could lie down again, an older woman in a colorful outfit came near his bench. She glanced around the library grounds. Finally her eyes stopped on the sign out front.

"Henderson Memorial Public Library," she read aloud. "Boy, have things changed!"

She shook her head, as if in disbelief, then walked over and scratched Wishbone under the chin.

"Well, I bet you're waiting for somebody, now, aren't you?" she asked.

Wishbone lifted his head higher for her. "Oh, yes, *that's* the spot. There's a good place on my back, too. Look for the big black circle." Wishbone wagged his tail. "Have we met, madam?"

The woman sat down beside him. "You know, I had a little fella who'd wait for me when I was a young girl."

His ears up and his head cocked, Wishbone yipped. "'Little fella'? Tell me more."

The woman scratched behind Wishbone's ear, making his hind foot thump on the bench in the same way as if he were actually scratching.

Alert! His mind snapped to attention. *Embarrassing move! Stop the leg. STOP the leg!*

The woman smiled at Wishbone. "My little fella would sit out here for as long as it took me to find the right book." She stood up and gazed toward the library door. "So many years have passed since I was last here."

Wishbone lay down. "What a nice lady." He went into his watchdog mode again. "Well, enjoy your trip to the library, ma'am!" Wishbone watched her walk inside, then closed his eyes. *ZZZZZZZZZZZZZZZ . . .*

Joe sighed as he walked back and forth in the reference section, scanning the shelves. He ran his fingertips across the book spines. *This would be a lot easier if I knew what I was looking for,* he thought.

Stopping his fingers at a set of encyclopedias, Joe grabbed three volumes at random. Then he turned and grabbed a paperback dictionary from the shelf behind him.

This is as good a place as any to start, he thought.

As Joe walked over to sit down at the table where he'd left his backpack, a grandmotherly-aged woman in a colorful outfit entered the library. Her flowered vest had some of the same darker colors as her purse and shoes. Joe watched curiously as she stood in the entranceway and gave the place the once-over.

Who is she? he wondered. Joe slid the top encyclopedia toward himself. Without even looking down, he randomly flipped it open. He couldn't remember ever seeing this lady around Oakdale. She looked sort of important—like a teacher, maybe.

Joe dug around in his backpack and pulled out his notebook paper and a pencil. He watched the woman walk over to the model house on display in the center of the library. She bent down for a closer look.

Plopping an elbow on the table, Joe rested his chin in the palm of his hand. *I should be looking for a project idea,* he thought, *not sitting here staring into space.* Lost in thought, he thumped his eraser on the encyclopedia. He'd never get an idea at this rate.

Joe forced himself to look down at the open book. ALABAMA was printed in bold letters at the top of the page. *No good—that's still around,* he thought, flipping through more pages. He reached the end of the volume. His mind wandered to the hockey game Sam had planned. *Who's going to play?* he wondered. *Hopefully, not Damont Jones.*

"Oh, excuse me!"

Joe looked up. The older lady had turned away

from the display and was apologizing to Joe's mom, the librarian.

"I'm so sorry I bumped into you," she said kindly. "I wasn't watching where I was going." She slid her purse straps from one arm to the other. "I guess I'm sort of preoccupied."

Like me, Joe thought.

Ellen smiled. "There's no harm done. I was just on my way to my desk. May I help you find something?"

The woman shook her head. "Thank you, but no. I just stopped in to see the library. I wanted to see if it had changed as much as everything else in this town has."

Joe watched her glance from wall to wall.

"There are so many books now! It's not like when I was young." A smile spread across her face. "It's hard to believe this is where I used to come every Saturday."

Wow! Joe thought. He liked to read, but he didn't think he'd want to spend *every* Saturday here.

"Oh, how long ago was that?" asked Ellen.

"Goodness!" The woman chuckled. "It's been close to fifty years."

"Oh, my!" Ellen reshelved a stray book in the rack next to her.

The woman reached out and gently spun the globe sitting atop the same shelf. "I left Oakdale forty years ago to practice medicine in Chicago." She smiled. "My parents were so proud. I was the very first black person from Oakdale to become a doctor." Her smile widened. "That was quite a rarity for those days, especially for a woman." She fingered her purse straps. "I retired last year, just after my husband passed away. I thought it was high time for me to revisit my roots."

I knew she was someone important, Joe thought.

Ellen folded her hands in front of her and nodded. "Well, welcome back! And feel free to look around as long as you like . . . Dr. . . . ?"

"Brown. Thelma Brown."

Ellen extended her hand. "It's a pleasure to meet you, Dr. Brown. I'm Ellen Talbot, and I hope you thoroughly enjoy your visit." Her voice took on a serious tone. "And I'm sorry about your husband."

"Thank you, Ellen. I sure do miss him. He was a sweet man." She nodded at the books. "And he loved spinning yarns. I expected to see his name on a book one day, but he never seemed to find the time to put his stories to paper."

As Ellen nodded, the phone on the reference desk began to ring. "Oh, will you excuse me, please?" She glanced toward the phone. "I have to get that."

Dr. Brown smiled. "Of course."

Hurrying to her desk, Ellen took the call.

Without an excuse to stall, Joe finally looked down at his paper. "Still blank," he mumbled. Then he drew in a deep breath and exhaled loudly. He picked up the dictionary. But before he even opened it, he glanced up and saw Dr. Brown heading toward him.

She smiled. "Since we're the only ones here this morning, I'm guessing that's your dog out by the front door."

"Uh . . . yes, ma'am," Joe replied, smoothing a ragged corner of the dictionary. "His name is Wishbone."

Dr. Brown winked. "He looks like a keeper."

"He sure is." A smile spread across Joe's face. "He's the best."

"You know, when I was young, I had a dog that was the best, too. He was a beautiful golden retriever named Champion." She chuckled. "He was a champion at being lovable and stealing laundry off the neighbor's clothesline."

Joe laughed. "That sounds sort of like Wishbone. He likes to dig holes in our neighbor's yard."

Dr. Brown tilted her head. "I hope your neighbor is understanding."

"Uh . . . pretty much so," Joe said.

Nodding, Dr. Brown walked on, continuing her tour of the library. Joe opened up the dictionary and went back to searching out an idea for his social-studies paper.

Outside the library, Wishbone basked in the sun, enjoying every minute of his nap on the library bench. But a crow flying low over his head cawed and startled him. His head popped up; the fur on his back bristled.

"Who's there?" he called.

But Wishbone was alone . . . except for the crow on the roof, watching and waiting.

Wishbone thought of Rip Van Winkle in the Catskills, alone on a mountaintop. At least Rip had thought he was alone, until he was startled by that strange-looking fellow. Where in the world did he come from? Maybe that was the key to his mystery.

Chapter Five

"Hello!" Rip called to the man climbing up the hillside. Now the stranger had a head, but only one leg. "Helllooo!" he called louder, wagging his tail uncertainly as he peered into the glen.

The fellow coming toward him made no attempt to wave or speak.

"Okay," Rip said, "so his hearing's not as keen as mine. I guess that's to be expected when your ears come and go."

Glancing to the side of the glen, Rip noticed a fine stream of water trickling between some boulders. He licked his lips. *So near, yet so far*, Rip thought. His tongue was as dry as a month-old T-bone.

Before reaching Rip, the fellow stopped and set down the small keg that he had carried under his arm. His hand disappeared as a ray of sun stretched through the leaves and touched it. The man leaned forward, and as his hand entered the shadows, it reappeared. With a great heave, he put down the large keg that had been on his shoulder. He gestured for Rip to come to him.

"Me?" Rip did a quick check over his shoulder to see if the man was motioning to someone behind him. As he suspected, not a soul was there—just tree after tree after tree. "Hmm. Me, it is," Rip said, taking a puppy-sized step forward.

Waiting silently, the stranger motioned again. For a second his elbow disappeared in a spot of sunlight, leaving his wrist unconnected to the rest of his arm.

"That's quite a load you have there," Rip called, taking a few more small steps and cautiously wagging his tail. "Although your own weight seems to . . . uh . . . change quite a bit. Ha-ha!"

As the stranger stepped away from the trees and into a pool of sunlight, he completely disappeared.

"Hello? Helllooo? Neat trick," Rip said, looking around nervously. "Could you show me how it's done?" That might really come in handy on bath day!

The stranger appeared again in the shade of a pine tree, but still he said nothing. More than a bit uneasy, Rip dropped his tail down. He continued slowly to wag it, to show he was of a friendly nature.

Helping him is the neighborly thing to do, thought Rip. *He must be new to the village, someone who has lost his way.* No, Rip could not, in good conscience, leave the fellow to wander alone in the wild mountains; the man's good luck might . . . er . . . disappear if he should venture too close to that bear.

But Rip cocked his head as another doubt burrowed

its way into his thoughts. Wouldn't he have heard about any newcomers from Derrick Van Bummel or Brom Dutcher that morning at the King George Inn? They had spent an hour speaking of such things. *Well,* he thought, *maybe this guy is just an old stray.* If that was the case, he really needed Rip's help.

A low, thunderlike rumble split the air; Rip responded with a jump and a yelp. His heart beat fast and hard in his furry chest. Rip looked at the fluffy gray clouds above him. Then he held up his paw to check the humidity.

"Perhaps we're going to have a thundershower— not surprising, way up here, especially at this time of year."

But even as he said it, Rip realized the few clouds above were not dark storm clouds.

The strange man, entirely visible now, didn't say a word. But again he motioned to Rip.

As was his nature, Rip gave in to his kinder thoughts. With a friendly hello bark, he trotted down the hillside toward the man. "I'm sure he means me no harm." But upon approaching the stranger and sniffing, Rip again reconsidered. There was another oddity about the man that Rip could not deny. It all came down to Rip's keen nose.

Rip raised his nose and sniffed high. He sniffed low. He sniffed deep. No matter how hard or where he sniffed, he could not smell the man. No scent of fear. No scent of dirt, or sweat, or food, or tobacco. Absolutely nothing.

Okay, stay loose and stay cool, Rip thought, trying to hide his feeling of concern. He wagged his tail. "So, you need a little help lugging the old refreshments up to a party, huh?" Rip stood face to face with the fellow. "Well, it just so happens I have some time on my . . . uh . . . well . . . hands. Ha-ha! I'm your . . . er . . . man. Lead on."

The man bent, picked up the small keg, and turned. Rip held out his paws. But the stranger tucked the keg under his own arm. He started to trudge up a dry gully path that led toward the trickling water.

"Hmm. I was actually going to take the small keg, but . . . okay." Rip stood on his hind legs and, with a grunt, began rolling the large keg up the path with his front paws. The contents inside sloshed with each turn.

Ahead of Rip, the stranger moved in what seemed to be slow motion—every swing of his arm, every step of his feet—smooth and flowing. One by one, each tree the man passed rustled, as if the wind had blown on that tree alone.

"Okaaay . . ." Rip cast a glance to his left, wondering if *he* had the same effect on the trees. Nope. "Hey . . . uh . . . where are we going?" Rip called.

Looking over his shoulder, the stranger gestured for Rip to keep following him.

Rip kept rolling the keg with his front paws. "So, what's your name?" he asked cheerfully. He waited, but the fellow never answered. "Where are you from? Helllooo! Feel free to jump right in and interrupt me anytime you want." Rip sighed. "No? Questions too tough for you, huh? Well, okay, let's try another. What's in the keg? Cider? Ale?"

Silently the man continued his ascent, with parts of his body disappearing, then reappearing.

"Do you think I ask too many questions?" Rip asked.

Again the man gave no response.

"Have you always been this gabby?" Rip asked. He couldn't help wondering why this odd fellow needed kegs of ale carried up the wild mountain.

At that moment, as the stranger turned to look at Rip, thunder crashed through the mountain again.

"Whoa!" Rip nearly jumped out of his hide. "That thunder catches me off guard every time." He cast a suspicious glance at the near-cloudless sky. "No comment, huh?"

Great, thought Rip. *I've had more satisfying conversations with a fire hydrant!*

"Ugh." Rip grunted and leaned all of his weight into the keg. "This . . . ugh . . . thiiing . . . is getting harder . . . ugh . . . and harder to push, and there are some really . . . ugh . . . great trees around here. How about if we . . . ugh . . . maaake a pit stop?"

The stranger kept walking, but Rip stopped.

"Whew!" He balanced the barrel on a flat rock jutting out from the hillside. "And could you check your pockets for snacks? I'm working like a dog here, and it's making me hungry." He shook as best he could, while keeping the keg in place with his paws. "And how are you at back rubs? My shoulders are a little stiff from all this uphill pushing stuff."

When the fellow failed to answer, Rip sighed.

"Okay. Guess I'll take that as a 'no.'"

Grunting, Rip leaned forward and gave the keg an extra-hard push. No sooner had he started rolling it uphill again when the stranger stopped and put down the smaller keg.

"You mean we're here?" Rip asked, relieved his job was almost done. In his excitement he produced a burst of power that nearly rolled him right over the barrel. "Oh!"

Catching himself, he gave his keg a final nudge so it came to rest alongside the smaller one. He looked up. There stood the fellow with his right side in the sun, so only one side of him was visible. *You may be tall,* Rip thought, *but you're only half the man I am. Ha-ha!*

He smiled. "Well, stranger, I was glad to help out, but I really need to be off now. . . . Hey!"

Rip caught sight of a hollow through a large split in the side of the gully.

"Would you look at that?" He jumped on top of the big keg and stretched his neck for a better view. A group of men were playing ninepins in the clearing. "It wasn't thunder I've been hearing—it was bowling balls!"

Ninepins is a game similar to bowling, only the ball is smaller and held in the hand, and only nine pins are used, not ten. Bowling pins are arranged in a triangle formation. Ninepins are arranged in a diamond shape.

As Rip watched the men, their arms and legs faded in and out of sight, just as his guide's had. "Okay, fellas," he said, "let's see if you guys can keep your heads."

Chapter Six

Rip continued to peer into the open space at the men bowling ninepins, as a thin, low fog began to swirl around the edges of the clearing. The men's arms and legs disappeared and then reappeared as they met the sun's rays reaching through the split in the gully. Rip moved his own paw in and out of the light, but nothing happened. "Hmm . . . solid as a rock."

One of the fellows rolled a ball at the pins, creating another thunderous crash as the ball struck the pins.

"Hey, this is great!" Rip ran through the divide and into the clearing. "It must be league day! Okay, I'll stick around for one game, but then I really—"

Solemn-faced, the men all turned and looked at Rip.

Abruptly, Rip dropped to his haunches. "Was it something I said?"

Without uttering a word, or changing their expressions, the men turned back to their game.

"Guys? Gentlemen?" Rip wagged his tail. Waiting for a reply, he studied them. They were dressed in the same old-fashioned clothing as Rip's guide—dusty pants that ended just below the knees, and tattered coats. Swords hung at their sides.

Rip sniffed the air. These men, too, were scentless. It was odd. Everything in the world had an aroma, and Rip had a wonderful nose. Why, then, couldn't he smell these men?

As Rip continued to watch, he noticed that one fellow seemed to be the leader of the group. Silently, the men looked to him for guidance. It was he who nodded for the next player, and it was he who pointed out who should set up the pins.

"Hmm." Rubbing his chin with his paw, Rip checked out the top dog even further. He was dressed not unlike the others, but his face seemed older, and more weather-beaten. It was difficult to tell for sure, though. All the men wore rather long hair, and all but one wore beards that hid their pale faces. Some had wide moustaches, too; many of them grew so long that they drooped.

Then it hit Rip like a ton of dog biscuits! This odd group of men were dressed just like the sailors in the old painting in the church pastor's house. The painting had been brought over to America from Holland by the very first settlers in the area.

The fellow without a beard, who looked a bit younger than the others, rolled a ball at the pins. "I'll get it!" Rip called, chasing after it. He came to an abrupt stop when the fellows turned and stared. *I guess that ball would be pretty hard on the teeth*, Rip thought. He wagged his tail. "Maybe I'll just wait for my turn."

The commander of the group put a ball down in front of him.

"All right, boys. Watch and learn!" Rip called out.

He removed his musket from his shoulder, leaned it against a tree, then nosed the ball straight ahead. He stepped back and watched it hit the pins. *Crash!*

"Look at that! A strike!" Rip flipped in the air, then made a perfect four-point landing. He looked around at the strangers, who were still somber and silent, with body parts partially missing. "Am I showing too much enthusiasm?"

Another ball was set in front of him. With his nose, he pushed it straight toward the pins, too. A thunderous peal ripped through the silence as the ball hit the pins.

"Woo-hoo! Another strike!" Rip pawed the air. "Hey, loosen up, guys. You look as if you've been rolling gutter balls all afternoon!"

The men looked at one another, puzzled.

Rip wagged his tail. "Whatsa matta? Catskills got your tongue? Ha-ha!"

Again the men exchanged looks of puzzlement.

"Oooh . . . tough crowd . . ." Rip looked around. Someone had moved the kegs into the clearing. Spotting a number of mugs on a tree stump next to the small keg, Rip trotted toward it. "Okay, then, drinks for everybody. Come on, fellas!"

Rip slid a mug over, then opened the spigot on the small keg with his paw. Some sort of cider flowed into the mug beneath it. Rip sniffed. Now, *this* he could smell! And it had a mouth-watering aroma.

"Step right up, gentlemen," Rip said, filling mug after mug to the brim. "No need to be shy. There's plenty to go around." He chuckled. With his paw, he pushed another mug under the spigot.

One by one, the strange men gathered around. All of them completely visible, they picked up mugs of cider. Without a word, they sat and began to drink.

Rip smiled. "I was hoping for a bit of conversation now," Rip said to the men, "but I guess you're all the strong, silent type. And it seems you're all . . . er . . . *solid* citizens now—if you get my drift."

The men came back to Rip for refills from the keg. Then they returned to their ninepins game.

Rip watched them play for a while. "Hmm . . . everyone always bowls a strike," he mused.

Finally Rip turned back to the keg.

"Maybe I'll try a wee bit of this brew myself," he decided. "I still have quite a thirst from that long climb up the mountain." He drew himself a full mug, then lapped up a sample. "All right. This stuff is *good*."

He sat down a moment to scratch his ear. Then he got up and took another taste.

"This stuff is equal to the very best beverage of Holland." Stretching out his tongue, he took another drink . . . and another . . . and another. Through blurry eyes, he noticed the sun had dipped behind the mountains. Although the tree-studded land around him was as dark as tar, the clearing was nicely lit. *Almost glowing.* And not by sunlight. "Oh, boy."

As Rip licked the cider from his whiskers, he began to get sleepy. He tried to walk off the feeling. His legs seemed to tangle, and he felt like he had eight to keep straight instead of four. His head felt as heavy as a cannonball.

Rip shook, trying to rid himself of the feeling. Gradually, he moved slower and slower, and his head dropped lower and lower. He called out to the strange men: "Hey, fellas? I could really use a hand . . ."

Rip gently dropped to his side. With his head resting on a mound of grass, he fell into a deep sleep.

This time Rip slept for twenty years. . . .

Chapter Seven

"Playtime!" Wishbone raced across the front yard, around Joe and Ellen. Then he shot through the piles of leaves they were raking together.

"Wishbone!" Joe stopped working and held his hand up to shield his eyes from the sun. "We'll never get done if you keep scattering the leaves all over."

"It looks as though he has some energy to burn," said Ellen.

"Very good, Ellen." Wishbone leaned down on his

elbows and barked at Joe. "Come on, buddy. Let's play tag." He turned and raced away. "You're it!" Glancing over his shoulder, he noticed Joe still leaning on his rake. Wishbone circled back and barked again. "No, huh? How about you, Ellen? Want to play?"

But Ellen wouldn't chase him, either.

Wishbone lay down on Joe's pile of leaves for a moment. Then he jumped back up. "Okay. I'm sure I can find something else to entertain me. Let's see what you guys have buried in here." Wishbone began to dig, sending leaves sailing into the air.

"Wishbone!" Joe and Ellen called at the same time.

Abruptly, Wishbone dropped to his haunches. "Whatever it was, I didn't do it." He looked at Joe and Ellen, then at the leaves he'd scattered. "Oh . . . you mean this. I was looking for treasure. You know, if I found anything, I'd share it with you. We're partners, right? And partners don't get upset with each other for just one little mistake. Right?" He wagged his tail. "Say *right*, Joe, say it. Come on."

Instead, Joe nodded over Wishbone's head to a dark blue car driving slowly into their cul-de-sac. "I wonder who that is," Joe said.

As they watched, the car slowed even more. Then it turned into their driveway.

"Company!" Wishbone wagged his tail. "That means snacks. How about coffee cake, Ellen? That's always good. And it creates lots of crumbs." He stepped closer to her. "Or what about finger sandwiches? Hold the fingers and please double the bologna on mine, thank you."

"It's Dr. Brown," Ellen said. She laid down her rake and headed toward the car.

Joe followed. "The lady from the library?"

"Yes, Joe." Ellen stepped up and held the car door open for her. "What a pleasant surprise, Dr. Brown! What brings you out to Forest Lane?"

"Snacks, Ellen!" Wishbone barked. "She's here for snacks! Everybody to the kitchen!" He started toward the front door, but when no one followed him, he stopped. "Okay, maybe in a minute or two." Wishbone wagged his tail and trotted over to greet Dr. Brown, too.

A smile spread across Dr. Brown's face as she got out of her car. "This truly is a surprise, Ellen—much more than you know." She looked over at the front porch. "Finally, I'm seeing something in this town that hasn't changed much." Her glance returned to Ellen and Joe. "I grew up in this very house," she said.

Ellen smiled in surprise. "What a small world!"

"Wow!" Joe said. "This is where you lived with your dog, Champion?"

"This is it," said Dr. Brown. "We spent many happy days playing together on this very lawn."

"Aha!" Wishbone sat up tall, waiting to be noticed. "Now I know who buried those prehistoric soup bones in the backyard."

"Hello, Wishbone. Nice to see you again." Dr. Brown bent to pet him. Then she pointed to the side yard. "That garage is where Champion slept the night he tangled with a skunk." She made a sour face. "He came home smelling something awful."

"Ooh, tough break," Wishbone said.

Dr. Brown continued. "My parents wouldn't let him come inside the house. I was sure he'd die of a broken heart, all alone in the garage. From the very first night we got him, he'd always slept on the floor next to my bed."

"I hope he had a nice soft rug!" Wishbone said.

"I begged my parents to let me bathe him so he could come inside, but they refused." She smiled. "Finally they explained. We needed to bathe him in tomato juice to get rid of the odor. And we couldn't do that until the store opened in the morning." She sighed and shook her head. "I'm not sure who was more lonely—Champion, or me. It was a very long night."

Joe raised his eyebrows. "And did the tomato juice work?"

"It sure did." Dr. Brown smiled. "He really hated that bath, though."

"That's not a surprise," Wishbone said. "Baths in water are bad enough." He turned and ran to the steps. "Now, come on, Ellen, invite her in. I'm hungry."

"It was the last time Champion ever came home smelling like skunk."

"Wishbone hasn't met up with a skunk yet," Joe said, bending to stroke his fur. "Hey, where'd he go?" Joe looked around.

Ellen smiled. "He's on the porch. . . . And hopefully he never will tangle with one."

"You can bet on it, Ellen," Wishbone said.

"There probably aren't many skunks around here these days," Dr. Brown said. She looked over at the adjoining houses. "Look at all those lovely plants next door. Someone is quite a gardener."

"Wanda Gilmore." Ellen brushed a bug away from her face. "Do you remember the Gilmores?"

"I should say so!" Dr. Brown sounded pleased. "Wanda still lives there?"

"Uh-huh." Ellen nodded.

"That's the yard I told you about at the library," Joe said. "The one Wishbone likes to dig in."

"Oh, my!" Dr. Brown chuckled. "I guess you could say he has good taste."

"It's the perfect place to bury my treasure." Wishbone wagged his tail. "Soft soil, easily accessible, and a place Bruno the Doberman wouldn't think to look for my stuff." He paused. "Those pink flamingos standing guard over there couldn't care less what I do. Now, speaking of my good taste, how about if we go inside and get something that tastes good? . . . Ellen?"

Dr. Brown moved her purse from one arm to the other. "I can't believe Wanda still lives there. Why, the last time I saw her, she was just a toddler."

"Believe me," Wishbone said, "she's a lot bigger now."

"Would you like to come in for some coffee?" Ellen asked.

"Thank you, Ellen!" Wishbone said.

"We'd love to hear more about the house. And Oakdale." Ellen glanced up the street. "And Wanda should be back soon. I'd like to invite her over before you have to leave. I'm sure she'd want to see you."

"A Wanda Warning! Thank you again, Ellen." Wishbone hurried to the front door. "And don't forget about Champion. We want to hear more about him, too."

"I'd be delighted to stay." Dr. Brown walked with Joe and Ellen to the porch. "You don't know what an unexpected treat it is to be invited in. I didn't want to intrude on anyone. I'd just planned on driving by for a look at the place. I had a wonderful childhood here."

Joe raised his eyebrows. "It's hard to believe you lived here, too—before us."

Dr. Brown turned to him and winked. "Believe it. Have you found the secret hiding place upstairs yet?"

Joe looked surprised. "No."

"Think of it, Joe." Wishbone wagged his tail. "A secret hiding place—right in our very own house! What a surprise."

I bet Rip Van Winkle felt a little surprised himself when he woke up from his marathon nap in the mountains.

Chapter Eight

Rip blinked open his eyes, then squinted against the glaring sun. He pulled himself out from under a thick blanket of leaves, then sat on his haunches. "Ooooh, my head!"

Adjusting his hat with his paw, he looked around.

"So many leaves have fallen—the wind must have kicked up quite a storm last night." Last night! That meant he'd spent the whole night on the mountain!

Frantically, he turned and looked at the sun. It was in the east—a rising sun. Morning!

"Oh, boy! I'm in Dame Van Winkle's dog house now! What excuse shall I give her for staying away the entire night?" He nosed a tender shoulder. "And if a fit of the rheumatism should lay me up, I shall have a blessed time with her. Never will I hear the end of it."

He recalled what happened before he fell asleep. He remembered the strange man with the kegs, leading him up the gully path. He thought about the clearing and the gloomy party of silent men playing ninepins. *And he recalled the drink of ale!*

Anxiously, Rip rose to all fours. He groaned and wiggled his shoulder. "I'm so stiff my bones are creaking like an old gate. These mountain beds do not agree with me."

Upon looking around further, Rip realized he stood on the grassy mound where he'd first seen the stranger in the glen.

"But the glen was not covered with leaves then. It was a beautiful green." He eyed the nearby trees, which were now mostly bare. "Never before have I seen them stripped so fast. It's so strange!"

With a shake, Rip removed the last remnants of leaves from his fur.

"Where is everybody? Helllooo! Helllooo! I guess the bowling team's left. And they didn't even leave a trophy." He looked around. "Hmm . . . now where did I put my musket?"

No sooner were the words out of his mouth than he spotted a gun poking out of the leaves. Rip picked up the musket in his teeth and leaned it against a nearby tree.

"This is not mine!" he growled. "Mine was a clean, well-oiled musket." He ran his paw along the barrel. "This gun is covered with rust, and the lock is falling off!" Lowering his head, he eyed the wooden gun butt even more carefully. "Look at all those holes! The stock is worm-eaten!"

Rip turned abruptly in search of the men.

"I think my former bowling buddies have played a trick on me," he grumbled. "They stole my gun and left me this useless firearm.

"Fellas?" Rip barked loudly. "I think someone took my musket by mistake. I'll give you yours if you give me mine."

Rip cocked his head and listened for footsteps. But the only sounds he heard were those of the insects crawling through the leaves. He called again, but not one man showed himself.

"So it's hide-and-seek," said Rip, remembering their disappearing-in-the-sun trick. "With the Body-Parts-Я-Us team." He slung the rusty musket onto his back. "My first spot to check will be the hollow where we played ninepins."

The stiffness in Rip's shoulder gave him an uneven walk as he made his way to the edge of the mound. His glance swept over the shadows for signs of the men. Then Rip looked to the waterfall on the side of the narrow valley. No longer was it just a fine stream of water!

"What?" he said in total surprise.

Rip rubbed a paw across his eyes, then looked again.

"This can't be!" he said, astonished. He watched a wide stream gush over the edge and frothily flow from rock to rock. The waterfall completely hid the section of gully where he and his mysterious guide had climbed yesterday.

With some difficulty, Rip made his way down into the glen. He pawed through the underbrush, and he put his nose to the ground and sniffed.

"Why can't I detect my own scent from yesterday? I may just have to take this nose of mine in for a thousand-mile checkup!

"And where did all this thick growth of bushes come from?" He moved along through patches of birch, sassafras, and witch hazel trees. He kept sniffing. "Look at all the yellow blossoms on the witch hazel." He nosed one. "These appear late in the fall, not now." A lone partridge flew up from the brush, startling him. Rip barked. "That really sends my heart into double-time."

Rip pushed on. Ahead was the mountain stream, wide and foaming, filling the glen below.

Hurrying forward, he stopped only once, to free a paw tangled in the wild grapevines growing between the trees. "I will trot right up to those fellows and demand the return of my musket!"

Finally, he reached the part of the gully that yesterday had opened to the hollow. Rip slipped behind the waterfall and searched the area with his eyes. He reached up with his front paws and pushed.

"Oh, boy, I'm in trouble now."

Where there had been the opening, now there stood a solid rock cliff. A torrent of water gushed over it. Rip searched the cliff again with his eyes. Not one trace of the opening to the hollow remained.

Chapter Nine

"Helllooo? Knock-knock?" Rip stared at the rock wall. The cold spray from the waterfall washed over him. "What is going on?" He shook off the water droplets from his fur. "And I thought yesterday was weird."

Turning, Rip made his way from the waterfall back to the trees. His stiffness seemed to have eased somewhat. Strangely, however, his walk was still slower than normal. It felt as if he had weights strapped to all four legs, holding him back. Suddenly his stomach growled like an angry dog. He glanced up at the sun, now higher in the sky.

"What should I do? The morning is quickly passing by. I'm famished. I must get home if I do not wish to starve among the mountains. And I do not!"

He sniffed.

"The air smells different today than yesterday. Perhaps it's all the decaying leaves." Rip pawed the ground. "Decaying leaves? Leaves do not decay overnight!"

71

He sat down for a moment and looked around.

"Is this odd, or what? The season seems to have changed from early fall to near winter in one day. Impossible!

"Helllooo!" Rip called once more to the men, wagging his tail hopefully. "I give up. Ally, ally, in come free! Show your faces! Or an arm. How about just a foot?"

But his only answer was the cawing from a flock of crows, high above him in a bare tree. There were so many that Rip thought they looked like black leaves. But instead of fluttering in the breeze, the crows stood quite still, except for an occasional bob of their heads. Secure in their perch, they seemed to look down on Rip and sneer at his confusion.

"Excuse me. It's not polite to stare," Rip barked at them.

The crows flew off, leaving Rip alone with his unanswered question.

"What am I to do?" he asked. "I want my own musket so I can go home. Yet home is where Dame Van Winkle waits with her broom." He snapped at a fly buzzing around his head. "Alas, it is unfortunate that a harsh temper will not mellow with age." He shook his head. "A sharp tongue is the only tool with an edge that grows sharper with constant use. That woman's tongue should be considered a lethal weapon!"

Rip sighed and searched for the path leading down the mountain.

"I will stand tall and take my punishment like

a . . . er . . . man. After all, home is where Judith and young Rip wait for me." A smile crossed his face. "The hours we spend together are a joy to me."

Rip put his nose to the ground.

"Now where is that path?" Sniffing, he zigzagged through the bare, gray trees. "It's vanished, just like my musket."

A flash of movement in a shady spot up ahead caught Rip's eye. He stopped and glanced around.

"Fellas? Yoo-hoo."

A squirrel scurried out from the spot and dashed across to another tree.

"Alas." Rip sighed. "Just a critter. Perhaps I am stuck with this rusty musket," he said. As he spoke, his stomach growled again. "I'm so hungry, my stomach sounds like the bear I heard yesterday."

After one last glance into the shadows, Rip continued down the mountain, careful to listen for the real bear.

At the first faint sound of the Hudson River, a sense of comfort came over Rip. He stopped and scratched his brown ear.

"Soon I will be at my village, and life will not be so mysterious. Perhaps I can visit a neighbor and receive some food before I return to the anger of Dame Van Winkle." He adjusted his hat. "A half-full stomach will help make her tongue-lashing tolerable."

But as Rip descended the mountain and neared the village, another strange thing occurred. Just ahead, a dog trotted along the riverbank toward him.

"Hello there, fella!" Rip called. He raised a paw and waved. Then he realized the dog was unfamiliar to him. "Where did you come from, pup? I've not seen you around here before."

The dog lowered his head and tail. He growled at Rip, circling wide to avoid him in passing.

"It cannot be!" Rip said, his heart heavy in his chest. "Never has a village dog taken a stand against me! Never . . . Something is *very* wrong."

Chapter Ten

When Ellen opened the front door, Wishbone led everyone inside the house. "To the kitchen, people!" He went on ahead. Then he turned and glanced over his shoulder. Ellen and Dr. Brown were following him, but Joe stood still, staring curiously up the staircase.

"Energy, Joe—we need food for energy." Wishbone wagged his tail. "Then we'll find the secret hiding place."

"Come on, Joe," Ellen called. "Have some lemonade. After we have coffee and visit, I'm sure Dr. Brown wouldn't mind showing you that special hiding place."

"Mind? Are you kidding?" Dr. Brown asked as they entered the kitchen. "I'd love it."

Joe smiled. "It's a deal."

Wishbone stood in the middle of the kitchen. "And the cute little dog should sit where, Ellen?"

"Please sit down, Dr. Brown." Ellen nodded toward the kitchen table. Then she went to open a cabinet.

Joe poured himself a glass of lemonade, then

added ice. He sat down at the table, next to Dr. Brown. Ellen brewed some coffee. Then she pulled two mugs from the cabinet, picked up the coffeepot, and poured. She looked to the table. "Cream or sugar, Dr. Brown?"

"Helllooo!" Wishbone said. "Gee, Ellen, I'm not *too* famished or anything. Oh, well . . . I'll just find my own seat." He walked over and sat next to Joe's chair. "I'm in the mood for crumbs, pal. Big ones."

"I'd like a little sugar in my coffee, please." Dr. Brown glanced around the kitchen, a contented look on her face. "My mother cooked many wonderful meals in here. Every Sunday she made the best pot roast with gravy. And once a week she made up a double batch of the most wonderful oatmeal cookies."

Wishbone watched Dr. Brown breathe in deeply and smile.

"You know, I can almost smell those cookies right now," she said.

Joe and Ellen chuckled. "Maybe it's because Joe and I made oatmeal cookies last night," Ellen said, setting a mug of coffee in front of Dr. Brown.

"Oh!" Dr. Brown laughed, too. "I bet you're right."

Ellen went and put some of the cookies on a plate. She carried them to the table and sat down. As the three of them each took one, Joe looked longingly toward the staircase.

"Thinking about that secret hiding place?" Dr. Brown asked.

"Food *and* adventure—my kind of day!" Wishbone wagged his tail.

76

"I sure am," Joe said, taking a bite of his cookie, then setting it down.

"Helllooo! The dog is hungry, too. Okay, I guess I'll have to change my tactics." He sat up and begged.

"Isn't he cute!" Dr. Brown reached out and scratched Wishbone between the ears. "It looks like he wants a cookie, too."

Wishbone pawed the air. "Well, thank goodness someone around here can read body language."

Joe jumped up. "I'll get his ginger snaps."

"I can live with that." Wishbone followed him to the cabinet and waited.

Joe opened the box. Then he held out three dog cookies in the palm of his hand.

"Thank you." Wishbone took one. "One . . . mmm . . . ginger snap. Two . . . mmm . . . Three . . . Wait! Don't put them away yet. How about another one? That's an economy-size box, Joe. You get more for the money."

Joe stuck the box back in the cabinet and returned to the table.

"Is that a firm 'no'? Okay." Wishbone trotted back and sat next to Joe again. "All right, then, now for those crumbs. Do not lean over the table to eat your cookie, Joe. Let me repeat that. *Do not lean over the table.*"

"I suppose Oakdale has changed quite a bit in forty years," Ellen said, placing both hands around her mug.

Dr. Brown reached up and fingered the strand of pearls around her neck. "*Everything's* different. I hardly recognized anything downtown. But this house . . ." She looked around the kitchen again. "It's as if it were frozen in time. I was so glad to see the green trim outside." She smiled. "It's just like I remember it."

Ellen picked up her cup. "Would you like to go for a tour?"

Dr. Brown nodded. "That would be nice."

"I love it when a plan comes together." Wishbone quickly searched for any cookie crumbs that might have fallen from their laps when they stood up. "Terrific cookies, Ellen, Joe. Just what the doctor ordered."

Dr. Brown walked toward the dining room. Joe, Ellen, and Wishbone followed. Suddenly Wishbone trotted ahead of everyone.

"Make way for the guide," he announced. "I've sniffed out every inch of this place. I know it like the back of my paw!" He kept up his quick pace. "Here we have the dining room—lots of space, beautiful living area . . . and the study's this way. It's a great room!" Glancing over his shoulder and noticing the others weren't following, Wishbone sat. "Okay, I'll wait."

As Dr. Brown strolled through the living room, Wishbone noticed her face brightening.

"So many memories," she said. She ran her hand along a window frame. "One summer I caught the mumps from my brother, Robert." She held her hands close to the sides of her face. "My cheeks were as big as apples. Of course, Robert was all better by that time." She pointed to the yard. "I'd sit here by the window and watch the other kids play. I was miserable—it even hurt to swallow." She closed her eyes for a second. "But good old Champ stayed right here by my side until I was well again."

"Oh, how sweet." Ellen slipped a hand into her pants pocket and leaned against the door frame.

"Yeah," Joe said. "Sounds like Wishbone."

Wishbone sat taller. "Some things never change, Joe—like canine loyalty."

Dr. Brown turned away from the window, running her hand along the back of the sofa as she walked past.

"Did your folks build the house?" Ellen asked.

"Yes." Dr. Brown nodded. "I believe it was built in 1919, the same year I was born."

"Wow! That was before my time," Wishbone said. "Let's see, in dog years you're seven times . . . Wow! Doesn't she look great, Joe?"

Continuing around the room, Dr. Brown seemed to be happily remembering all her years growing up in the house. "My father was an architect, and he designed everything in here . . . even the stained-glass windows."

"I really love those," Ellen said, following Dr. Brown toward the study.

"Come on, Joe," Wishbone said. "Onward!" As soon as they entered the study, Wishbone jumped up into the red chair over near the bookshelves. "And this is *the* chair."

Sitting on the edge of her computer desk, Ellen rested her mug on her knee. "This is my favorite room."

"This is my favorite chair," Wishbone said.

Dr. Brown smiled. "It was mine too, Ellen." She

touched the bookshelf. "This was always bursting at the seams with books. I used to curl up in a big chair and just read and daydream and imagine that I was the hero in each of those wonderful stories."

Wishbone wagged his tail. "I liked this woman's style the moment I laid eyes on her."

Dr. Brown turned to Joe. "You've been so patient. Would you like to go upstairs now and see the hiding place? It's in my old room."

"You bet." Joe grinned.

"And I bet I know exactly which room that is," Ellen said, leading the way.

Wishbone hopped out of the chair and dashed ahead of Dr. Brown and Joe. "Right this way, folks. Onward and upward. And as you walk up the stairs, please notice the fine wood paneling, left and right— all original, I might add."

Wishbone raced ahead, with Joe on his tail. They ran into Joe's room ahead of the others.

"Quick, Joe," Wishbone said, running across the floor. "Dirty clothes! Pick them up. Thank you."

As Wishbone jumped on the bed, Joe spotted the clothes on the floor and quickly tossed them aside. They landed on top of a basket full of balls in the corner.

"Perfect timing, Joe," Wishbone said.

Dr. Brown smiled as she entered the room. "I might have known you'd have my old room, Joe."

Joe raised his eyebrows. "The secret hiding place is in here? Where?"

"Yeah, where?" Wishbone looked around.

Nodding, Dr. Brown pointed to a board between the window seat and the built-in bookcase. "Unless it's been fixed, that board comes out. I used to hide all my treasures there." She chuckled. "Especially the ones I didn't want my brother, Robert, to find!" She nodded again at Joe. "Go ahead, check it out."

Joe kneeled at the window seat. "This one?" He pointed to the wide board running up and down.

"That's the one," Dr. Brown said.

"Oh, *that* secret hiding place." Wishbone jumped off the bed and trotted over to Joe. "Ha-ha-ha! You know, I knew this was here all along. I just wanted you to find it for yourself." Wishbone moved in closer for a better sniff. "You believe that, don't you, Joe?"

Joe grabbed the edges of the board with both hands and pulled. "It seems to be stuck." He grunted as he struggled to wiggle it free.

"Your face is turning red, Joe," Wishbone said. "Why don't you get something to wedge in there, like maybe . . . hmm . . ."

Joe reached up and grabbed a ruler from the bookcase.

"Like maybe a ruler!" Wishbone sat down.

Ellen and Dr. Brown stood, watching from behind.

"This should pry it open," Joe said. Sticking the ruler under the edge of the board, he wiggled and pushed. Finally, it slipped underneath the board, popping the bottom section free. Joe smiled. "Here it comes." He pulled and the board came off easily.

Thick cobwebs covered an opening in the wall. "There it is!" Joe sounded pleased.

"Ah, treasure." Wishbone lowered his head for a better look, then sat back. "It looks dangerous. You go first."

Joe peered in through the cobwebs, then looked up at Dr. Brown. "There doesn't seem to be anything in there."

"I may have cleaned it out long ago," she said.

Wishbone stepped forward and sniffed the opening thoroughly. "Hello? Wait a minute! I smell something!"

Nudging Wishbone aside, Joe reached in with his hand.

"Oh, excuse me," Wishbone said, moving out of Joe's way.

Joe reached in farther. "Wait! I think I feel something!"

Ellen and Dr. Brown exchanged smiles.

Joe pulled out a small cloth bag with a drawstring. After he loosened the string, he poured out two small spheres, one a little larger than the other.

"Let me see." Wishbone moved in for a better look. "Wow! It's a . . . it's a *something!*"

Joe rolled the spheres around in his hand. "A marble and a ball bearing?" He handed them to Dr. Brown.

Her face lit up immediately. "No, Joe, two marbles." She held up the smaller one. "This one with the swirls is called a glassie, and this bigger one is my prize steelie shooter."

"Cool!" Joe said.

"Hmm . . ." Wishbone eyed the marbles. "I'll stick with my own treasures, thank you."

Dr. Brown sat on the window seat. Glancing down, she admired the treasure in her hand. "Marbles were our version of video games, Joe. Just like your games today, we had to shoot straight. But we got to keep everything we hit!" She held up the shooter. "I won hundreds of marbles with this little gem. Life wasn't any less exciting back then, Joe . . . just different." She put her hand in her lap and closed her fingers around the marbles. "Looking at these makes me think of something I haven't thought of in years."

Ellen tilted her head. "What's that?"

Wishbone and Joe looked on eagerly as they waited for her to answer.

Dr. Brown turned her glance to the window and the yard below. "The time capsule! I wonder if it's still there."

"What time capsule?" Joe's eyebrows shot up.

Dr. Brown put two fingers to her cheek.

"A thinking pose, if I ever saw one," Wishbone said.

"Oh, goodness." She chuckled. "That must have been about 1929, or 1930. My brother, Robert, and I put everything in a little metal box and buried it between two trees out front."

Joe sat back on his knees. "Neat. What did you put in it?"

Dr. Brown tilted her head. "Oh, just little things we had around the house. I don't remember anything in particular." She eyed the marbles in her hand again. "It might be fun to see what I really did put in that box."

In a flash, Joe was on his feet. "Well, come on, let's go find it!"

"Ellen?" Dr. Brown asked.

Ellen drank the last of her coffee. "I'm up for a treasure hunt."

Wishbone wagged his tail. "Buried treasure? You're going to need someone who can dig. Hmm . . . let me see, who can I think of . . . ? Oh, me!"

Gazing out the window, Dr. Brown raised her eyebrows. "It might be hard. The trees look different now."

Wishbone jumped on the window seat and

looked outside, too. "I bet *everything* in the yard has changed since you were here."

Wishbone thought of Rip Van Winkle and all the changes he'd found when he had awakened. Not only had the opening in the wall disappeared, but he'd been growled at by a village dog! What was going to happen next?

Chapter Eleven

Rip's tail hung low as he watched the growling dog hurry out of sight. "This has been one strange day." He shook his head in disbelief, pointed his nose toward the village, and walked on.

Soon he met a man and a woman enjoying a stroll.

"Good day," Rip yipped, and tipped his hat, as they approached. He was much surprised that their faces were unfamiliar to him. And their clothes, too, were like none he'd ever seen. *But,* he thought, *at least they keep themselves together solidly in the shade* and *the sun.* He sniffed the air. They each had a scent about them. That was more than he could say about yesterday's strangers!

The woman cast her eyes to the side, while the man put his arm around her shoulder. Guiding her, he moved her to his other side, away from Rip.

Rip turned and stared after them. They acted as if he were a flea-infested stray! Why, just thinking about their reaction made him itch! He scratched his neck and ears, then chewed at a spot on his tail.

As Rip continued on again, he met others along the way.

"Good day to you." Rip tipped his hat.

"Hello. Nice to see you."

Slowly, he became alarmed. Not one face was recognizable to Rip; and not one person, in return, recognized him. The people either hurried away or skirted around him altogether. None returned his greeting or his wave.

Cocking his head, Rip brought a paw to his face and stroked his chin. At that instant he was met with another unexplainable surprise.

"Oh, boy." Rip stroked his face again to be sure. "Somehow, my beard has grown a foot long! How can that be!"

He shook his head hard, to clear his mind. The wispy end of his beard flew up into his face. It was as gray as a December cloud!

Rip's thoughts swam in his head, dog-paddling every which way but in the right direction. "Why are things not as I remember?" he asked, frustration filling his voice. He slapped his side. A great plume of dust billowed up from his coat. He coughed and fanned away the cloud of dust with his paw. Looking down he noticed—*really noticed*—his clothes for the first time since awakening.

"So many missing buttons." He held up his front leg for a closer look at his sleeve. "And look at all these holes—there are so many that even I will not fault Dame Van Winkle for saying I'm ragged as a beggar. True, it is!

"Helllooo!" Rip looked around him. "Something's wrong here. Yoo-hoo! . . . Anyone? Could somebody tell me about last night?"

After shaking repeatedly to dust himself off, he set off again, as fast as he could go. Imaginary weights still seemed to pull at all four of his legs. Yet, at times he was able to break into a trot.

As he entered the outskirts of his village, a troop of children was playing at the edge of the lane. Rip wagged his tail as he approached them from behind.

"Lads! Playing marbles, are you? This is a most-welcome sight!"

The children turned to face him. Rip jumped and flipped for them, but sadly he made it only halfway around. His heart missed a beat as well. For, as he looked from face to face, not one of the youngsters seemed familiar. And where were their smiles?

"Look at that beard!" one young lad cried. "It's as matted and dirty as unspun wool." He pointed a finger at Rip. "Old man has a fun-ny beard. Old man has a fun-ny beard!"

Soon others joined in the taunting.

"Stop!" Rip barked, holding up a paw and wagging his tail slowly. "Is there not one here among you who knows who I am?" He searched their faces hopefully. Perhaps the lads could set him straight. "Am I not your friend? Do I not bring you toys I have made with my own two hands? Do I not spin stories for you? Tell me true."

Their faces wrinkled into deeper frowns and scowls as they shook their heads no. One of the bigger lads stood and circled Rip, catlike. Suddenly the lad reached out and tugged Rip's coattail.

"A beggar you are, to be sure. You're trying to play tricks on us." Stepping closer, the lad held his nose high and pinched it closed with his fingers. "And you're badly in need of a bath!"

Actually, the people who lived in the colonies during this time bathed only about once a month themselves.

No way! Rip thought, backing away. *I think I'll get going while the getting is good.* As he turned and hurried off, the children's laughter followed him. "Alas. It's a lot more fun being laughed *with,* than laughed *at.*"

His stomach growled, reminding him of his hunger.

"I shall make haste to the Van Hatters'. Perhaps Dame Van Hatter will give me another of her tasty johnnycakes."

But as Rip trotted toward the lane that rimmed the village, his ears twitched and his tail drooped. He came to an abrupt stop.

"A new house on the corner!" he barked. He looked past it. "Another new house! And another."

He rushed toward them, then slowed to read the names above the doors.

"Vandervelder, De Groot, Tjoelker. None do I know.

Am I, and the village, too, bewitched?" He raised a paw and pointed. "There stand the Catskill Mountains, and there runs the Hudson River." He turned. "Every hill and dale is precisely as it has always been. . . ." He looked back at the houses, puzzled. "Surely this is my native village, which I left yesterday."

Rip rubbed a paw across his face.

"The ale last night has addled my poor head."

More new houses lay ahead, but Rip turned and took a shortcut to the Van Hatters'. He stopped at the front window.

"Hey! Who broke the lattice I just fixed?"

Standing on his hind legs, Rip pressed a paw to the windowpane. Suddenly the door to the house flew open and a tall, thin man stepped out.

"What do you want?" he asked, pulling a corncob pipe from his mouth.

Rip dropped down to all fours. "Edward Van Hatter, is that you?" he asked unsurely. *Wow!* he thought. *This guy has changed overnight as much as I have!*

The fellow took a step toward Rip, towering over him like a giant. He pointed the stem of his pipe to the carved nameplate above the door. "Can't you read, old man? 'Vanderford.' Now, get out of my yard. Do your begging elsewhere." Then he went inside and slammed the door.

Well! Rip thought. He was not *begging*. Why, he wasn't even sitting up!

Dashing up the lane, he cut across yards and fields. This way, or that? Sometimes he had to stop and sniff. The land had changed. Some trees and bushes had been replaced by houses. Other foliage had grown so big that he didn't recognize it.

All four legs pumped hard as Rip headed toward home. Not one house he passed looked the way he remembered it. Not one face in the windows was recognizable. And not one dog gave him a friendly tail wag. All barked, while some even bared their teeth and growled as he neared.

"I'm on my way," Rip said, hurrying. "I don't have to be hit over the head with a newspaper to get your point. You'll not find me wanting to know if your bark is worse than your bite."

With some difficulty, he found the lane that led up to his farm. With silent awe he approached his house. *Any second now,* he thought, *I'll be hearing Dame Van Winkle's shrill voice.*

"Yoo-hoo!" he called. "Lambchop?" With his teeth he picked a lone wildflower from the grass. *This will make a good peace offering,* he thought.

But as he trotted up the path to the house, the sight before him made him bark in surprise. The flower fell from his mouth.

"The house has fallen into decay," he said. "Alas, the roof has caved in!" Tall weeds scratched his underbelly as he walked forward. "The windows have shattered, and the door is off its hinges."

Rip entered the house but stayed close to the doorway.

"Oh, my, this place is a real mess! Hmm . . .

Dame Van Winkle has always kept the house sparkling clean. Spotless. Perhaps the children have been playing outdoor games indoors."

He looked at the fireplace, which now supported a bird's nest instead of a kettle.

"Helllooo! Judith! Young Rip! Where are you? Home I am, Dame Van Winkle!"

The lonely chambers rang for a moment with his voice. Then, again, all was silent. The house was empty, forlorn, and apparently abandoned.

"Hmm . . . It seems my scolding has been delayed." Rip smiled. "Okay, maybe I'll just trot on down to the King George Inn. I'm sure my good friends there will know what's going on."

Chapter Twelve

Rip hightailed it to the inn, passing stranger after stranger along the way. "I've never seen so many people! The population is thrice what I remember."

He wagged his tail as he neared the inn. Men, women, and children milled about in the street.

Rip dipped and bobbed his head, trying to spot the inn. "That will certainly be a welcome sight."

But when the crowd parted and the building came into view, Rip stopped abruptly. His ears pointed straight up in surprise. A large, rickety wooden building stood in place of the King George Inn! The front windows, large and gaping, were broken out. Torn petticoats and old hats hung where the glass should have been. Rip stared, his mouth hanging open in a pant. A sign hung over the door. It read: THE UNION HOTEL: JONATHAN DOOLITTLE, OWNER.

Pawing his chin, Rip looked to the side of the hotel. The great tree that used to shelter the little Dutch inn was gone, too. He would miss that tree in more ways than one! In its place there now stood a tall, naked pole. On the top fluttered a red, white, and blue flag of stars and stripes.

"Hmm," Rip said, "that's not familiar at all! But—" He wagged his tail excitedly as he recognized the ruby face of King George on the sign by the door. "At last—something that hasn't changed!"

But after moving closer, and upon further scrutiny, Rip realized that something *was* different about the picture. In fact, many things had changed. The red coat worn by the king was now blue and yellow. And he wore a *hat,* cocked to one side. In his hand he now held a sword instead of a scepter.

Wishbone here. A scepter is a rod-shaped weapon carried by royals. It doesn't have a blade like a sword does.

Underneath the picture was a sign painted in large letters. It read: GENERAL WASHINGTON. Rip repeated the name in his head. Why, he'd never even heard of this Washington fellow.

Rip sniffed the air and eyed the crowd of folks standing by the door. "Nope. Don't know any of them, either." The very mood of the village seemed changed. A busy, bustling tone had replaced the dull and drowsy atmosphere Rip was used to.

With a glance behind him, his blood quickened. He hadn't noticed until now, but somewhere along the way people had begun to follow him. Now a crowd had gathered at his tail, whispering about his ragged clothes and long, unkempt beard.

Where is Nicholas Van Vedder? Rip wondered, as he wove his way in and out of all the legs. Looking this way and that, he searched for signs of Nicholas's pipe smoke. He spotted plenty of rising puffs, but none belonged to his friend. "Nicholas?" he called.

Listening carefully, Rip also searched the crowd for the schoolmaster rattling forth the contents of an old newspaper.

"Yoo-hoo! Derrick Van Bummel! I'm back. Guys?"

But in place of Rip's old-time friends stood a lean, ill-natured fellow with his pockets full of pamphlets. As he distributed them to the assembled crowd, he shouted, "Remember the Boston Tea Party! Remember Bunker Hill! The heroes of '76! The freedoms we have won! We have our liberty!"

Some of the crowd replied by clapping. Others shouted hoorays.

A tea party for all of Boston? Rip thought. *That must have been some guest list! Too bad I missed that wingding. I bet there were plenty of goodies.*

The man continued his loud remarks, speaking out about members of Congress, and citizens' rights.

Rip looked on, bewildered. *A politician?* he thought. *And everyone, except me, seems to know what he's talking about. Maybe I should have listened more carefully when Van Bummel was reading from the newspapers.* Rip sighed.

"Elect me to Congress and I'll preserve the liberties that this flag stands for!" said the politician. He pointed to the red, white, and blue flag.

Whose flag is that? Rip wondered. *And where is our British flag?*

"Hey, old man!"

Rip heard the call from the crowd, but he paid it no mind. Then someone laid a hand firmly upon his shoulder, startling him.

"Ye with the old muzzle—I'm talking to ye," said a very plump man beside him.

The crowd hushed. Everyone, even the politician, stared at Rip.

Rip pawed at his whiskered muzzle. "Whoa! Let's not get personal here!"

The man wrinkled his brow and nodded to the musket slung across Rip's shoulder.

"Oh! You mean *that* muzzle." Rip wagged his tail.

More of the crowd pushed closer, eyeing him curiously from head to foot.

"On which side did ye vote?" the man asked Rip.

"Vote?" Rip cocked his head. He didn't have a clue as to what the man meant. "Helllooo! Could you run that by me again?"

A tall, red-haired man pulled Rip aside. Bending down, he tipped Rip's hat up and whispered in his spotted ear. "He wants to know if you are a Federal or a Democrat."

Rip looked at him, more puzzled than ever. He scratched his neck with his hind foot. "A *what* or a *what?*"

Whispers floated through the air as the crowd waited for Rip to answer. An old gentleman in a wig and a pointed, cocked hat made his way toward Rip. "Out of my way." Using his elbows, he shoved people to the right and left as he passed. "Coming through." The man planted himself firmly before Rip. With one hand on his hip, and the other resting on his cane, he bent and stared into Rip's eyes. The look was so intense, it seemed to Rip that the man was looking into his very soul.

Rip wagged his tail nervously. "Okay. I can see we're not quite on the same wavelength here."

"What brought you to the election with a gun on your shoulder, and a mob at your heels?" the man demanded. He poked his cane on the ground to emphasize each word as he spoke. "Do you mean to start a riot in the village?"

Rip took a step back, away from the tip of the cane. *Let's watch the toes,* he thought. The wall of legs behind him prevented him from moving any farther. "Alas! gentlemen and good dames," he barked, alarmed as he looked up into the scowling faces. "I am a poor farmer. A family man. I am a native of this place, and a loyal subject of King George the Third!"

An angry shout rose up from the crowd; arms flailed in the air. "A Tory! A Tory!" the people shouted. "He sides with the king and thinks England should still rule the colonies!"

More angry shouts arose.

"He's a spy!" came another cry.

Hands reached out toward him, clawing the air. "Grab him! Hang the traitor!"

"Oops, wrong answer." Rip dropped to his stomach and searched for an escape route through the crowd. But the villagers had closed in around him, forming a thick wall of legs.

"Quiet! Quiet! Silence, I say!" It was with great difficulty that the old man in the cocked hat restored order. He looked sternly at the crowd until all fell silent. Then, turning, and bending ever so slightly, he gave the same cold look to Rip. "I demand to know who you are seeking to find, and what you came here for."

Rip looked up into the sour face looming over him. *Boy, I wonder if this guy was ever a dog catcher,* Rip thought.

"No harm do I mean you," Rip said humbly, glancing from the fellow to the crowd. "I'm searching for my neighbors." He stood and wagged his tail slowly, hoping the crowd could be persuaded to be friendly. "My friends spent hours drinking ale on this very spot. And I was with them."

"Well," said the man standing in front of him, poking his cane at the ground again. "Who are they? Name them."

Rip wagged his tail faster. "Nicholas Van Vedder, the landlord of the inn . . . Where might I find him?"

A silence followed as the people looked at one another, shook their heads, and shrugged. Finally, the old man raised a bony finger in the air. "Nicholas Van Vedder!" he replied in a thin voice. "Why, he's been dead and gone for eighteen years! It's true! There was a wooden tombstone in the churchyard that used to tell all about him." He scratched his head. "But that rotted years ago, and is gone too."

Rip's heart pounded hard against his furry chest. Nicholas Van Vedder, dead for eighteen years? A shiver traveled down his spine and out to the tip of his tail. "Where is Brom Dutcher?" he asked hesitantly, afraid of the answer he might receive.

"Oh, a good Whig he was," said the old man. "He went off to the army at the beginning of the Revolution."

A Whig was a colonist favoring independence from England. It's sort of like me wanting to be free from the leash! The Revolution was the American Revolution—the war that made America independent from England.

The crowd parted slightly as the old man slowly worked his way closer to Rip. "Some say he was killed at the battle of Stony Point. Others say he was drowned in a storm at the foot of Antony's Nose. I don't know for sure—but he never came back again."

Thoughts swam in Rip's head. "Where, then, is Van Bummel, the schoolmaster?"

The old man wagged his finger slowly in the air and bobbed his head as he thought. "He went off to the war, too, and he became a great militia general."

"And now he's a member of Congress!" thundered the politician.

War? Congress? Antony's Nose? Rip couldn't believe all the changes in his life. Alas, he was alone in the world. And what a strange world it had become, he thought. He could not explain the enormous lapses in time. Nor did he understand the matters of war. Rip sighed. He had no more courage left to ask about any more of his friends. He pawed his face, then looked around at the faces in the crowd. "Does nobody here know Rip Van Winkle?" he called out hopelessly.

"Oh, Rip Van Winkle!" exclaimed two or three, nodding. "Oh, to be sure!"

Rip wagged his tail. "Okay, fellas, now we're getting somewhere!"

One woman pointed across the way. "That's Rip Van Winkle yonder, leaning against the tree."

As the crowd parted slightly, Rip looked toward the tree, surprised. Suddenly his collar was too tight; it was hard to breathe.

Poor Rip! Just when he thought he found someone who knew him, and could maybe explain things, *another* Rip Van Winkle pops up. Spooky!

Let's get back to Joe, Ellen, and Dr. Brown, and see if Dr. Brown can find her time capsule. Hopefully, she won't be as confused as Rip. I'm ready for a good dig!

Chapter Thirteen

"Follow me!" Wishbone jumped down from the window seat and ran down the stairs. He heard the footsteps of Ellen, Dr. Brown, and Joe behind him. Just as Wishbone reached the bottom step, the doorbell rang. "Somebody get that, please." He sat on the edge of the blue carpet near the door and waited.

Joe reached the landing first and opened the door.

"Thank you." Wishbone wagged his tail. "David, Sam—you're just in time. We're going on an adventure—in our own yard! We're looking for a time capsule. Want to help?"

"Hi, guys." Joe moved aside so David and Sam could step in.

"Hi," Sam and David replied in unison, as Joe shut the door.

"Want to go do something?" Sam adjusted her baseball cap. "After today's game, maybe we should practice hockey."

Joe turned and glanced at Ellen and Dr. Brown,

who were almost down the stairs. "Actually, we're going to search for a time capsule. Want to help?"

David looked at Sam, and they both nodded. "Sure," David said.

Ellen smiled. "Hi, kids."

"Hi, Mrs. Talbot." Sam and David both spoke at the same time, but not at the *exact* same time, so it sounded like, "Hi hi, Mrs. Mrs. Talbot Talbot."

"Timing is everything, guys," Wishbone said.

Joe looked at Dr. Brown, who was standing beside Ellen. "Oh, Dr. Brown, these are my friends, David and Samantha."

Dr. Brown's smile widened. "Pleased to meet you."

Sam and David returned her greeting.

"Now, what's this about a time capsule?" Sam asked, kneeling to tie her shoe.

"Door, please." Wishbone stood up and stared at the door until Joe pulled it open. "Thank you." He trotted out to the lawn, then turned and looked back. "Hurry, people. The dog is ready and waiting."

Shielding his eyes from the sun as they walked outside, Joe explained things to Sam and David.

Wishbone paced impatiently. "Faster, Joe, faster."

"That's really neat," David said, sitting on the porch steps.

"Yes," Sam agreed, plopping down beside him. "I wonder who lived in our house before us."

"Your dad might know," Ellen said.

Wishbone watched Dr. Brown. While her glance

104

bounced from the trees to the shrubs, she walked halfway across the yard, then hesitated. Turning, she looked all around her. "Have I gone crazy?" As she glanced around again, a frown wrinkled her forehead. "The yard seems changed! There are more trees now." She motioned with her hand toward the street. "And this paved circle wasn't here when I was a girl."

"Oh." Ellen nodded, a look of understanding on her face.

Suddenly David's eyebrows shot up. "What's your time capsule made of?"

"David, you've got an idea!" Wishbone said.

Dr. Brown fingered her pearls again. "I believe it was a metal box."

"Come on, guys." David jumped up. "I think I can help her."

As Joe and Sam followed him, Joe waved to Ellen and Dr. Brown. "We'll be right back."

"Guys?" Wishbone watched them run toward David's house.

"Okay." Ellen sat down on the porch steps, while Dr. Brown continued looking around.

"Don't worry about inviting the dog along, guys," Wishbone called after the kids. "I'll just wait here for you." He went and sat by Ellen's feet.

Dr. Brown pointed past the kids, to David's house. "That house wasn't built then, either." She shook her head. "I simply can't remember which two trees the box is buried between." She looked at Ellen. "Maybe they were cut down years ago."

"You may be right!" Ellen petted Wishbone, then scratched behind his ears.

"Oh, yeah!" Wishbone leaned into her fingers. "As long as my digging has been postponed, I can't think of a better way to pass the time." He cocked his head. "Over to the right, Ellen. Ahh. Thank you. Oh, look—Joe, Sam, and David are coming back."

"Look." Ellen stood and nodded. "The kids are coming back."

"I just said that." Wishbone stood and wagged his tail. "David's carrying a big . . . a big . . . What *is* David carrying?"

David hurried over to Dr. Brown and held out his hand and the *thing*. "This metal detector should find the box right away." He turned on the detector. Followed by Sam and Joe, David slowly scanned the ground between a set of trees in Joe's front yard. "Nothing here." He moved on and scanned the ground between two more trees. Suddenly the machine beeped. "Look! I found it already!" David grinned.

Wishbone circled them, then lay down near the steps. He put his head on his paws. "I don't think so, David. I happen to know there's a perfectly good chew bone buried there."

"Are you sure?" Samantha asked David eagerly.

"I'm telling you, Sam, don't get too excited," Wishbone said.

David nodded and pointed to the gauge. "See, this thing is almost definitely metallic."

Kneeling, Joe felt around in the grass. Suddenly

he grinned and held up his hand. "It's my locker key!"
He stood up and slapped David on the shoulder.
"Thanks for finding it for me," he said teasingly.

David made a face. "Yeah, right."

Samantha ran her hand around one of the trees in
the area David had just checked. "Their trunks are so
thin—these two trees don't look old enough."

"Sam's right," Ellen said.

"Don't be too disappointed, David," Wishbone
said. "Sometimes I don't find the right tree the first
time, either." Wishbone trotted into the grassy circle
in the middle of the street. "Speaking of trees, I think
I'll find one myself." He got up and started to sniff
around the base of a tree trunk. "Okay, who's been
here? Fritz!"

Sam touched Dr. Brown's arm, then nodded
toward Wishbone. "Hey, maybe Wishbone's on to
something. Those two trees could be it—they look old
enough."

"Let's give it a try," said Dr. Brown, brightening.
"David?"

The group headed across the yard toward Wishbone. Slowly, David started to scan the ground between
the two trees.

Wishbone sighed. "You're welcome to look, but
I've already checked out the area. . . . I said I've already
checked out the area. Oh, David . . ."

David made a face. "Nothing."

Wishbone gave him his best *"What did I tell
you?"* look.

Dr. Brown squinted and slowly looked around again. She sighed. "Everything is different."

Wishbone watched Ellen reach out and put a hand on Dr. Brown's arm.

David put the metal detector to the ground again and moved it back and forth. As he took a step forward, the machine beeped again. He grinned and bent down, then made a face. "It's only a quarter," he said.

"Don't sound so disappointed," Wishbone said. "A few more of those and you could get a nice chew bone for a friend."

"Hey!" In a flash, David's smile was back. "Maybe we could try subterranean sonar!"

Joe raised his eyebrows. "Try *what?*"

"Whoa! By the looks on their faces, everyone is as confused as you are, Joe," Wishbone said, then lay down.

"Subterranean sonar," David said. "I could rig a device to send high-pitched sound waves into the ground. With the right monitoring gear, we would be able to see the relative size and shape of any buried objects."

Samantha looked amazed. "You could make something like that?"

David shrugged. "Sure. I think so."

But to Wishbone, David didn't look so sure at all.

Sighing, Joe looked across to Dr. Brown and Ellen. "There's got to be an easier way."

Ellen shrugged.

Wishbone rested his head on his paws. "Yeah, preferably something that doesn't involve high-pitched sounds."

A faint clank caused Wishbone to raise his head.

"What's that?" He looked toward Wanda's house. "Hmm . . ."

Wanda stood on her lawn, stabbing the metal rod of one of her flamingos into the ground.

Wishbone sat up. "Hey! How did you get home without me noticing? It must have been when we were busy breaking into the secret hiding place."

Cocking his head, Wishbone watched Wanda struggle to poke the rod into the same patch of grass. *Plunk!* Each time the rod went halfway down, then stopped as it hit something. Muttering, Wanda yanked the flamingo up, then tried again.

Wishbone wagged his tail. "Let's see here. A big tree by her driveway, and a spot of grass that seems to have something hard under the dirt. "Could it be? Hey, Wanda, wait for me!" Wishbone raced over to Wanda's yard and started digging at her feet. "This is what I call fun!"

Ellen's voice broke Wishbone's concentration. "Joe, you'd better get Wishbone."

"Wishbone!" Joe called out.

Wishbone glanced up long enough to see Joe heading his way. "Oh-oh. Gotta hurry. Excuse me, Wanda." He nosed her shoe.

Wanda moved back as if she'd just stepped in a pile of something gross.

"Why, Wanda, I'm hurt!" Wishbone said. He kept digging.

"Joe! What is Wishbone doing?" she asked, putting a hand on the brim of her sun hat.

Joe made a face as he dropped to his knees. "I don't know, Ms. Gilmore." He looked down. "Wishbone, what are you doing?"

Wishbone dug faster. "Don't worry. I'll get to the bottom of this."

Wanda put her hands on her hips. "Ellen, he's up to something."

"Yes, I know. I'm coming," said Ellen.

Wishbone paused to look up. "Oh, here come Ellen and Dr. Brown. And Sam and David, too. An audience!"

Wanda waved her hands in the air. "Your canine roto-tiller is destroying my lawn again!"

"I hear panic in your voice, Wanda. Really, things will be okay." As everyone gathered around, Wishbone cleared his throat and tried to sound British. "Today on *Digging Up Your Neighbor's Yard,* I'm going to show you how to unearth rare and precious objects. My lovely assistant, Wanda, has graciously allowed us to use her yard."

Dr. Brown stepped closer. "He's quite a mover and a shaker."

"That's me," Wishbone said. "A mover and a shaker." He continued digging. "It's here, I know it's here. I *know* it's here. . . . Okay, where is it? . . . Aha!" Finally, Wishbone's nails scratched against metal. "Bingo!" He stopped digging and stepped back.

Joe reached into the dirt with both hands and pulled out a square metal box. It was caked with dirt.

Wanda's eyes opened wide. She gasped.

Joe held the box out toward Dr. Brown. "Is this the time capsule?"

Dr. Brown took the box and gently brushed some of the dirt away. She smiled. "Yes, Joe, this is a little piece of the past."

"I'll take that smile as a thank you," Wishbone said. He looked at the box. "Now, let's see what's inside!"

Well, things turned out well for Dr. Brown, but the jury is still out on Rip. . . .

Chapter Fourteen

The man in the cocked hat poked his cane at the ground by Rip's front feet. "I demand to know who you are!"

Rip shook his head. He was at his wits' end. "I'm not myself—I'm somebody else." With his paw, he pointed across the way to the tree. "That's me yonder—no, no, that's somebody else who got into my skin! I was myself yesterday, but I fell asleep on the mountain. And during the night, while I slept, they switched my gun." He swept his paw through the air, drawing attention to the buildings. "All this has changed, and I'm changed, too. And I can't tell what my name is, or who I am!"

The bystanders raised their brows and passed looks back and forth. Some nodded. Others winked. Still others tapped fingers to their temples.

One young woman drew imaginary circles in the air with her index finger. "He's daft, he is," she whispered, then laughed.

The children followed the example of the woman by drawing circles around their temples and giggling at him.

Helllooo! Rip thought. *My hearing is great, thank you. If you can't say anything nice, don't say anything at all.*

From the back of the crowd came more whispers. "Secure the old man's gun!" someone said.

Rip cocked his hat, perked up his ears, and listened carefully.

"Yes," uttered another. "We must keep the crazy coot from doing any mischief. I say we lock him up and throw away the key!"

The scent of their fear filled Rip's nose. "Yoo-hoo! We need to talk." Rip looked up just as a pair of big, meaty hands reached for the scruff of his neck. "I don't think so," he said.

He dove through an opening between two boots. With his tail low, he pushed forward, through all the skirts and boots. People turned and twisted and lifted their feet as he squeezed past their ankles.

"Grab him!" someone ordered.

A woman screamed and twirled as Rip brushed by her skirt and sped into a wide-open area. "I'm outta here!" He pumped his four legs hard and fast.

"He's touched, for sure!" someone yelled. "And he's getting away! Catch him!"

Rip ran and ran. Shouts followed him. The crowd wasn't far behind. He zipped up one road and down another. He zigged here and zagged there. His mouth hung open; his breath came hard and fast and his tongue lolled to one side.

The shouts were farther away now. But Rip kept running; the houses he passed blurred together. Turning, he headed up a hill. He could barely hear the crowd now. Still, he pumped his four legs hard. Then, before he knew it, he'd run into a patch of tall weeds and grass. Even with his keen hearing, the shouts of the crowd were but a whisper now.

Rip stopped to catch his breath. "Uh-oh!" He dropped to his belly and hid in the tall grass. Just ahead, two people were unexpectedly near. In his hurry to escape the angry mob, Rip hadn't even looked at what was in front of him!

On his left, an old man hobbled along happily. In the other direction, kneeling nearby in some shorter grass, was a young woman holding a small child in her arm. Clasped in her hand was a bouquet of fall wildflowers.

Adjusting his hat, Rip looked through the weeds. This time he really *saw* his surroundings. Wooden tombstones poked out of the ground, one after another. Rip shivered, raised his tail, then stood for a better look. "Now I get it—I'm in the churchyard cemetery! But where's the church?"

The woman turned, a look of surprise on her face as she saw Rip. Then the look melted into a smile. "Ye startled me." She put the flowers on the grave. Then she stood and walked toward Rip. "Are ye a stranger to the place? Do ye need help finding a grave?"

Rip dropped his tail and took a step back. *Should I turn tail and run?* he wondered. *But how far could she get chasing me with a baby in her arm?*

He glanced around the cemetery again and shook his head. "There are so many more tombstones than I remember." He pointed at the hillside with his paw. "And the church is gone."

She nodded. "It was taken by fire years ago," she said. "We built the new church right in the village, but the graveyard remains here."

The young woman shifted the child to her other arm, the arm nearest Rip. As she did so, the baby began to fuss and whimper. Puckering up, the baby cried out and flung his arms around his mother's neck. "There, now." The woman gently bounced him up and down in her arms. "Hush, Rip. This man will not hurt ye."

Rip pawed his muzzle. "Helllooo! I don't think I heard you right. Did you call your child 'Rip'?"

"Yes." She nodded. "'Tis his name."

As Rip looked at the yawning child, the truth began to dawn on him. He wagged his tail. "And what is your name, my good woman?"

She shifted the baby again. "Judith Gardenier."

His heart beat faster—as if it, too, were being chased. *Gardenier,* he thought. *As in "Delmond Gardenier"?* "And your father's name?" Rip asked hopefully, jumping on a nearby tree stump.

"Ah, poor man. Rip Van Winkle was his name. But it's been twenty years since he last went away from home with his gun. I was but a little girl when he left." She kissed her baby, who was fast asleep.

Rip wanted to reach out a paw to her, but he stopped himself. "Uh . . . was that your father's grave you put the flowers on?" The fur on his neck stood on end as he thought of seeing a tombstone bearing his own name.

She shook her head. "My mother's grave, it is." She took a deep breath. "She died long ago doing what she liked most."

Rip gave her a questioning look. "And what was that?"

"She died while having a fit of anger at a New

England peddler." Judith smiled faintly. "The poor fellow. I'm not sure which scared him more—the whacks my mother gave him with her broom, or the sting of her words."

Well, at least Dame Van Winkle died happy, Rip thought. *That's a comfort.*

Suddenly he heard voices coming up the other side of the hill. He could not hold back his news any longer. Wagging his tail, he quickly reached out and placed a paw on Judith's arm. "*I* am your father. I am Rip Van Winkle."

Judith gasped and pulled away from his touch. She placed a protective arm across her baby's back.

"True, it is!" Rip said. He glanced to the hillside as the villagers came over the rise, yapping like hounds on a hunt. Judith's reaction was more painful to him than if a cat had put claws to his heart.

"There he is!" someone from the mob shouted. "Grab him!"

Rip gave Judith a pleading look as the others advanced toward him. "Give me a chance," he begged. "I *am* Rip Van Winkle. I can prove it."

Chapter Fifteen

Rip wagged his tail slowly as he waited for his daughter's reply. Judith stared deep into his eyes. Then she reached out and touched his shoulder. She stepped between him and the crowd, which was coming toward him.

"Stop!" She held up one hand, the way an instructor might do in obedience school. When the crowd stopped, Judith put her arm under her baby again for support. "This man says that he can prove he's my father. I want to hear what he has to say."

The crowd murmured but kept its distance.

Rip gave his daughter a nod of thanks. Then he turned to face the villagers. His nose twitched; the scent of their fear was still strong. "Yesterday," Rip said, "when I went into the mountains, it wasn't really yesterday at all."

The murmuring got louder. Rip watched as the old man who had been walking around the cemetery joined the front of the crowd.

Speaking above the murmurs, Rip continued. "I met strange men there—ghosts, I think . . ."

The crowd laughed.

"Stop!" Rip barked. "Let me finish!" His heart pounded against his furry chest as he waited for them to quiet down. He wanted to growl at their rudeness, but he didn't. "We played ninepins and drank ale," he said. "I fell asleep, and the next thing I knew, it was morning . . . only, it was a morning twenty years later."

"And what were these fellows' names?" asked a plump woman suspiciously. She didn't believe him at all. "What were they doing in the mountains?"

Rip looked from face to face. He felt all their eyes drilling into him, like a thousand cat bites. "I do not have an answer. They spoke not a word."

Laughter rose from the crowd again.

"Helllooo!" Rip said loudly. "These guys were ghosts—you know, now you see me, now you don't?"

"How does that prove ye are my father?" Judith asked, her face and voice filled with uncertainty.

Rip pushed his hat up with his paw. "Are you not Judith Gardenier, wife of Delmond Gardenier?"

"Why, yes," said Judith, paling with surprise. "I did not tell ye my husband's name."

Rip wagged his tail. "On the day I left, Delmond Gardenier was just a lad, close in age to you. I gave him a dog I had carved with my own two . . . uh . . . hands."

Judith was staring at him now, a look of confusion

on her face. "It's true," she said to the others. "When my father didn't return from the mountains, Delmond and the other boys told everyone they'd seen him that very day. And Delmond showed off the dog this man speaks of."

"And you, my daughter, had a doll that I had carved for you. On the day I left, you made her a suit of clothes and rushed outside to show me. Then your mother took you into the house. That was the last I saw of you."

"Oh!" Judith gasped. "Ye are my father!" She rushed forward. Keeping one arm under her child, she hugged Rip with her other arm. His hat fell to the ground.

"Oh, boy, a group hug!" Rip said, careful not to stick his wet nose on the baby's face.

The crowd moved closer. The man with the cane and cocked hat walked over and grabbed the old man who had been strolling through the cemetery. With quick steps, he guided him roughly toward Rip. "Let's see what old Peter Vanderdonk has to say! He'll know what's true. He's the oldest man around. And he's a descendant of the village historian—the one who wrote about the country in the early days!"

The crowd murmured, then quieted. The man with the cocked hat crossed his arms and tapped his foot impatiently. "Well, Peter Vanderdonk, what have ye to say?"

With a paw, Rip picked up his hat and anxiously awaited this fellow's opinion.

Peter Vanderdonk pushed his glasses up higher on his nose. Then he put himself nose to muzzle with Rip. He squinted. "Yes, yes," he said in a shaky voice, "'tis Rip Van Winkle. I'm sure of it."

Rip heard the crowd gasp. "Yoo-hoo!" he said. "I tried to tell you so."

The plump woman stepped forward and pointed toward the mountains. "What about his ghost friends? How do ye explain that?" she growled.

"Well . . ." Peter Vanderdonk rubbed his chin. "There is a story in one of the village history books that talks about strange spirits haunting the mountains." He pointed a finger in the air. "It's believed that Hendrick

122

Hudson comes back every twenty years with his crew from the *Half Moon*," he said, bobbing his finger up and down. "He comes to keep a guardian eye upon the river called by his name."

In 1609, Hendrick Hudson sailed the *Half Moon*, a Dutch ship, into a river that would later bear his name—the Hudson River. His son was part of his crew. Although the crew returned safely to their home port from this voyage, their next sailing proved disastrous. Part of the crew mutinied. Hudson, his son, and seven others were set adrift at sea and were never seen again. No wonder their spirits aren't at rest!

Rip watched the crowd. They seemed mesmerized by Peter Vanderdonk's story.

Peter Vanderdonk nodded. "My father had laid eyes on these men, too. He told me they wore old-fashioned breeches, and they played ninepins in the mountains." As he made his next remark, his voice rose along with the finger he wagged in the air. "And . . . I myself heard them one summer afternoon. The sound of their ninepins game sounded exactly like distant claps of thunder."

Rip jumped up and flipped. "Those are the guys!"

A man from the crowd pushed his way forward. "Well, if Peter Vanderdonk says it's true, then true it is!" He raised his fist into the air.

"Yes! Yes!" Shouts arose from most of the villagers.

Rip wagged his tail and looked at the people. The plump lady scowled at him. "Okay, I can see a couple of frowns out there," he said. "Somebody still doesn't believe me." Rip wagged his tail faster. "It's all true. Really."

The crowd started to break up. Smiling, villagers slapped one another on the back. Slowly, they turned and started back down the hill.

Judith scratched the fur between Rip's ears. "I believe ye, Father."

"Well, that's good enough for me." He pawed the air. "Now, is there someplace we could get a bite to eat? Twenty years is a long time to go without a meal."

Rocking her child in her arms, Judith nodded at Rip. "I will take ye home and fix ye a meal fit for a king." She smiled. "No, it will be better. It will be fit for a president!"

Rip slept through a lot of changes. Wars took place while he was asleep. One war was the American Revolution. The people in the American colonies thought King George III of England was taxing them unfairly. So they revolted and then broke free from England. After getting independence, George Washington became their top dog . . . er . . . rather, president, in 1788.

They started off, but Judith suddenly stopped. "Oh!" She had a surprised look on her face.

"What is it, daughter?" Rip asked.

"My doll, Father—the one ye made!" She tilted her head. "Only now do I remember! When ye went away and never came back, I put her under a loose floor plank in our house. We *must* stop at the old place and get her."

Rip knew exactly which plank Judith was talking about. Only last week—rather, last week plus twenty years—Dame Van Winkle had hounded him about fixing it. It was the third plank from the door.

"Lead the way," Rip said, trotting along beside her. They followed the crowd down the hillside. "See you later, people," Rip called, giving them a wave of his paw. He was happy to see many turn and wave back.

"See ye later, Rip Van Winkle," someone called. "Welcome home."

When Judith and Rip got to the old house, Rip stopped in front of the door. He blocked Judith from entering. "You wait outside, away from the house. It's unsafe. I do not want you or my grandson put in any danger."

Judith nodded. "Yes, Father."

Rip watched her move back from the rickety house. Then he stepped inside and went carefully over to the third plank. He dug at it with his toenails until an edge popped up. Grabbing the board in his teeth, he pulled it away. In the hole lay a small, cloth-wrapped bundle, covered with cobwebs. Rip brushed away the cobwebs with his paw. Using his teeth, he pulled on the edge of the wrapping. Whatever was inside began to unwind. Out rolled the doll.

"I found her!" Rip called.

With his keen ears he heard Judith gasp. Rip quickly sniffed out the area, and he dug at the dirt with his paws. But the doll was the only thing there. Grabbing it in his mouth, he hurried outside to Judith.

A wide smile brightened her face. "Thank ye, Father." Holding her child tightly as she leaned down, Judith took the doll from Rip's teeth.

"Happy to be of service." He wagged his tail. "Now, what's for dinner?"

She laughed. "Food, and plenty of it! Delmond is a good husband and a fine farmer," she said proudly. "Ye will live with us? Please, Father?"

Rip wagged his tail. "Well, what can I say? It works for me."

As they walked on, Rip occasionally put his nose to the ground and trotted off. *Trees! I love them,* he thought happily, stopping to sniff every trunk. Then he would quickly and happily trot back to Judith's side.

"Delmond will be surprised to see ye," Judith said. "And pleased. So will Rip."

Confused, Rip cocked his head and looked at the baby in her arms. The baby had already seen him. He continued staring until suddenly it was as if someone had shone a light into the doghouse—he could see things very clearly! "Now I get it," Rip yelped happily. He flipped in the air. "Rip! My *son,* young Rip?"

Laughing, Judith nodded. "Only he is no longer *young* Rip. He is a man now. An artist. He, too, lives

126

with us, and helps Delmond with the farm. But his true love is painting pictures for the family."

Rip stopped and, with his teeth, tugged a piece of twig from his fur. "The lad was always good at picturing," he said proudly.

As they approached the Gardenier house, Rip ran ahead and sniffed out the land. *Lots of grass to roll in,* he thought happily. It felt cool beneath his paws. He could see by the size of the pumpkins growing in the nearby field that the soil was rich and moist.

"Helllooo! Anybody home?" he barked. He scattered a cluster of clucking chickens as he ran through them.

In a moment Delmond and young Rip came from behind the house, each with a tool in hand. With a second look, Rip noticed young Rip's "tool" was a small paintbrush. *It must be for picture painting,* he thought. *It is too little to paint a house.*

Rip Van Winkle jumped into a small cart that stood in the yard. Another jump put him atop an overturned pail in the cart. He stood eye to eye with his son. Why, his son was the Rip Van Winkle who had been pointed to in the village! Rip wagged his tail. And now that Rip was close enough, he could see that the young man was the splitting image of himself. However, the man had only two legs, no tail, and just enough fur to cover his head. Except for those differences, they could have been twins.

Young Rip looked dumbfounded. "Ye look like me, but old!" he said. His voice was no more than a whisper.

Rip pawed the air. "I am your father, come back from the mountains." Rip watched the mouths on the two men drop open. "Hey, guys? Uh . . . you're gonna catch flies. And, believe me, they're not the tastiest things around."

Rip watched the two men look at each other.

"Okay. I can see you don't believe me." He removed his hat and faced his son-in-law. "Delmond, do you still have the dog I carved for you?" He turned. "And you, young Rip—Judith tells me you are now picturing with paint. When you were a lad, you used clouds."

Quick as lightning flashes, both men had their arms around Rip, scratching the fur between his ears.

"This is good," he said. Soon Judith and her child were there, too. "All right! Another group hug," Rip said. "Two in one day. How lucky can I get?" His tail went into high-speed wag. "This calls for a celebration. Let's eat!"

And eat they did. Judith set out a huge meal, while Rip explained his night in the mountains to his son and son-in-law.

"And now, people, we have a problem," Rip said between bites of meat.

Everyone but the baby stopped and stared at him. Rip felt bad, because their faces looked almost sad.

"No, no. You've got it all wrong," he said, wagging his tail. "We can work this out. It's only a small problem. We have three Rips living in the same house. How do we know which Rip should come when being called?"

"You are right," said Delmond. "That could be confusing."

The others nodded and murmured their agreement, except for the very youngest Rip.

Judith bent over and kissed the baby. "From this day forward, my son shall be known as 'young Rip,' for he is the youngest," she said. Judith raised her brow and nodded at her brother. "Ye shall be known as 'Rip the painter.' And ye, Father, shall now be known as 'Father.'" She smiled warmly at him.

"That'll work." Rip gulped down his last piece of meat, then waited while Judith put more in his dish.

But to the people of the village, he was, from then on, known as "Old Rip Van Winkle, the one who met the ghosts." Rip didn't mind. In fact, he rather liked the attention the name brought him. And as he took to his old walks and habits, he soon found some of his cronies. But they had not been asleep for twenty years, so they needed more time to rest than Rip did.

So Rip made friends among the children. Soon these children loved him as much as the lads from twenty years ago had. His heart leaped with joy, and sometimes he did, too, whenever he heard shouts from them—shouts of "Rip Van Winkle! Rip Van Winkle, tell us a story!"

And he always obliged. He'd sit silently for a moment and let them scratch the fur between his ears. Then he'd take a deep breath, point a paw to the mountain, and in a spooky voice begin: "Ghosts there are, way up high. . . ."

Although Rip much preferred the company of children, one day he went to the village inn. He jumped up and took his place once more on the bench just outside the inn's door. "Hey, anybody want to know the dirt about the early days of King George the Third? The guy didn't even learn to read until he was ten!"

One by one, people stopped to listen. In return, villagers began to offer Rip bits of information about the past.

"I'm all ears," he said.

Day after day, Rip returned to the bench. Before long, he was into the regular track of village gossip. He became known as one of the patriarchs of the village and a storyteller who weaved tales of the old times before the war.

"Yoo-hoo! Got a minute?" He told his story to every stranger who arrived at the hotel. At first, his story changed on some points. When people frowned at these changes, Rip waved his paw in the air as if he were erasing his words. "I'm just confused. It was not long ago that I was awakened from a very deep sleep."

It didn't take long before every man, woman, and child knew Rip's story by heart. Some pretended to doubt the reality of it. They insisted that Rip had been out of his head with fever. But most of the old Dutch villagers gave his story full credit.

From then on, whenever a thunderstorm struck the Catskills on a hot summer afternoon, the believers, young and old, would seek out Rip at the inn. "Tell us the story again," someone would say.

Rip, obligingly, would point his ears straight up and wait for the next crash of thunder. "'Tis Hendrick Hudson and his crew from the *Half Moon*," he'd say. "Playing ninepins in the clearing, they are . . . bowling strikes . . ."

Then Rip would point his paw upward, to the eerie glow on the mountainside. The villagers would turn and look, and listen to his story one more time.

Chapter Sixteen

Wishbone watched Joe head for the Talbots' front door, the time capsule in his hands. He wagged his tail and turned to Sam, David, Ellen, Wanda, and Dr. Brown. "Come on, people." Then he ran after Joe.

Soon they were all in the living room. Joe held out the box toward Sam. "Will you hold this so I can go get some newspaper for the coffee table?"

"Sure." Sam grabbed onto the cleanest part of the box with her fingertips and waited for Joe to return.

After laying out newspaper, Joe put the box on the table. He brushed off the top and sides of the box, letting the dirt fall on the newsprint.

"That's right, Joe," Wishbone said. "We don't want any of that dirt going to waste." He jumped up on the couch and looked over to the coffee table. "Okay. Good view. This is the spot for me." Wishbone looked around. "Dr. Brown, you sit here on the couch next to me. Joe, you can sit in the chair to my left."

Wishbone sighed as Wanda sat down in the chair next to him.

"Nobody ever listens to the dog," he said.

Ellen, Sam, and David sat on the floor by the table.

"Wanda, thanks for letting us dig up your yard," Dr. Brown said. She moved over so Joe could sit on the couch between her and Wishbone.

Wishbone happened to look down as Dr. Brown crossed her ankles. He wagged his tail. "Hey, look, everybody. She's wearing purple Hush Puppies. Cute, huh?"

Wanda smiled at Dr. Brown. "Oh, well . . ." She paused. "I guess it served a higher purpose."

"This box is in pretty good shape." Sam leaned close to the table and scratched her fingernail across the top of the box. "But what's this stuff all over it?"

Wishbone leaned forward as far as he could without falling off the couch. "Open-open-open."

"My brother dipped the whole thing in paraffin to make it more waterproof," Dr. Brown said. "I hope it worked."

Joe picked up the box and handed it to her. "You do the honors, Dr. Brown."

"Thank you, Joe," Wishbone said. He watched Dr. Brown struggle to break the wax seal.

Opening the latch, she looked as excited as a new puppy on Christmas morning. "There are the marbles I was talking about, Joe." She took them out, quickly looked at them, then passed them to Joe. She looked down. "Oh, and here's a picture of me and Champ." She reached into the box and brought out the picture.

"Champ? Where? Let me see." Wishbone walked across Joe's lap to get a good look at the photo. "Ah, he's a handsome devil . . . he shares my noble bearing." Wishbone stood tall.

Dr. Brown handed the picture to Joe, who handed the marbles to Wanda. "Here's one of the cars from my brother's collection." She pulled out a metal car and handed it to David. "And look," Dr. Brown said. "Here's Champ's contribution to the time capsule—an old rubber bone."

"Boy, it looks as if that's been chewed on a time or two," Wishbone said. "Exactly how big were Champ's teeth?"

Dr. Brown pulled out a yellowed newspaper front page from 1930, glanced at it, then set it on the table.

"What's this?" Sam asked, picking up the paper.

"It must be from the day we buried the box," Dr. Brown said. "It's about whatever was going on then."

Sliding to the end of the cushion, Joe leaned toward Sam and read the headline aloud: "'HOBROCK INDUSTRIES OPENS NEW PLANT.'" He looked up. "Hey, Mom! It's about the Hobrock plant. Wow! Look at all the smoke billowing from those smokestacks."

Sam turned the paper so everyone could see the picture that went with the article.

Dr. Brown smiled. "Oh, that was a big day in this town."

Ellen rested an arm on the coffee table. "Well, you

know they're closing it this month—Environmental Protection Agency violations."

Dr. Brown clicked her tongue. "Oh, what a shame. A lot of our friends worked at that plant." She reached into the box and pulled out a number of newspaper clippings and quickly sorted through them. "There are so many stories in this box. . . ." She passed them on to Ellen. "Oh!" Smiling, Dr. Brown pulled out a weathered baseball program. "This is from an Oakdale Oaks baseball game—the Negro League."

"Oakdale had a baseball team?" Joe sounded surprised.

Dr. Brown chuckled. "Of course. And every Friday night my father would take us to the baseball game over at Legion Field."

Joe sighed. "I wish we had a baseball game to go to every Friday night."

"Really! Me, too," Sam said.

David nodded. "That would be cool."

"Mom!" Joe jumped up, throwing Wishbone off balance.

"Okay, pal, take it easy, before someone gets hurt. That 'someone' could be me!" Wishbone said.

"Mom!" Joe repeated. "There's the idea for my social-studies paper—a baseball team."

"Good, Joe." Ellen smiled. "And you've got your source right here." She gestured to the couch. "You can interview Dr. Brown."

Excitedly, Joe turned to her. "Can I?"

Dr. Brown put the time capsule back on the table. "That would be the highlight of my visit to Oakdale, Joe."

"Yes! This paper will be totally fun." Joe grinned.

"And then the three of us can put together a time capsule," Sam said, pointing to David and Joe. "You, too, Wishbone." She grinned. "This will be great—start thinking about what you want to put in it."

Wishbone scratched his ear. "Give up one of my squeaky toys? I don't think so. Maybe a bone. A very old bone. Or how about if I put in one of Wanda's plants? . . . No?" He sighed. "I'll have to sleep on it. And I know just where I'll do it." He jumped off the couch. "Excuse me. Pardon me, coming through."

Wishbone trotted into the study and jumped into his big red chair. He circled the cushion, then curled up and tucked his tail close to his body.

Ah, let's see, he thought. *What would be the worst thing about sleeping for twenty years? Couldn't eat . . . couldn't chase cats . . . uh, couldn't dig up Wanda's yard. Nope, twenty minutes should be just fine. Aaaahhh . . . ZZZZZZZZZZZ. . . .*

About Washington Irving

Besides being a writer, Washington Irving spent part of his adult life being a lawyer, a businessman, and a United States diplomat to England and Spain. He was born in 1783 and became interested in writing in his teens. His first published work appeared in 1802 in a newspaper edited by his brother. It was in the form of a letter.

Irving's first book, *A History of New York from the Beginning of the World to the End of the Dutch Dynasty*, was written under the name of Diedrich Knickerbocker. It was published in 1809. Although the book offended some New Yorkers, it was a major comic triumph. Washington Irving wrote many more books and short stories; two of his best-known tales are the short stories "Rip Van Winkle" and "The Legend of Sleepy Hollow." These works marked the acceptance of the short story as an important literary form in the United States.

Irving's last work was a five-volume biography titled, *The Life of George Washington*. Irving died in 1859, not long after completing the last volume. He was admired as a leading American author. He was also one of the first American authors to be acknowledged in Europe, as well as in the United States. Today he is not considered one of the most creative writers of his time. But his style, humor, and choice of subjects greatly influenced other writers.

About "Rip Van Winkle"

In 1815, Washington Irving left his home in New York and moved to England to help run a branch of the family's hardware business. When the company failed in 1818, Irving felt free to dedicate himself to literature. He stayed in Europe until 1832, traveling to many countries. Irving collected tales in each country he visited. Those tales as well as European traditions and European authors influenced his writing.

"Rip Van Winkle" was written in 1819–1820, while Washington Irving still lived in England. It was one of Irving's most important works. Although the story took place in America, it was based on a German folktale. "Rip Van Winkle" was first published in 1820 in a book of essays, stories, and other short pieces about the United States and England. The book, titled *The Sketch Book of Geoffrey Crayon, Gent*, also contains the short story called "The Legend of Sleepy Hollow," another of Washington Irving's most important works.

It's easy to see why the story of Rip Van Winkle has remained popular for nearly two hundred years. Like Wishbone, young and old alike can imagine themselves in Rip Van Winkle's shoes as he awakens after a twenty-year nap and searches for the key to his past.

About Vivian Sathre

Vivian Sathre grew up the youngest of seven children, with plenty of brothers and sisters to read to her. One of the stories that left a lasting impression on her was "Rip Van Winkle," by Washington Irving. As a child, Vivian couldn't help but wonder what her life would be like if she woke up after a twenty-year nap. So as an adult, she jumped—or should that be flipped?—at the chance to write the novelization of the Wishbone episode based on "Rip Van Winkle."

This is Vivian's eighth book for young readers. She loves writing for children—it allows her to pretend she's a child again. Depending on how old she wants to feel, she writes picture books, chapter books, and books for middle-grade readers. Her first novel, *J. B. Wigglebottom and the Parade of Pets*, nominated for the South Carolina 1995–1996 Children's Book Award, includes a strange dream, just as *Digging Up the Past* includes a strange dream for Rip Van Winkle. She admits that once in a while she has strange dreams, too.

Today Vivian is a full-time writer and feels lucky to have a career she loves. And she really enjoys writing for Wishbone. But writing means spending a lot of time alone at the computer, so she looks forward to her school visits. For Vivian, talking with kids is like having a six-ginger-snap day!

Vivian lives in a suburb of Seattle, Washington, with her family. And although Vivian had a number of dogs while she was growing up, she now has two house cats. But don't tell Wishbone!

Now Playing on Your VCR...

Two exciting **WISHBONE®** stories on video!

Ready for an adventure? Then leap right in with **Wishbone™** as he takes you on a thrilling journey through two great action-packed stories. First, there are haunted houses, buried treasure, and mysterious graves in two back-to-back episodes of *A Tail in Twain*, starring **Wishbone** as Tom Sawyer. Then, no one is more powerful than **Wishbone**, in *Hercules* exciting new footage! flea dip! It's **Wishbone**

Hercules...or rather *Unleashed*, featuring It's more fun than a on home video.

WISHBONE™

Available wherever videos are sold.